GED

PREPARATION FOR THE
HIGH SCHOOL EQUIVALENCY EXAMINATION

LITERATURE AND THE ARTS

NEW GED TEST 4

ELIZABETH ROMANEK

Project Editor
Ann Upperco

CONTEMPORARY
BOOKS, INC.
CHICAGO ▪ NEW YORK

Library of Congress Cataloging-in-Publication Data

Romanek, Elizabeth.
  GED preparation for the high school equivalency
examination literature and the arts.

    1. Literature—Examinations, questions, etc.   2. Arts
—Examinations, questions, etc.   3. General educational
development tests—Study guides.   4. High school
equivalency examination—Study guides.   I. Upperco, Ann.
II. Title.   III. Title: Literature and the arts.
PN62.R66   1987   700'.7'6   87-9292
ISBN 0-8092-5040-3

Published by Contemporary Books, Inc.
180 North Michigan Avenue, Chicago, Illinois 60601
Manufactured in the United States of America
International Standard Book Number: 0-8092-5040-3

Published simultaneously in Canada by
Fitzhenry & Whiteside
91 Granton Drive
Richmond Hill, Ontario L4B 2N5
Canada

Editorial Director
Caren Van Slyke

Editorial
Sarah Schmidt
Karen Schenkenfelder

Production Editor
Patricia Reid

Art Director and Cover Design
Georgene G. Sainati

Illustrator
Rosemary Morrissey-Herzberg

Art & Production
Princess Louise El
Marilyn Vevang
Lois Koehler

Typography
Lisa A. Waitrovich

Cover photo © Image Bank

ACKNOWLEDGMENTS

Excerpt on page 2 from "The Dazzle of Lasers" by W. Marbach, et al. Copyright 1983 by Newsweek, Inc. All rights reserved. Reprinted by permission.

Excerpt on page 3 from *The Adventures of Huckleberry Finn* by Mark Twain. Published by Bantam Books, Inc. Reprinted by permission.

Poem on page 4: "Ballad of the Landlord" by Langston Hughes. Reprinted by permission of Harold Ober Associates, Incorporated. Copyright 1951 by Langston Hughes. Copyright renewed 1979 by George Houston Bass.

Excerpt on page 5 from *West Side Story* by Arthur Laurents and Leonard Bernstein. Copyright © 1957 by Leonard Bernstein and Stephen Sondheim. Copyright © 1956, 1958 by Arthur Laurents, Leonard Bernstein, Stephen Sondheim, and Jerome Robbins. Reprinted by permission of Random House, Inc.

Excerpt on page 6 from "Let's Not Use Vietnam Vets as an Excuse for TV Violence" by Frank Bies. Reprinted with permission from *TV Guide Magazine* © 1986 by Triangle Publications, Inc., Radnor, PA. Reprinted also with permission of the author.

Excerpt on page 12 from *Black Elk Speaks* by John G. Neihardt, copyright John G. Neihardt 1932, 1959, 1961, etc., published by Simon & Schuster Pocket Books and the University of Nebraska Press. Reprinted by permission.

Excerpt on page 13 from *Balanchine's Complete Stories of the Great Ballets* by George Balanchine and Francis Mason. Copyright © 1954, 1968, 1975, 1977 by Doubleday & Company, Inc.

Excerpt on pages 14–15 from "Tuesday, March 27" in *Blue-Collar Journal: A College President's Sabbatical* by John R. Coleman (J.B. Lippincott Co.) Copyright © 1974 by John R. Coleman. By permission of Harper & Row, Publishers, Inc.

Excerpt on page 16 from "Death of a Maverick Mafioso." Copyright © 1972 Time Inc. All rights reserved. Reprinted by permission from *Time*.

Excerpt on page 18 from *Long Lance: An Autobiography of an Indian Chief* by Chief Buffalo Child Long Lance. Reprinted by permission of Henry Holt & Co.

Excerpt on pages 19–20 from "Why I Want a Wife" by Judy Syfers. Copyright 1970 by Judy Syfers. Reprinted by permission.

Excerpt on pages 20–21 from *Modern Black Stories*, edited by Martin Mirer, © 1971 published by Barron's Educational Series, Inc., 113 Crossways Park Drive, Woodbury, NY 11797.

Excerpt on page 22 from "Vietnam, Vietnam" by Pete Hamill. Courtesy *Vanity Fair*. Copyright 1985 by The Condé Nast Publications, Inc. Reprinted by permission of the publisher and Pete Hamill.

Excerpt on page 24 from "How to Write a Letter That Will Get You a Job" by Nona Aguilar. Reprinted from the March, 1977 issue of *Family Circle Magazine*. © 1977 The Family Circle.

Excerpt on page 24 from *Working: People Talk About What They Do All Day and How They Feel About What They Do* by Studs Terkel. Copyright 1972, 1974 by Studs Terkel. Reprinted by permission of Random House, Inc.

Excerpt on page 27 from *Barrio Boy* by Ernesto Galarza. © 1971 by University of Notre Dame Press.

Excerpt on pages 28–29 from "Lynette Woodard, Harlem Globetrotter" by Michele Kort. Copyright 1986 by Michele Kort. Reprinted by permission.

Excerpt on pages 29–30 from *The Road to Wigan Pier* by George Orwell. U.S. Rights: Reprinted by permission of Harcourt Brace Jovanovich, Inc. Canada Rights controlled by the Estate of the late Sonia Brownell Orwell, and Secker and Warburg Ltd. Reprinted by permission.

Excerpt on page 35 from "Thank You, M'am" by Langston Hughes in *The Langston Hughes Reader*. Reprinted by permission of Harold Ober Associates, Incorporated. Copyright © 1958 by Langston Hughes. Copyright renewed 1986 by George Houston Bass.

Excerpt on pages 37–38 from "The Most Dangerous Game" by Richard Connell. Copyright 1924 by Richard Connell. Copyright renewed 1952 by Louise Fox Connell. Reprinted by permission of Brandt & Brandt Literary Agents, Inc.

Excerpt on page 39 from "A & P" in *Pigeon Feathers and Other Stories* by John Updike. Copyright 1962. Reprinted by permission of Alfred A. Knopf, Inc.

Excerpt on page 40 from *The Stories of John Cheever*, published by Alfred A. Knopf. © 1958, 1986 by John Cheever. Reprinted by permission of International Creative Management.

Excerpt on page 42 from "Parker's Back" by Flannery O'Connor. Copyright © 1965 by the Estate of Mary Flannery O'Connor. Reprinted by permission of Farrar, Straus & Giroux, Inc.

Excerpt on page 45 from *A Sense of Where You Are* by John McPhee. Copyright © 1965, 1966, 1967, 1968, 1969, 1970, 1971, 1972, 1973, 1974, 1975, 1976 by John McPhee. Reprinted by permission of Farrar, Straus and Giroux, Inc.

Excerpt on page 48 from "Schools" in *Consumer Resource Book*. Published by Better Business Bureau of Chicago and Northern Illinois, Inc. Reprinted by permission of the publisher.

Excerpt on page 50 from "The Bridge" by Gay Talese. Reprinted by permission of Gay Talese.

Excerpt on pages 51–52 reprinted from *The Wheel of Love* by Joyce Carol Oates by permission of the publisher, Vanguard Press, Inc. Copyright © 1970, 1969, 1968, 1967, 1966, 1965 by Joyce Carol Oates.

Excerpt on page 53 from *A Story Teller's Story* by Sherwood Anderson. Reprinted by permission of Harold Ober Associates, Incorporated. Copyright 1924 by B.W. Huebsch, Inc. Copyright renewed 1951 by Eleanor Copenhaver Anderson.

Form on pages 57–58 from *Business Communications* by Michael E. Adelstein and W. Keats Sparrow. Copyright 1983 by Harcourt Brace Jovanovich, Inc. Reprinted by permission.

Excerpt on page 59 from "Giving Power to Words" by Philip Swain. Copyright © 1945 AAPT. Reprinted by permission of the *American Journal of Physics*.

Excerpt on page 63 from "The World House" by Martin Luther King, Jr. from *Where Do We Go From Here: Chaos or Community?* Copyright 1967 by Martin Luther King, Jr. Reprinted by permission of Harper & Row, Publishers, Inc.

Excerpt on page 64 reprinted by permission of Joan Daves, from *I Have a Dream*. Copyright © 1963 by Martin Luther King, Jr.

CONTENTS

TO THE STUDENT

Introducing the GED Interpreting Literature and the Arts Test

Part of preparing for a test is working through the doubts and questions that you have. Perhaps it has been a long time since you took an important test. Maybe you are not sure what is required to pass the GED Interpreting Literature and the Arts Test, or you are nervous about the test-taking situation.

This book has been designed so that you can succeed on the test. It will provide you with instruction in the skills you need to pass the test as well as plenty of GED-type practice. If you work carefully through this book, you should do well. The material on pages xv–xvi will give you advice on how to use this book.

What Kind of Test Is This?

The GED Interpreting Literature and the Arts Test consists of prose passages of two hundred to four hundred words and poetry passages of eight to twenty-five lines. Each passage is followed by four to eight multiple-choice questions. These questions require you to interpret selections from popular literature, classical literature, and commentaries about literature and the arts that will be covered in this book. You will read a prose, drama, or poetry passage and answer questions based on it. To answer successfully, you will need to:

- be able to interpret prose and poetry passages

- be able to show that you can:
  - understand what you read
  - apply information to a new situation
  - analyze elements of style and structure in passages

Actually, you already do many of these different kinds of thinking in daily life. In this book, we will help you apply these skills to passages of literature and commentaries on the arts.

What Does the Test Look Like?

There are forty-five multiple-choice questions, and you will be given sixty-five minutes to complete the test. To get an idea of what the test is like, look at the posttest at the end of this book. This posttest was based on the real GED Test.

What's on the Test?

The GED Interpreting Literature and the Arts Test can be broken down into the content areas it covers and the skills it tests.

These subjects make up the content of the test.

Popular Literature	50%
Classical Literature	25%
Commentaries about Literature and the Arts	25%

These essential subjects are covered in Chapters 4–8 of this book. They include selections of fiction, nonfiction, poetry, drama, and commentaries about literature and the arts.

Remember that you are being tested on your ability to think about certain ideas and concepts. You will be asked to do more than just find an answer that was given in a passage.

Thinking skills that you will be tested on include:

Understanding Ideas	60%
Applying Ideas	15%
Analyzing Ideas	25%

Chapters 1–3 of this book focus on these thinking skills and all of the activities and questions in this book will help you answer these types of questions. However, when you answer a question, you shouldn't be concerned about which thinking skill is being tested. The chart above is intended simply to show you how the Literature Test may differ from other tests you have taken.

Questions About the Five GED Tests

The following section answers some of the questions asked most frequently about the GED Tests.

Q: WHAT DOES *GED* STAND FOR?

A: *GED* stands for the Tests of General Educational Development. The GED is a national examination developed by the GED Testing Service of the American Council on Education. The credential received for passing the test is widely recognized by colleges, training schools, and employers as equivalent to a high school diploma.

While the GED measures skills and knowledge normally acquired in four years of high school, much that you have learned informally or through other types of training can help you pass the test.

The GED Test is available in English, French, and Spanish, on audiocassette, in Braille, and in large print.

Q: WHAT SHOULD I KNOW TO PASS THE TEST?

A: The test consists of five examinations in the areas of writing skills, social studies, science, literature and the arts, and mathematics. The chart below outlines the main content areas, the breakdown of questions, and the time allowed per test.

The GED Tests

Test	Minutes	Questions	Percentage
Writing Skills Part I	75	55	Sentence Structure 35% Usage 35% Mechanics 30%
Part II	45	1 topic	
Social Studies	85	64	History 25% Economics 20% Political Science 20% Geography 15%* Behavioral Sciences 20%
Science	95	66	Biology 50% Physical Sciences 50%
Literature and the Arts	65	45	Popular Literature 50% Classical Literature 25% Commentary 25%
Mathematics	90	56	Arithmetic 50% Algebra 30% Geometry 20%

*In Canada, 20% of the test is based on geography and 15% on behavioral sciences.

On all five tests, you are expected to demonstrate the ability to think about many issues. You are also tested on knowledge and skills you have acquired from life experiences, television, radio, books and newspapers, consumer products, and advertising.

In addition to the above information, keep these facts in mind:

1. Three of the five tests—literature, science, and social studies—require that you answer questions based on reading passages or interpreting cartoons, diagrams, maps, charts, and graphs in these content areas. Developing strong reading and thinking skills is the key to succeeding on these tests.

2. The Writing Skills Test requires you to be able to detect and correct errors in sentence structure, grammar, punctuation, and spelling. You will also have to write a composition of approximately two hundred words on a topic familiar to most adults.

3. The Math Test consists mainly of word problems to be solved. Therefore, you must be able to combine your ability to perform computations with problem-solving skills.

Someone once said that an education is what remains after you've forgotten everything else. In many ways, this is what the GED measures.

Q: CAN I TAKE THE TEST?

A: Each year, more than 700,000 people take the GED Test. In the United States, Canada, and many territories, people who have not graduated from high school and who meet specific eligibility requirements (age, residency, etc.) may take the test. Since eligibility requirements vary, it would be useful to contact your local GED testing center or the director of adult education in your state, province, or territory for specific information.

Q: WHAT IS A PASSING SCORE ON THE GED?

A: Again, this varies from area to area. To find out what you need to pass the test, contact your local GED testing center. However, you must keep two scores in mind. One score represents the minimum score you must get on each test. For example, if your state requires minimum scores of 40, you must get at least 40 points on every test. Additionally, you must meet the requirements of a minimum average score on all five tests. For example, if your state requires a minimum average score of 45, you must get a total of 225 points to pass. The two scores together, the minimum score and the minimum average score, determine whether you pass or fail the GED.

To understand this better, look at the scores of three people who took the test in a state that requires a minimum score of 40 and a minimum average score of 45 (225 total). Julie and Sarah did not pass, but Ramon did. See if you can tell why.

	Julie	Sarah	Ramon
Test 1	44	42	43
Test 2	43	43	48
Test 3	38	42	47
Test 4	50	40	52
Test 5	50	40	49
	225	207	239

Julie made the total of 225 points but fell below the minimum score on Test 3. Sarah passed each test but failed to get the 225 points needed; just passing the individual tests was not enough. Ramon passed all the tests and exceeded the minimum average score.

Generally, to receive a GED credential, you must correctly answer half or a little more than half of the questions on each test.

TO THE STUDENT   **xiii**

Q: **WHAT HAPPENS IF I DON'T PASS THE TEST?**

A: You are allowed to retake some or all of the tests. Again, the number of times that you may retake the tests and the time you must wait before retaking them are governed by your state, province, or territory. Some states require you to take a review class or to study on your own for a certain amount of time before taking the test again.

Q: **HOW CAN I BEST PREPARE FOR THE TEST?**

A: Many libraries, community colleges, adult education centers, churches, and other institutions offer GED preparation classes. Some television stations broadcast classes to prepare people for the test. If you cannot find a GED preparation class locally, contact the director of adult education in your state, province, or territory.

Q: **I NEED TO STUDY FOR THE OTHER TESTS. ARE THERE OTHER MATERIALS AVAILABLE?**

A: Contemporary Books publishes a wide range of materials to help you prepare for the tests. These books are designed for home study or class use. Contemporary's GED preparation books are available through schools and bookstores and directly from the publisher, at Contemporary Books, 180 North Michigan Avenue, Chicago, Illinois 60601.

Now let's focus on some useful test-taking tips. As you read this section, you should feel more confident about your ability to succeed on the GED Interpreting Literature and the Arts Test.

Test-Taking Tips

1. **Prepare physically.** Get plenty of rest and eat a well-balanced meal before the test so that you will have energy and will be able to think clearly. Last-minute cramming will probably not help as much as a relaxed and rested mind.

2. **Arrive early.** Be at the testing center at least fifteen to twenty minutes before the starting time. Make sure you have time to find the room and to get situated. Keep in mind that many testing centers refuse to admit latecomers.

3. **Think positively.** Tell yourself you will do well. If you have studied and prepared for the test, you should succeed.

4. **Relax during the test.** Take half a minute several times during the test to stretch and breathe deeply, especially if you are feeling anxious or confused.

5. **Read the test directions carefully.** Be sure you understand how to answer the questions. If you have any questions about the test or about filling in the answer form, ask before the test begins.

6. **Know the time limit for each test.** The Literature Test has a time limit of 65 minutes.

    Some testing centers allow extra time, while others do not. You may be able to find out the policy of your testing center before you take the test, but always work according to the official time limit. If you have extra time, go back and check your answers.

7. **Have a strategy for answering questions.** You should read through the reading passages or look over the pictorial materials once and then answer the questions that follow. Read each question two or three times to make sure you understand it. It is best to refer back to the passage or illustration in order to confirm your answer choice. Don't try to depend on your memory of what you have just read or seen. Some people like to guide their reading by skimming the questions before reading a passage. Use whichever method works best for you.

8. **Don't spend a lot of time on difficult questions.** If you're not sure of an answer, go on to the next question. Answer easier questions first and then go back to the harder questions. However, when you skip a question, be sure that you have skipped the same number on your answer sheet. Although skipping difficult questions is a good strategy for making the most of your time, it is very easy to get confused and throw off your whole answer key.

    Lightly mark the margin of your answer sheet next to the numbers of the questions you did not answer so that you know what to go back to. To prevent confusion when your test is graded, be sure to erase these marks completely after you answer the questions.

9. **Answer every question on the test.** If you're not sure of an answer, take an educated guess. When you leave a question unanswered, you will *always* lose points, but you can possibly gain points if you make a correct guess.

    If you must guess, try to eliminate one or more answers that you are sure are not correct. Then choose from the remaining answers. Remember, you greatly increase your chances if you can eliminate one or two answers before guessing. Of course, guessing should be used only when all else has failed.

10. **Clearly fill in the circle for each answer choice.** If you erase something, erase it completely. Be sure that you give only one answer per question; otherwise, no answer will count.

11. **Practice test-taking.** Use the exercises, reviews, and especially the posttest in this book to better understand your test-taking habits and weaknesses. Use them to practice different strategies such as skimming questions first or skipping hard questions until the end. Knowing your own personal test-taking style is important to success on the GED.

HOW TO USE THIS BOOK

If you are a student about to prepare for the GED Tests, you are to be admired. You have decided to resume an education that had been cut short. It is never easy to get back on track after you have been derailed. While it may not be easy, it will not be impossible. It will require determination and a lot of hard work.

This book will guide you through the types of questions you can expect to find on the Literature Test. To answer some questions successfully, you will need to recall ideas that you may have heard or read about previously. You may be surprised at what you already know about literature and the arts.

If you read newspapers, magazines, and novels, you are already on the road to success. If you do not read very much, now is the time to start. Not only will you improve your understanding of literature, you will also set a pattern for lifelong learning.

1. Before beginning this book, you should take the pretest. This will give you a preview of what the Literature Test includes, but more importantly it will help you identify which areas you need to concentrate on most. Use the chart at the end of the pretest to pinpoint the types of questions you answered incorrectly and to determine what skills you need special work in. You may decide to concentrate on specific areas or to work through the entire book. We strongly suggest that you do work through the whole book to prepare yourself best for the actual test.

2. This book has a number of features designed to help make the task of test preparation easier, as well as effective and enjoyable. These features include:

   • a preliminary "warm-up" section of three chapters that isolates the three reasoning skills—*comprehension, application,* and *analysis*—and provides you with plenty of practice in applying these skills; this section includes a broad sampling of passages from all three subject areas on the GED Interpreting Literature and the Arts Test; these sections are indicated by the symbol

   • content chapters that cover the essential concepts that you need to know; these chapters are indicated by the symbol

   • questions from the three levels of reasoning skills in a format similar to the GED Test

- high-interest selections from popular literature, classical literature, and commentaries about literature and the arts; these selections include excerpts from fiction, nonfiction, poetry, and drama

- a variety of exercise types to maintain your interest—matching, fill-in-the-blank, true/false, multiple-choice, and short essay

- writing exercises that provide an opportunity to practice critical thinking about literature; these exercises also provide practice for the essay portion of the GED Writing Skills Test; these are indicated by the symbol

- over 500 practice questions for strengthening reading, interpreting, and thinking skills

- an answer key for each chapter that explains the correct answers for the exercises; if you make a mistake, you can learn from it by reading the explanation that follows the answer and then reviewing the question to analyze the error. Answers to GED Practice exercises are coded by skill level.

3.   After you have worked through the eight chapters in this book, you should take the posttest. The posttest is a simulated GED Test that presents questions in the format, level of difficulty, and percentages found on the actual test. The posttest will help you determine whether or not you are ready for the GED Test and, if not, what areas of the book need to be reviewed. The posttest evaluation chart is especially helpful in making this decision.

INTERPRETING LITERATURE AND THE ARTS PRETEST

Directions: Before beginning to work with this book, take this pretest. The purpose of this pretest is to help you determine which skills you need to develop in order to pass the GED Interpreting Literature and the Arts Test.

The Interpreting Literature and the Arts Pretest consists of twenty multiple-choice questions. These questions are based on passages of fiction and nonfiction prose, poetry, drama, and commentaries on literature and the arts.

Answer each question as carefully as possible, choosing the best of five answer choices and blackening in the grid. If you find a question too difficult, do not waste time on it. Work ahead and come back to it later when you can think it through carefully.

When you have completed the test, check your work with the answers and explanations at the end of the section.

Use the Evaluation Charts on page 8 to determine which areas you need to review most. For the best possible preparation for the GED Literature Test, however, we advise you to work through this entire book.

Pretest Answer Grid

1 ① ② ③ ④ ⑤	8 ① ② ③ ④ ⑤	15 ① ② ③ ④ ⑤
2 ① ② ③ ④ ⑤	9 ① ② ③ ④ ⑤	16 ① ② ③ ④ ⑤
3 ① ② ③ ④ ⑤	10 ① ② ③ ④ ⑤	17 ① ② ③ ④ ⑤
4 ① ② ③ ④ ⑤	11 ① ② ③ ④ ⑤	18 ① ② ③ ④ ⑤
5 ① ② ③ ④ ⑤	12 ① ② ③ ④ ⑤	19 ① ② ③ ④ ⑤
6 ① ② ③ ④ ⑤	13 ① ② ③ ④ ⑤	20 ① ② ③ ④ ⑤
7 ① ② ③ ④ ⑤	14 ① ② ③ ④ ⑤	

Passage 1

WHAT ARE THE APPLICATIONS OF THE LASER BEAM?

Science-fiction writers invented it first. In his 1898 classic, "The War of the Worlds," H. G. Wells imagined an invasion of Martians who nearly conquered
5   planet Earth with weapons firing lethal beams of light. In the 1930s, Buck Rogers fought his way through the pages of comic books armed with a ray gun. It took scientists decades to catch up. Not
10   until 1960, nearly 50 years after Albert Einstein first described the basic principle, did Theodore Maiman, a 33-year-old engineer at Hughes Research Laboratories, build a homely four-inch cylinder
15   containing a ruby rod encircled by a flash tube: the world's first working laser.

More than two decades later, the laser has wrought a technological revolu-
20   tion. Lasers are an indispensable tool for delicate eye surgery, and doctors are using lasers experimentally to destroy cancerous tumors, unclog diseased arteries and even treat herpes. Just as they pro-
25   vide new tools for health care, however, they also make possible new engines of destruction: recently Dr. Edward Teller, the father of the hydrogen bomb, called on President Reagan to urge that the
30   United States build a space-based laser-weapon system that would use a nuclear bomb to fire brutally intense laser X-rays against enemy missiles in flight.

Today pilots flying the new Boeing
35   767 and 757 aircraft navigate with the aid of new laser gyroscopes. Supermarkets use lasers to ring up prices at the checkout counter by "reading" the universal bar codes like the one on *News-*
40   *week*'s cover. Powerful lasers cut and weld steel in factories from Detroit to Tokyo. Artists and filmmakers are beginning to use lasers for animation: at Lucasfilm, George Lucas, the creator of
45   "Star Wars" and its sequels, has a team of computer wizards developing a machine that uses a computer-driven laser to draw animated images on film; a second film, with human actors, is then
50   merged by laser with the graphics into a single seamless whole.

—Excerpted from "The Dazzle of Lasers" in *Newsweek*

1.   Who built the world's first working laser?

(1)   H.G. Wells
(2)   Buck Rogers
(3)   Albert Einstein
(4)   Theodore Maiman
(5)   Edward Teller

2.   What idea summarizes the second paragraph?

(1)   Lasers are an indispensable tool for delicate eye surgery.
(2)   The laser has wrought a technological revolution.
(3)   Doctors are using lasers experimentally to unclog diseased arteries.
(4)   Lasers provide new tools for health care.
(5)   America should build a space-based laser system.

3.   Why do filmmakers use lasers?

(1)   to create dazzling special effects
(2)   to compete with computer technology
(3)   to develop new machines for scientists
(4)   to create sequels for their films
(5)   to publicize their latest movies

4.   You could expect that the author of this passage would probably also be enthusiastic about

(1)   innovations in supermarket management
(2)   applications of computer technology
(3)   the merits of science fiction novels
(4)   the military defense budget
(5)   the latest Lucasfilm release

Passage 2

WHAT DO YOU NOTICE ABOUT HUCK'S RELATIONSHIP WITH HIS FATHER?

As for his clothes—just rags, that was all. He had one ankle resting on t'other knee; the boot on that foot was busted, and two of his toes stuck through, and he
5 worked them now and then. His hat was laying on the floor—an old black slouch with the top caved in, like a lid.

I stood a-looking at him; he set there a-looking at me, with his chair tilted
10 back a little. I set the candle down. I noticed the window was up; so he had clumb in by the shed. He kept a-looking me all over. By and by he says:

"Starchy clothes—very. You think
15 you're a good deal of a big-bug, *don't* you?"

"Maybe I am, maybe I ain't," I says.

"Don't you give me none o' your lip," says he. "You've put on considerable
20 many frills since I been away. I'll take you down a peg before I get done with you. You're educated, too, they say—can read and write. You think you're better'n your father, now, don't you, because he
25 can't? *I'll* take it out of you. Who told you you might meddle with such hifalut'n foolishness, hey?—who told you you could?"

"The widow. She told me."
30 "The widow, hey?—and who told the widow she could put in her shovel about a thing that ain't none of her business?"

"Nobody never told her."

"Well, I'll learn her how to meddle.
35 And looky here—you drop that school, you hear? I'll learn people to bring up a boy to put on airs over his own father and let on to be better'n what *he* is. You lemme catch you fooling around that
40 school again, you hear? Your mother couldn't read, and she couldn't write, nuther, before she died. None of the family couldn't before they died. *I* can't; and here you're a-swelling yourself up like
45 this. I ain't the man to stand it—you hear?

—Excerpted from *Huckleberry Finn* by Mark Twain

5. What do the phrases "a-looking" (lines 8 and 12) and "clumb in" (line 12) tell you about the narrator of this story?

   (1) that he doesn't get along with his father
   (2) that he speaks a foreign language
   (3) that he speaks standard English
   (4) that he cannot read or write
   (5) that he speaks in dialect

6. What is the main topic of conversation between Huck and his father?

   (1) the widow's meddling
   (2) Huck's education
   (3) the mother's death
   (4) the family's background
   (5) the father's behavior

7. The purpose of the dialogue is

   (1) to explain why sons should obey their fathers
   (2) to reveal the problems of a single parent
   (3) to imply that Huck and his father should study grammar
   (4) to dramatize the conflict between Huck and his father
   (5) to ridicule Huck's and his father's upbringings

8. What social problem discussed in this passage is also being addressed today?

   (1) illiteracy
   (2) child abuse
   (3) alcoholism
   (4) juvenile delinquency
   (5) kidnapping

Passage 3

HOW DOES A LANDLORD
REACT TO HIS TENANT?

Ballad of the Landlord
Landlord, landlord,
My roof has sprung a leak.
Don't you 'member I told you about it
Way last week?

5   Landlord, landlord,
These steps is broken down.
When you come up yourself
It's a wonder you don't fall down.

Ten Bucks you say I owe you?
10   Ten Bucks you say is due?
Well, that's Ten Bucks more'n I'll pay you
Till you fix this house up new.

What? You gonna get eviction orders?
You gonna cut off my heat?
15   You gonna take my furniture and
Throw it in the street?

Um-huh! You talking high and mighty.
Talk on—till you get through.
You ain't gonna be able to say a word
20   If I land my fist on you.

Police! Police!
Come and get this man!
He's trying to ruin the government
And overturn the land!

25   Copper's whistle!
Patrol bell!
Arrest.

Precinct Station.
Iron cell.
30   Headlines in press:

MAN THREATENS LANDLORD

• •
•

TENANT HELD NO BAIL

• •
•

JUDGE GIVES NEGRO 90 DAYS IN COUNTY
JAIL

—by Langston Hughes

9. Stanza 6 (lines 21–24) is told from whose point of view?

(1)   the landlord's
(2)   the tenant's
(3)   the poet's
(4)   the bill collector's
(5)   the janitor's

10. You can conclude that the landlord is

(1)   hot-tempered
(2)   conscientious
(3)   friendly
(4)   negligent
(5)   poor

11. Why does the landlord threaten to evict the tenant?

(1)   The tenant turned off the heat.
(2)   The tenant destroyed the stairwell.
(3)   The tenant threw the furniture on the street.
(4)   The tenant caused the roof to leak.
(5)   The tenant refused to pay $10.

12. The tenant's language in the first four stanzas (lines 1–16) most closely resembles

(1)   an apartment lease
(2)   a complaint letter
(3)   an eviction notice
(4)   a police report
(5)   a newspaper story

Passage 4

HOW DO TONY AND RIFF FEEL ABOUT A GANG CALLED THE JETS?

TONY: Now go play nice with the Jets.

RIFF: The Jets are the greatest!

TONY: Were.

RIFF: Are. You found somethin' better?

5 TONY: No. But—

RIFF: But what?

TONY: You won't dig it.

RIFF: Try me.

TONY: O.K. . . . Every single damn night
10 for the last month, I wake up—
and I'm reachin' out.

RIFF: For what?

TONY: I don't know. It's right outside
the door, around the corner. But
15 it's comin'!

RIFF: *What* is? Tell me!

TONY: I don't know! It's—like the kick I
used to get from bein' a Jet.

RIFF: . . . Or from bein' buddies.

20 TONY: We're still buddies.

RIFF: The kick comes from people,
buddy boy.

TONY: Yeah, but not from being a Jet.

RIFF: No? Without a gang you're an
25 orphan. With a gang you walk in
twos, threes, fours. And when
your gang is the best, when
you're a Jet, buddy boy, you're
out in the sun and home free
30 home!

TONY: Riff, I've had it. *[Pause]*

RIFF: Tony, the trouble is large: the
Sharks bite hard! We got to stop
them now, and we need *you*!
35 *[Pause. Quietly]* I never asked the
time of day from a clock, but I'm
askin' you: Come to the dance
tonight . . . *[TONY turns away]*
. . . I already told the gang you'd
40 be there.

TONY: *[After a moment, turns to him
with a grin]* What time?

RIFF: Ten?

TONY: Ten it is.

—Excerpted from *West Side Story*
by Arthur Laurents

13. The word *kick* (lines 17 and 21) refers to
 (1) a football punt
 (2) a drug-induced sensation
 (3) a thrilling experience
 (4) illegal money
 (5) a leg movement

14. Why does Riff say, "Without a gang you're an orphan" (lines 24–25)?
 (1) to suggest that Tony's parents are dead
 (2) to analyze why city kids feel abandoned
 (3) to imply that Tony's parents ignore him
 (4) to compare a gang to a family
 (5) to show that gangs recruit orphans

15. What is Riff's tone of voice when he asks Tony to go to the dance?
 (1) mean
 (2) quiet
 (3) angry
 (4) bossy
 (5) sad

16. Why does Tony decide to attend the dance?
 (1) He's enthusiastic about belonging to a gang.
 (2) He hasn't gone out for the last month.
 (3) He wants to find a girlfriend.
 (4) He doesn't have anything better to do.
 (5) He values his friendship with Riff.

Passage 5

HOW ARE VIETNAM VETS DEPICTED ON TV?

What a difference a decade makes. Ten years ago, Vietnam vets were the scourge of prime time. On television and in films such as "The Enforcer" and
5 "Taxi Driver," they invariably were cast as psychopathic bustouts and homicidal maniacs. Driven by their war experiences to acts of deranged violence, they had to be unceremoniously blown away by the
10 likes of Kojak and Clint Eastwood.

No sooner had the Nation begun acknowledging that Vietnam veterans performed honorably during the war than television conveniently recycled them
15 into acceptable forms. With the advent of *Magnum, P.I.*, Vietnam vets went from heavies to heroes. The Mohawk-cropped Travis Bickle of "Taxi Driver" has been transformed into the Mohawk-cropped
20 B.A. Bicarus of *The A-Team*.

On the surface at least, shows like *Miami Vice* and *The A-Team* amount to little more than routine action-adventure entertainment. But the underlying tenor
25 of all these programs—the portrayal of the hero as the violent social misfit— ought to raise serious concerns about television's current depiction of Vietnam veterans.

30 The most prolific portrayer of the Vietnam vet as teledetective has been Stephen Cannell, the executive producer and co-creator of *Hunter*, *Riptide*, and *The A-Team*. Cannell's shows, by pictur-
35 ing Vietnam vets as romantic heroes, have helped chip away at the social prejudices against them. "It is an improvement," says Vietnam combat veteran William Broyles, the former editor of
40 *Newsweek* and author of "Brothers in Arms," a book about the Vietnam experience. "I'd rather see television romanticize us than vilify us. Even if the characters function in complete ignorance of
45 what we're like, or what it was like for us over there." But the new, improved stereotypes are no more representative of the 2.6 million Americans who served in Vietnam than were the homicidal mani-
50 acs of a decade ago.

—Excerpted from "Let's Not Use Vietnam Vets as an Excuse for Violence" by Frank Bies

17. The details in the passage are arranged
 (1) to trace the process of producing a TV adventure series
 (2) to classify different types of war heroes
 (3) to explain Vietnam vets' reactions to combat duty
 (4) to compare and contrast the changing TV portrayals of Vietnam vets
 (5) to analyze the effects of TV violence on viewers

18. Which statement best summarizes William Broyles' opinion of Vietnam vets' TV roles?
 (1) The characters provide routine action-series entertainment.
 (2) Although unrealistic, the romantic characterization is an improvement.
 (3) The characterization reflects America's social prejudices.
 (4) The characters' violent behavior stems from their war experiences.
 (5) The characters show that Vietnam vets performed honorably.

19. The critic regards Stephen Cannell's TV shows as
 (1) insincere
 (2) unbiased
 (3) inaccurate
 (4) disrespectful
 (5) patriotic

20. Which of the following examples also illustrates an unfair representation of a group?
 (1) Courtroom dramas depicting lawyers as analytical
 (2) Westerns depicting American Indians as savage
 (3) TV series depicting women as professionally successful
 (4) Detective films depicting private investigators as shrewd
 5) Hollywood movies depicting men as caring fathers

PRETEST ANSWERS AND EXPLANATIONS

1. **(4)** The concluding sentence of the first paragraph explains that Maiman invented the first working laser.

2. **(2)** The first sentence of the second paragraph directly states the main idea of the paragraph.

3. **(1)** You can infer from lines 42–51 that filmmakers such as George Lucas, the creator of *Star Wars*, use lasers to produce striking visual effects.

4. **(2)** The entire article enthusiastically discusses several applications of laser technology. Therefore, it is likely that the author would also be excited about the applications of computer technology.

5. **(5)** Huck, the narrator, speaks a regional English dialect that differs from standard English. You know from the passage that Huck and his father do not get along, yet that is unrelated to Huck's manner of speech. Lines 22–23 clearly state that Huck knows how to read and write.

6. **(2)** The focus of their discussion mainly concerns the father's reaction to Huck's education.

7. **(4)** The dialogue dramatizes the conflict between Huck and his father. Huck's father is strongly opposed to Huck's schooling.

8. **(1)** In the concluding paragraph, the father states that no one in the family could read or write. Today, many Americans are also illiterate.

9. **(1)** You can conclude that the landlord is responding to the tenant's threats. In lines 19–20, the tenant tells the landlord, "You ain't gonna be able to say a word / If I land my fist on you." As a result, the landlord calls, *"Police! Police! / Come and get this man!"*

10. **(4)** According to the tenant, the landlord hasn't repaired the leaking roof or the broken steps. Therefore, you can conclude that the landlord is negligent.

11. **(5)** In lines 9–12, the tenant states that he refuses to pay "ten bucks" until the landlord fixes "this house up new." The landlord apparently believes that this overdue payment is grounds for eviction.

12. **(2)** Like a person would do in a complaint letter, the tenant directly states his grievances.

13. **(3)** Tony and Riff use the word *kick* figuratively, not literally. The kick from belonging to a gang or being with people refers to a thrilling experience.

14. **(4)** Riff is indirectly comparing a gang to a family. He is suggesting that the bond among gang members is similar to the bond among blood relatives. He is saying that not belonging to a gang is like being an orphan.

15. **(2)** The stage direction *"[. . . Quietly]"* preceding Riff's request supports this response.

16. **(5)** In line 20, Tony says to Riff, "We're still buddies." You can conclude that Tony's decision to attend the dance is a personal favor to Riff.

17. **(4)** In the first paragraph, the author gives examples of how Vietnam vets were depicted ten years ago. The remaining paragraphs compare and contrast their more recent portrayals with their past portrayals.

18. **(2)** This answer restates William Broyles' opinion: "I'd rather see television romanticize us than vilify us. Even if the characters function in complete ignorance of what we're like, or what it was like for us over there" (lines 42–46).

19. **(3)** From the last sentence of the passage, you can conclude that the author thinks Cannell's TV shows inaccurately portray Vietnam veterans.

20. **(2)** Westerns depicting American Indians as savages unfairly characterize their behavior in American history.

PRETEST EVALUATION CHARTS

Use the chart below to determine the reading skills areas in which you need to do the most work. The questions on the GED Interpreting Literature and the Arts Test require you to understand literal comprehension (global and specific), inferential comprehension (global and specific), analysis, and application. These reading skills, covered on pages 9–84 of this book, are absolutely essential for success on the GED Literature Test. Circle any items that you got wrong and pay particular attention to areas where you missed half or more of the questions.

Pretest Reading Skills Chart

Skill Area		Item Number	Review Pages	Number Correct
Literal Comprehension	Main Idea/Global	2	9–30	_____/1
	Supporting Details/ Specific	1, 15, 18		_____/3
Inferential Comprehension	Main Idea/Global	6	31–54	_____/1
	Supporting Details/ Specific	3, 10, 11, 16, 19		_____/5
	Figurative Language/ Specific	13, 14		_____/2
Analysis	Style	5	55–84	_____/1
	Structure	7, 9, 17		_____/3
Application		4, 8, 12, 20	47–54	_____/4

Now circle the same numbers for the items that you circled in the chart above. This will give you additional information about the literature and the arts content areas in which you need the most work.

Pretest Content Areas Chart

Content Area	Item Number	Review Pages	Number Correct
Nonfiction Prose	1, 2, 3, 4	85–109	_____/4
Prose Fiction	5, 6, 7, 8	110–56	_____/4
Poetry	9, 10, 11, 12	157–87	_____/4
Drama	13, 14, 15, 16	188–220	_____/4
Commentaries on the Arts	17, 18, 19, 20	221–54	_____/4

1 LITERAL UNDERSTANDING

In their writing, authors sometimes directly state some of their information—ideas, facts, and details. Understanding what the author has told you directly is called *literal understanding*. This chapter will help you to build your reading skills in literal understanding. You will learn how to:

- ☐ Identify the main idea
- ☐ Summarize and restate information
- ☐ Recognize supporting details
- ☐ Understand a term in context

Identifying the Main Idea

When you are reading the newspaper, you immediately notice the headlines:

Police Crack Down on Drug Ring
Blizzard Paralyzes City
Funding for Day-Care Centers Slashed
Baseball Players Threaten to Strike
Lottery Winner Takes All: A Cool Million

Headlines attract your attention. They also alert you to the news story that follows. You expect the newspaper article to explain the headline in more detail. The following example demonstrates this relationship between a headline and a news story:

Woman Lifts Car Off Son

CALIFORNIA—Cynthia Burgess, a five-foot-three, 110-pound woman, lifted a Toyota weighing nearly a ton off her son, who was trapped under the car when the emergency brake was accidentally released. She described her show of strength as "no big deal."

Now answer the following questions about what you have just read:

1. According to the headline, what is the story about?

   _____

2. What is the woman's name?

   _____

3. What is her height and weight?

   _____

4. How much did the car weigh?

   _____

5. Why did she lift the car?

   _____

6. What was her reaction to this show of strength?

   _____

These are the answers to the questions: **1.** a woman who lifts her car off her son; **2.** Cynthia Burgess; **3.** five-foot-three, 110 pounds; **4.** nearly a ton; **5.** her son was trapped under it; **6.** it was "no big deal."

If you answered number 1 correctly, you understood that the headline announced the major point of the story. If you answered the remaining questions correctly, you grasped the basic facts relating to this amazing event.

The major point of a passage is called the *main idea*. Like a newspaper headline, the main idea expresses the central message—what the passage is about. A passage consists of several paragraphs focusing on one topic. On the GED Interpreting Literature and the Arts Test, you will have to understand the main idea of a passage. To develop your skill in identifying the main idea, you will begin with paragraph exercises. Then you will apply this skill to the longer reading selections called passages.

Identifying the Main Idea in Paragraphs

Understanding the structure of a paragraph will help you to identify the main idea. A paragraph usually consists of a **topic sentence** and several other sentences that explain or give details about the topic. The topic sentence may appear at the beginning or in the middle or even at the end of a paragraph. All of the sentences within the paragraph focus on the topic.

Suppose you were reading a paragraph on the topic of missing children. Within the paragraph, the author would focus on a single issue concerning the topic—what he wanted to discuss about missing children. The following sentences are examples of main ideas, each of which could be expanded into a paragraph:

The largest reported group of missing children are runaways.

A large number of children are kidnapped by relatives or friends, rather than strangers.

Stricter laws should be passed to punish people who abduct children.

Fingerprinting and videotaping are two ways that can help to identify missing children.

Grace Hechinger's book, *How to Raise Street Smart Children,* offers advice to families on facing the problems of child abduction.

Notice how each sentence makes a clear, definite statement about the topic of missing children. Authors often directly state the main idea when they are presenting information.

Now let's look at how the last main idea sentence can be developed into a paragraph:

> **Grace Hechinger's book, *How to Raise Street Smart Children*, offers advice to families on facing the problems of child abduction.** The author urges parents to discuss the subject of missing children openly. By honestly telling children about kidnappers, parents can teach their children how to avoid dangerous situations and to feel more secure. The author also suggests that parents establish rules to ensure their children's safety. Parents who want to protect their children from kidnappers will find this book invaluable.

As you can see, all the sentences in the paragraph relate to the main idea. They explain the author's purpose and highlight why the book is worth reading.

Recognizing the main idea helps you to organize your reading. Once you understand the major point of the paragraph, you can better understand how the remaining sentences are linked to the main idea.

To determine the main idea of a paragraph, follow this procedure:

1. Read the entire paragraph.

2. Ask yourself what the author is writing about. This is the topic.

3. Ask yourself what the author is expressing about the topic. This is the main idea.

Apply this procedure as you read the following paragraph about Marvel comic books:

> For a while everybody was laughing at Marvel because we were going after the college crowd. But I've always felt comics were a very valid form of entertainment. There's no reason to look down on telling a good story in the comic book medium. It's just a dialogue and illustrations, after all, like film, except it's harder than film because our action is frozen. If Ernest Hemingway had written comic books, they would have been just as good as his novels.
>
> —Stan Lee of Marvel Comics

Now answer the following questions:

1. What is the topic?

   _____

2. Which sentence generally states the author's attitude toward the topic?

   _____

The topic of the paragraph is comic books. The author summarizes his attitude about the value of comic books in the second sentence: "But I've always felt comics were a very valid form of entertainment." This statement directly tells you the main idea of the paragraph. The other sentences support the main idea. By comparing comic books with films and novels, these supporting sentences explain the merits of telling a story through comic books.

Exercise 1: Main Idea in Paragraphs

Directions: For further practice in identifying the main idea, first read the following paragraph. What repeated pattern does the writer, a Native American, observe in the world? The answer to this question is summarized in the main-idea sentence. Next, go back and underline the sentence in the passage that expresses the main idea. Then, on the lines provided, write the main idea in your own words.

> Everything the Power of the World does is done in a circle. The sky is round, and I have heard that the earth is round like a ball, and so are all the stars. The wind, in its greatest power, whirls. Birds make their nests in circles, for theirs is the same religion as ours. The sun comes forth and goes down again in a circle. The moon does the same, and both are round. Even the seasons form a great circle in their changing, and always come back again to where they were. The life of a man is a circle from childhood to childhood, and so it is in everything where power moves. Our teepees were round like the nests of birds, and these were always set in a circle, the nation's hoop. A nest of many nests, where the Great Spirit meant us to hatch our children.
>
> —Excerpted from *Black Elk Speaks* by John G. Neihardt

_____

_____

The first sentence, "Everything the Power of the World does is done in a circle," states the main idea. In writing the main idea in your own words, did you preserve the meaning of the original sentence? Your version should have explained that movements and objects in the world are based on the shape of the circle. Reread the paragraph and pay close attention to the examples that illustrate this observation. Then list six examples of circular objects or movements mentioned in the paragraph:

1. _____   4. _____

2. _____   5. _____

3. _____   6. _____

FOR ANSWERS AND EXPLANATIONS, SEE PAGE 270.

Identifying the Main Idea in Passages

A passage, like a single paragraph, also centers around one main idea. However, because a passage usually consists of more than one paragraph, the main idea is developed in more detail.

As mentioned earlier in this chapter, you will be required to understand the main idea of a passage on the GED Interpreting Literature and the Arts Test. The main idea provides the overall focus for the passage. Your comprehension of the main idea will give you a better understanding of the entire reading selection. You will see how specific statements and paragraphs are developments of the main idea.

To determine the main idea of a passage, follow this procedure:

1. Read the entire passage.

2. Ask yourself what the author is writing about. This is the topic.

3. Ask yourself what general statement about the topic is expanded in the passage. This is the main idea.

Apply this procedure as you read the following passage:

> It is strange that many people think ballet is a difficult thing to enjoy. Ballet isn't any harder to enjoy than a novel, a play, or a poem—it's as simple to like as a baseball game.
>
> Yet imagine a person who goes to a baseball game for the first time. He hasn't played the game, he doesn't know the rules, and he gets confused trying to watch everything at once. He feels out of place and annoyed because he isn't sure why everyone else is so excited.
>
> If he had played baseball himself, he wouldn't have this problem. But he doesn't have to play to enjoy. Once he knows what it's all about, once he understands why the players run and slide and leap and catch as they do, he begins to appreciate the game. He becomes familiar with its elements, he enjoys it. The same thing is true of ballet.
>
> —Excerpted from *Balanchine's Complete Stories of the Great Ballets* by George Balanchine and Francis Mason

Now answer the following multiple-choice question:

Which statement best summarizes this passage?

(1) A person who goes to a baseball game for the first time feels uncomfortable.
(2) A person appreciates baseball more if he understands the game.
(3) Reading a novel, a play, or a poem is an enjoyable experience.
(4) Ballet is as easy to like as a baseball game.
(5) Ballerinas are excellent athletes.

The second sentence of the first paragraph states the main idea as summarized in answer (4). Let's review the other choices and see why they are not main ideas:

(1) This sentence restates the main idea of the second paragraph only. It is not broad enough to be the central point of the entire selection.

(2) This statement is also too specific to be the main idea.

(3) This statement is mentioned in the first paragraph but is not developed in the rest of the passage.

(5) Although this statement is true, the author never discusses the athletic ability of ballerinas.

Main ideas of magazine articles are sometimes summarized in the titles. What would be an effective title for the passage you just read? On the following lines, write two descriptive titles that would tell the reader what the passage is about.

_____

_____

Exercise 2: Main Idea in Passages

Directions: The next passage is an excerpt from *Blue-Collar Journal* by John R. Coleman, a college president. He left his position for a year and worked blue-collar jobs. The following entry from his journal describes his experience as a kitchen helper. As you read the passage, notice how Coleman builds to the main idea. Then answer the questions.

Tuesday, March 27
One of the waitresses I find hard to take asked me at one point today, "Are you the boy who cuts the lemons?"
"I'm the man who does," I replied.
"Well, there are none cut." There wasn't a hint that she heard my point.
5   Dana, who has cooked here for twelve years or so, heard that exchange.
"It's no use, Jack," he said when she was gone. "If she doesn't know now, she never will." There was a trace of a smile on his face, but it was a sad look all the same.

10 In that moment, I learned the full thrust of those billboard ads of a few years ago that said, "BOY. Drop out of school and that's what they'll call you the rest of your life." I had read those ads before with a certain feeling of pride; education matters, they said, and that gave a lift to my field. Today I saw them saying something else. They were untrue in part; it turns out that you'll get called "boy" if you do work that others don't respect even if you have a Ph.D.

15 It isn't education that counts, but the job in which you land. And the ads spoke too of a sad resignation about the world. They assumed that some people just won't learn respect for others, so you should adapt yourself to them. Don't try to change them. Get the right job and they won't call *you* boy any more. They'll save it for the next man.

—Excerpted from *Blue-Collar Journal* by John Coleman

1. What is Coleman's job in the kitchen?

_____

2. Why does he get angry at the waitress?

_____

3. What is the main idea of this passage?

(1) You should adapt yourself to people who don't have respect for others.
(2) Respect is based on the kind of job you hold, not your education.
(3) People who disrespect you will call you *boy*.
(4) Billboard ads make fun of the less-educated.
(5) Education is essential for others to respect you.

FOR ANSWERS AND EXPLANATIONS, SEE PAGE 270.

As you read the journal entry, did you observe how the opening conversation leads to discussing the major point of the story—the significance of the word *boy*? Remember that the author may choose to place the main idea in the beginning, the middle, or the end of a passage. All other sentences and paragraphs relate to the main idea.

Writing Exercise 1

Building your skills in literal understanding relies on your ability to restate or summarize the information you read. To develop this skill, write a one-paragraph summary of the excerpt from *Blue-Collar Journal*. Your summary should contain the most essential points, including the main idea and important facts and details. Your answers from the previous exercise should help you to select and organize your information. On a separate sheet of paper, write your summary as though you were explaining the content of the passage to a friend.

ANSWERS WILL VARY.

Using the Entire Passage to Find the Main Idea

Sometimes an author does not directly tell you the main idea in one or two sentences. If this is the case, how can you identify the main idea? You will have to add up the key points and see how they are related. Then you should try to form a general statement that ties all this information together.

Use this process of determining the main idea as you study the next passage.

The scene could have been lifted right out of that movie. First, a night of champagne and laughter at Manhattan's Copacabana as Mobster Joseph ("Crazy Joe") Gallo, one of New York's most feared Mafiosi, celebrated his 43rd birthday. Then on to a predawn Italian breakfast at a gleaming new restaurant in the city's Little Italy area. Seated at his left at a rear table in Umbertos Clam House was his brawny bodyguard, Pete ("The Greek") Diopioulis; at Gallo's right, his sister Carmella. Across the table sat Gallo's darkly attractive bride of just three weeks, Sina, 29, and her daughter Lisa, 10. Quietly, a lone gunman stepped through a rear door and strode toward the table.

Both Gallo and Diopioulis were carelessly facing the wall instead of the door. The triggerman opened fire with a .38-caliber revolver. Women screamed. Joey and Pete were hit instantly. The Greek drew his own gun, began shooting back. So did one Gallo ally, seated at the front clam bar. Within 90 seconds, 20 shots ripped through the restaurant. Tables crashed over, hurling hot sauce and ketchup across the blue-tiled floor to mix with the blood of the wounded. The gunman whirled, ran out the same rear door and into a waiting car.

Gallo, wounded in a buttock, an elbow and his back, staggered toward the front of the cafe. He lurched through a front door and collapsed, bleeding, on the street. Carmella's screams attracted officers in a passing police car. They rushed Gallo to a hospital, but he died before reaching it.

—Excerpted from "Death of a Maverick Mafioso"
by *Time* staff

From the sentences listed below, circle the four statements that present the **most important** information in the passage.

(1)   The murder scene in the restaurant could have been taken from a Hollywood gangster movie.
(2)   Joseph Gallo was a mobster.
(3)   Gallo's 29-year-old bride was attractive.
(4)   A gunman shot Gallo.
(5)   Hot sauce and ketchup spilled on the floor.
(6)   Gallo died before reaching the hospital.

Sentences (3) and (5) are not central to the story's purpose. Sentences (1), (2), (4), and (6) are the most important. Write the main idea of this passage in a statement combining the information in these four sentences:

_____

_____

_____

Check to see if your words convey a message similar to the following statement:

The main idea of this passage is that the dramatic murder of mobster Joseph Gallo occurred like a scene taken from a movie.

The entire passage details the story of Gallo's killing. The main idea could be expressed in many ways.

Recognizing Supporting Details

As you have already read, identifying the main idea focuses your attention on the most important point expressed in the passage. You also observed that authors develop the main idea by including additional information. Specific statements relating to the passage's central message provide you with a more complete picture of what the author is saying. These specific statements are called *supporting details*.

In your conversations with friends, you often use supporting details to explain or clarify a general comment. If you were telling someone that you enjoyed watching a certain TV show, you might give an example of your favorite episode. You could also describe the major characters, offer reasons why the show is so entertaining, or report facts about the actors. Similarly, examples, reasons, facts, and descriptions are ways in which an author supports the main idea.

The GED Interpreting Literature and the Arts Test will determine your ability to understand information that is directly stated in the supporting details. In this section you will improve your skill in comprehending the types of specific statements that back up the main idea.

Examples

When using specific *examples*, authors cite instances that illustrate the main idea. You can more clearly understand the meaning of a general statement when you are shown an example. As you read the following paragraph, notice how the examples explain the main idea:

> Many of Grimm's fairy tales end violently. In "Cinderella," birds peck out the eyes of the evil stepsisters. The wicked stepmother in "Snow White and the Seven Dwarfs" is forced to dance in red-hot iron shoes, which eventually kill her. The title character in "Rumpelstiltskin," a dwarf, commits suicide by tearing his body apart.

The first sentence introduces the main idea. The rest of the paragraph names three examples of violent endings in fairy tales. Using your own words, restate the information given in each example. Write your responses next to the title of the fairy tale.

1. "Cinderella": _____

_____

2. "Snow White and the Seven Dwarfs": _____

_____

3. "Rumpelstiltskin": _____

_____

The next passage also shows how an example supports the main idea.

Exercise 3: Supporting Details

Directions: Read the passage and then answer the questions.

> In the civilization in which we live, a man may be one thing and appear to be another. But this is not possible in the social structure of the Indian, because an Indian's name tells the world what he is: a coward, a liar, a thief, or a brave.
>
> When I was a youngster every Indian had at least three names during his lifetime. His first name, which he received at birth and retained until he was old enough to go on the war-path, was descriptive of some circumstance surrounding his birth. As an instance, we have a man among the Blackfeet whose name is Howling-in-the-Middle-of-the-Night. When he was born along the banks of the Belly River in southern Alberta, the Indian woman who was assisting his mother went out to the river to get some water with which to wash him. When she returned to the teepee she remarked: "I heard a wolf howling across the river." "Then," said the baby's mother, "I shall call my son 'Howling-in-the-Middle-of-the-Night.' "
>
> —Excerpted from *Long Lance: An Autobiography of an Indian Chief* by Chief Buffalo Child Long Lance

1. What does the passage say about the meaning of Indian names?

_____

_____

2. According to the second paragraph, what is the significance of an Indian's first name?

_____

_____

3. According to the passage, why was one man named "Howling-in-the-Middle-of-the-Night"?

_____

_____

FOR ANSWERS AND EXPLANATIONS, SEE PAGE 270.

Writing Exercise 2

Some people have nicknames that describe their appearance or personality. For instance, Al Capone, a notorious Chicago gangster, was called "Scarface Al" because his face was severely scarred.

Write a brief paragraph on a separate sheet of paper in which you explain how someone received a nickname. You may use a friend, a relative, or a famous person as an example.

ANSWERS WILL VARY.

Reasons

Imagine you are watching a television commercial about a computer training school. To persuade you to enroll, the TV announcer says:

"Excellent job opportunities exist for both men and women in the computer industry."

"Since most businesses use computers, a variety of interesting positions are available."

"Computer professionals receive high salaries."

"Working with computers can be both a challenging and rewarding career."

Each statement discusses why you should attend computer training school. Statements that answer the question "Why?" are called *reasons*. Main ideas that explain a viewpoint, an opinion, or an action are often supported by reasons.

In the following passage, Judy Syfers, the author, pokes fun by illustrating the value of having the support of a traditional wife in the home. As you read the passage, identify the main idea and the reasons the author gives to support it.

Why do I want a wife?

I would like to go back to school so that I can become economically independent, support myself, and, if need be, support those dependent upon me. I want a wife who will work and send me to school. And while I am going to school I want a wife to take care of my children. I want a wife to keep track of the children's doctor and dentist appointments. And to keep track of mine, too. I want a wife to make sure my children eat properly and are kept clean. I want a wife who will wash the children's clothes and keep them mended. I want a wife who is a good nurturant attendant to my children, who arranges for their schooling, makes sure they have an adequate social life with their peers, takes them to the park, the zoo, etc. I want a wife who takes care of the children when they are sick, a wife who arranges to be around when the children need special care, because, of course, I cannot miss classes at school.

—Excerpted from "Why I Want a Wife" by Judy Syfers

Go back and underline the main idea sentence. Then circle four reasons the author gives to support her main idea.

You should have underlined the first sentence, "Why do I want a wife?" Each sentence in the second paragraph lists at least one reason that answers this question.

As you probably observed, the preceding passage explains a typical wife's duties from the author's point of view. As the reader, you have the option of agreeing or disagreeing with the author's statements. In the next exercise, you will apply your ability to support your own opinion with reasons.

Writing Exercise 3

Answer *one* of the following questions by listing three reasons to support the opinion you choose. Use a separate sheet of paper.

1. Why do you agree with the author of "Why I Want a Wife"?

2. Why do you disagree with the author of "Why I Want a Wife"?

ANSWERS WILL VARY.

Facts

Newspapers report the facts of daily events. Encyclopedias are filled with facts about thousands of topics. The *Guinness Book of World Records* states amazing facts: the longest sentence ever written, the tallest man, the thinnest woman.

Facts are statements that can be proven. Authors develop their main ideas with facts when their purpose is to convey accurate information.

Exercise 4: Facts Relating to the Main Idea

Directions: To build your skill in locating specific facts within a passage, read the following biographical sketch of Ralph Ellison. Then answer the questions.

Ralph Ellison was born in Oklahoma City in 1914 and attended segregated schools where he developed a special interest in jazz and classical music. To further his ambition to become a composer of symphonic music, he went to

Tuskegee Institute in Alabama, majoring in music and composing. Becoming interested in sculpture he left Tuskegee after three years and went to New York City in 1936 to develop his talent. Then he became attracted to literature and came under the influence of Richard Wright, the noted novelist.

In the 1940's Ellison had a number of short stories and articles published in which he expressed again and again his belief that white America had to recognize the blacks as human beings. In 1952 his *Invisible Man* was published and recognized as a work of major importance. It won the National Book Award for Fiction in 1953. He is also the author of *Shadow and Act*, a collection of essays.

—Excerpted from *Modern Black Stories*
edited by Martin Mirer

1. What is the significance of the following dates?

    (1) 1914 _____

    (2) 1936 _____

    (3) 1952 _____

    (4) 1953 _____

2. What were Ellison's major subjects when he attended Tuskegee Institute?

    _____

3. What novelist influenced Ellison?

    _____

4. What belief did Ellison repeatedly express in his published short stories and articles? _____

    _____

5. What is the title of Ellison's collection of essays? _____

    _____

FOR ANSWERS AND EXPLANATIONS, SEE PAGE 270.

Descriptions

Police ask an eyewitness to a robbery questions about the thief's appearance. For example, they ask about height and weight, age, hair color, facial features, and clothing. The police jot down these notes:

> The thief was around six feet tall. Husky build. Probably weighs close to 200 pounds. In his late 20s, maybe 30. Reddish-brown hair. Fair complexion, freckles. Last seen wearing a wool plaid jacket and faded blue jeans. Bony face. Sharp features. Thin-lipped.

Then, based on the eyewitness's *description*, an artist draws a sketch of the suspect.

Similarly, when you read a description, you should try to see a picture created by the author's words. This is the author's purpose in developing a main idea through descriptive details. He wants you to visualize a person, place, object, or event.

In the following paragraph, Eudora Welty, a southern writer, describes a photograph of her grandfather. As you read the description, try to imagine a black-and-white snapshot of her grandfather.

> In our picture of Grandpa Carlen, his long beard and side whiskers are pure white, and seem to be stirred by some mountain wind. His large black hat is resting upside down on his knee and he sits in a straight-back bench. His right hand is holding, straight-up-and-down and thin as a rod, his staff; it looks four or five feet tall. The photograph is inscribed across the back in a strict hand, "To Chessie, if she will have it."
>
> —Excerpted from "Learning to See" by Eudora Welty

Can you see an image of Grandpa Carlen? What does he look like? What was his pose in the photograph? What objects are described? Reread the paragraph and underline specific phrases that answer these questions.

Observe in the following passage how the author, a Vietnam veteran, uses descriptive detail to support the main idea:

> Sometimes, in odd places, it all comes back. You are walking a summer beach, stepping around oiled bodies, hearing only the steady growl of the sea. Suddenly, from over the horizon, you hear the *phwuk-phwuk-phwuk* of rotor blades and for a frozen instant you prepare to fall to the sand. Then the Coast Guard chopper moves by, its pilot peering down at the swimmers, but your mind is stained with old images. Or you are strolling the sidewalks of a northern city, heading toward the theater or a parking lot or some dismal appointment, eyes glazed by the anonymous motion of the street. A door opens, an odor drifts from a restaurant; it's ngoc nam sauce, surely, and yes, the sign tells you this is a Vietnamese restaurant, and you hurry on pursued by a ghost. Don't come back, the ghost whispers; I'll be crouched against the wall, grinning, my teeth stained black from betel root.
> Vietnam.
>
> —Excerpted from "Vietnam, Vietnam" by Pete Hamill

You can identify the main idea by combining the first sentence with the last word of the passage: "Sometimes in odd places, it all comes back. . . .Vietnam." In other words, certain situations remind the author of his experience in Vietnam. When he is "walking a summer beach" or "strolling the sidewalks of a northern city," he sees, hears, or smells something that makes him recall Vietnam. On the following lines, identify a specific phrase that appeals to each one of these senses:

Sight: _____

Sound: _____

Smell: _____

Your responses might include seeing and hearing a Coast Guard chopper and smelling an odor coming from a Vietnamese restaurant. Notice how all the descriptive details in this passage contribute to your understanding of the main idea of the author's memories of Vietnam.

Understanding a Word in Context

In your everyday conversations, you often repeat in your own words what another person is telling you. Perhaps you are unsure about the way she is using a word or a phrase. Restating the definition in your own words helps you to understand the meaning.

The following dialogue between an interviewer and a job applicant illustrates this process of defining a term.

INTERVIEWER: Are you a cooperative person?

JOB APPLICANT: By "cooperative," do you mean getting along with my co-workers and boss?

INTERVIEWER: Well, that's part of it. Cooperation also means doing your share of the work and supporting the efforts of other employees.

JOB APPLICANT: In that case, I'm sure you'll find me to be a cooperative person. I've always related well to the people I've worked with and I believe in carrying my own weight. I learned the importance of cooperation when I played high school football. The coach and the other guys respected me because I was a team player.

INTERVIEWER: I like that example. Team players know the importance of cooperation in getting the job done well.

Did you notice that both the interviewer and the job applicant explain in their own words the meaning of *cooperative*? Although they each use different language in defining the term, they eventually agree about what cooperation means on the job. For example, the interviewer says, "Cooperation also means doing your share of the work and supporting the efforts of other employees."

On the following lines, write the job applicant's restatement of that definition.

_____

_____

Your restatement was correct if you included the phrases "getting along with my co-workers," "carrying my own weight," and "team player."

Imagine you were the job applicant. What words would you use to show the interviewer that you understand the meaning of cooperation? Write your version here:

_____

_____

An accurate restatement would use different language, but the meaning would remain the same.

Using Context Clues

Studying the context of a word means looking at the way it is used in a sentence or passage. The *context*, or surrounding phrases and sentences, will sometimes give you direct clues about the meaning of a word by restating the definition. The following example shows how an author restates a definition to make sure that you, the reader, clearly understand the way the author is using a particular word.

> Whether you're just getting back into the job market after years out of it or you're looking for a better job to advance your career, you can double your chances of success by using a "tailored" letter.
> What's a tailored letter? It's simply a brief letter highlighting background elements which most relate to the needs of a prospective employer. In other words, you "tailor" your experience to meet the needs of the person or company you want to work for. By following our simple guidelines, you can write a persuasive, concise letter that gets results.
>
> —Excerpted from "How to Write a Letter That Will Get You a Job"
> by Nona Aguilar*

In this excerpt, the word *tailor* has a special context. It is used to explain the type of letter you should write when you are applying for a job. In the fifth and sixth lines, notice that the author uses the phrase "in other words." This is a clue that the author is restating the meaning to make sure her message is clear to the reader. On the following lines, put into your own words what the author means by a *tailored* letter.

_____

_____

In Studs Terkel's book, *Working*, Nancy Rogers, a bank teller, describes her job:

> What I do is say hello to people when they come up to my window. "Can I help?" And transact their business, which amounts to taking money from them and putting it into their account.
>
> —Excerpted from *Working* by Studs Terkel

As used in this example, "transact their business" means

(1) telling customers about the bank's services
(2) depositing money in the customers' accounts
(3) balancing customers' checkbooks
(4) selling stocks and savings bonds
(5) cashing customers' paychecks

The correct answer is (2). *Depositing* is another way of saying "putting it" (money) into their account. Although the other answers describe ways of transacting business, they do not define the term according to the bank teller's explanation.

On the GED Interpreting Literature and the Arts Test, you will be asked multiple-choice questions about the meaning of a word or phrase that appears in the reading selection. You can derive the meaning of unfamiliar words or phrases from their context—the way they are used in relation to other words in the sentence or paragraph. Context clues can help you to figure out the definition without looking the word up in the dictionary.

Exercise 5: Identifying Context Clues

Directions: In this exercise, circle the context clues that help you to define the word in **boldface print**. Pay close attention to words or phrases that restate the meaning or give an example. Then write the meaning of the word.

1. Many characters in Charles Dickens's novels are **waifs**, homeless children who must fend for themselves.

    _____

2. John F. Kennedy had **charisma**. Old films of press conferences illustrate his magnetic and charming personality.

    _____

3. Leon received a **subpoena**, a legal document requiring him to testify in court.

    _____

4. The **extraterrestrial**—a creature from another planet—had three eyes, an oversized head, and green skin.

    _____

5. Isabel had a hard time following the **convoluted** plot of the murder mystery. The complicated story had numerous twists and turns in the action.

    _____

6. The Environmental Protection Agency found **toxic** chemicals in the city's water supply. Because these poisonous chemicals posed a health hazard, the agency advised residents to boil their drinking water.

_____

7. XYZ Company provides **tuition reimbursement** for courses relating to the employee's job. If a clerical assistant wants to take a bookkeeping class, the company will pay for the cost.

_____

8. *High School* is a **documentary** film. The characters in this movie are real students and teachers, not actors. All the scenes, such as a teacher asking a student for his hall pass, actually happened. Unlike a make-believe Hollywood production, this film shows you the true story of life in a large high school.

_____

9. During the Great Depression, thousands of Americans resorted to **panhandling.** Unemployed and poverty-stricken, they would walk the streets begging for money. This practice was expressed in the popular song "Brother, Can You Spare A Dime?"

_____

10. Rather than delivering sermons to a live congregation, **electronic preachers** use the airwaves to carry their religious message. They spread the gospel on TV and radio.

_____

FOR ANSWERS AND EXPLANATIONS, SEE PAGE 271.

GED Practice Sections

In the GED Practice section following every chapter in this book, you will have a chance to apply the skills you have learned. Each GED Practice section contains passages similar to those you'll find on the GED Interpreting Literature and the Arts Test. Like the excerpts on the test, each passage is preceded by a purpose question and followed by several multiple-choice questions.

The ***purpose question*** serves to focus your reading on the content of a passage; however, it is **not** the title of the selection. In addition to appearing before all GED Practice passages, a purpose question precedes every selection in chapters 4–8, as well as the pretest and posttest to this book. Use the purpose questions to help guide your reading and to answer the multiple-choice questions that follow each passage.

★ **GED PRACTICE** ★

Exercise 6: Chapter Review

Directions: Read the following passages and answer the multiple-choice questions. Use the purpose question to focus your reading.

Passage 1

HOW DO YOUNG BOYS PRETEND TO BE BULLFIGHTERS?

Once in a great while the older boys would also allow us to join them in the bullfights they organized in one corner of the pasture. The bulls, the matadores, and the picadores were the ten- to twelve-year-olds, and the master of the fight was the oldest of the gang. We were permitted to take part only as fans or
5 *aficionados*, to provide the yelling, the catcalls and the cheers. The master of the *corrida* directed us to sit on the ground on the upper slope of the bullring, which was entirely imaginary.

From behind a tree a trumpeter stepped to the edge of the ring. Blowing on a make-believe bugle he sounded a call and the bull rushed in—a boy with a
10 plain sarape over his shoulders, holding with both hands in front of his chest the bleached skull of a steer complete with horns. Between the horns a large, thick cactus leaf from which the thorns had been removed, was tied. It was at the cactus pad that the matadores and picadores aimed their wooden swords and bamboo spears.

15 If the fight went according to the rules, the master declared the bull dead after a few rushes, by counting the stabs into the cactus, and the dead bull was replaced by a live one. Sometimes a sword or a spear missed the cactus pad and poked the bull in the stomach or some more sensitive spot. If the bull suspected that the miss was on purpose and dropped his skull to charge the
20 torero with his fists, there was a free-for-all. We *aficionados* fell on one another with grunts and kicks, wrestling on the ground to increase the bedlam. If the commotion got out of the hands of the master of the *corrida*, there was always an adult watching from the village across the arroyo, who would walk over to the ring to scatter the rioters and send them home.

—Excerpted from *Barrio Boy* by Ernesto Galarza

1. Which of the following titles best describes this passage?

(1) Games Children Play
(2) Imitating a Bullfight
(3) Becoming a Man
(4) A Childhood Memory
(5) How Fights Start

2. The word *aficionados* in line 5 means

    (1) steers
    (2) wrestlers
    (3) fans
    (4) yells
    (5) troublemakers

3. In the second paragraph, the author gives details about

    (1) the reaction of the younger observers
    (2) the purpose of the bullfight
    (3) the rules for playing the game
    (4) how a boy disguised himself as the bull
    (5) how the game prepared the boys for adulthood

4. What happened when the "bull" thought he was intentionally poked in a sensitive spot?

    (1) An adult sent everyone home.
    (2) All the boys started fighting.
    (3) The fans started booing.
    (4) The master declared the bull dead.
    (5) The bull rolled over in pain.

Passage 2

WHAT HAS LYNETTE WOODARD ACCOMPLISHED?

The player they call "Wood" leaps high for a rebound, pulling it out of the air with a strength and surehandedness that declares to the other players, "It's *mine*." Then Wood returns to earth and begins dribbling the basketball to the opposite end of the court. Players reach out a hand to grab the ball, or try to
5 block Wood's progress with their bodies, but Wood is too quick and slithers past them without a pause. There are just two players left between Wood and the basket, and Wood simply darts between them, casually jumps a couple of feet off the ground, and with a flick of the wrist lays the ball over the rim of the basket and through the netting: Two points. Compliments and hand slaps to Wood for
10 a great move.

What's wrong with this picture? Nothing. Except that Wood, who is obviously "one of the guys" on this basketball court, is also the only woman on it.

Wood is Lynette Woodard, the woman who is bringing coed professional
15 basketball to the world, courtesy of the Harlem Globetrotters. Obviously, the Globetrotters saw the publicity value of such a bold move, especially since revenues and attendance figures for the 60-year-old basketball and comedy squad reportedly had been flagging.

But as much as it may mean to the Globetrotters financially, it could mean
20 even more to the cause of women in sports. It seems that people in this country sometimes need to see women perform on the same court as men before they can finally appreciate just how talented women can be. That's what happened when Billie Jean King played Bobby Riggs: their match generated a whole new audience for women's tennis. And perhaps seeing five-feet-eleven Lynette

25 Woodard hold her own on a basketball court with a bunch of guys will finally convince people of the merits of women's basketball.

"She's representing all the women athletes," said basketball player Lori Scot who had also tried out for the Globetrotters. "And we're well represented with Wood on the team."

—Excerpted from "Lynette Woodard" by Michele Kort

5. According to the passage, what is unique about Lynette Woodard?

    (1) She is five-feet-eleven.
    (2) She is the only woman playing on the Harlem Globetrotters.
    (3) She has an impressive jump shot.
    (4) She's not afraid to compete with men.
    (5) She is a high scorer.

6. The purpose of the first paragraph is to

    (1) explain how to score a basket
    (2) prove why women should play professional basketball
    (3) illustrate offensive and defensive moves in basketball
    (4) provide a play-by-play description of Woodard in action
    (5) persuade women to try out for the team

7. The term "publicity value" in line 16 refers to

    (1) the public's opinion of a player's skill
    (2) the TV and radio coverage of the team
    (3) the ability to attract an audience and increase ticket sales
    (4) a basketball player's popularity with the fans
    (5) techniques for promoting a celebrity's talent

8. The author used the example of Billie Jean King and Bobby Riggs to show that

    (1) tennis is as difficult to play as basketball
    (2) women can be as talented as men
    (3) competitive sports build character
    (4) more women should participate in sports
    (5) women's basketball should be taken more seriously

Passage 3

WHAT DO YOU NOTICE ABOUT COAL MINERS?

When the miner comes up from the pit his face is so pale that it is noticeable even through the mask of coal dust. This is due to the foul air that he has been breathing, and will wear off presently. To a Southerner, new to the mining districts, the spectacle of a shift of several hundred miners streaming out
5 of the pit is strange and slightly sinister. Their exhausted faces, with the grime clinging in all the hollows, have a fierce, wild look. At other times, when their faces are clean, there is not much to distinguish them from the rest of the population. They have a very upright square-shouldered walk, a reaction from

10   the constant bending underground, but most of them are shortish men and their thick ill-fitting clothes hide the splendor of their bodies. The most definitely distinctive thing about them is the blue scars on their noses. Every miner has blue scars on his nose and forehead, and will carry them to his death. The coal dust of which the air underground is full enters every cut, and then the skin grows over it and forms a blue stain like tattooing, which in fact it is. Some of

15   the older men have their foreheads veined like Roquefort cheeses from this cause.

—Excerpted from "The Road to Wigan Pier" by George Orwell

9. The purpose of this passage is to

   (1)   explain the dangers of coal mining
   (2)   tell you why miners are exhausted after work
   (3)   describe the physical appearance of a coal miner
   (4)   describe the way a coal miner walks
   (5)   warn miners to watch their health

10. According to the passage, why are the miners' faces so pale when they leave the coal pit?

   (1)   They are tired from working hard.
   (2)   They were breathing foul air.
   (3)   They aren't exposed to enough sunlight.
   (4)   They want to look strange and sinister.
   (5)   They feel faint from the heat.

11. Why do miners have permanent scars on their noses and foreheads?

   (1)   They always bang their heads against the low ceiling of the coal pit.
   (2)   They all tattoo their noses and foreheads with blue ink.
   (3)   Their noses and foreheads are covered with bluish-black coal dust.
   (4)   They bruise themselves when they are shoveling coal.
   (5)   Blue-stained skin forms over the coal miners' cuts.

12. Based on the passage, you can tell that the word *Roquefort* in line 15 is

   (1)   a growth on the skin
   (2)   the medical term for a wound
   (3)   the name of a coal-mining town
   (4)   a type of cheese
   (5)   a muscular pain

FOR ANSWERS AND EXPLANATIONS, SEE PAGE 271.

2
INFERENTIAL UNDERSTANDING

Inferential understanding is a way of thinking—a reasoning process you use to help you interpret your experiences. When you make an *inference*, you draw upon what you observe and know. Then you make an educated guess based on your observations and knowledge.

Making Inferences

Here is a familiar example that shows how you use your inference skills every day:

> You are driving along a main street. As you near the railroad tracks, you notice two flashing red lights. Bells clang as you watch the crossing gates fall, stopping traffic. You hear a distant whistle.

What would you infer about this situation? You would probably conclude that a train is approaching. Why?

Go back and trace the reasoning process you used to arrive at this conclusion. Certain clues guided your thinking. Flashing red lights, clanging bells, falling crossing gates, a distant whistle—all these clues hinted to you that a train was approaching.

Based upon your observations and knowledge, you made an educated guess. You assumed your inference was correct, although nobody told you directly. Actually seeing the train speeding by would prove that you were right.

The inferences that you make depend largely upon your powers of observation—your ability to spot important details or clues. The next example illustrates how specific clues support an inference:

Observation: A man wearing dark glasses taps his cane against the pavement. His German shepherd leads him across an alley.

Inference: The man is blind.

Clues: 1. Wears dark glasses
2. Walks with a cane
3. Is directed by a German shepherd, probably trained as a Seeing Eye dog

All these clues make the inference believable. There is sufficient evidence to infer that the man is blind.

Exercise 1: Clues That Support an Inference

Directions: In the following exercises, you will apply your skills in detecting clues which support inferences. Carefully study the observations. Then list the clues that show why the inference for each observation is valid.

1. **Observation:** During the second quarter of a football game, the referee blows his whistle. The tackled quarterback lies motionless on the field. Two men with a stretcher rush from the sidelines and carry him away.

   Inference: The quarterback is injured.

   Clues: _____

   _____

2. **Observation:** Employees in the office gather around a secretary and say, "Congratulations!" She holds out her left hand and shows them her diamond ring.

   Inference: The secretary was recently engaged.

   Clues: _____

   _____

3. **Observation:** As a woman walks toward the door of a small clothing store, a high-pitched alarm goes off. The store manager races after the woman and grabs her arm. A sweater, stuffed inside the woman's coat, drops to the floor.

   Inference: The manager caught the woman shoplifting.

   Clues: _____

   _____

4. **Observation:** After a concert people in the audience loudly clap their hands and cheer. Some stand and yell, "Bravo! Bravo!"

   Inference: The audience enjoyed the performance.

   Clues: _____

   _____

5. **Observation:** A black limousine heads a long line of cars moving steadily through traffic. Although it is early afternoon, all the car headlights are turned on.

   Inference: These cars are part of a funeral procession.

   Clues: _____

   _____

FOR ANSWERS AND EXPLANATIONS, SEE PAGE 271.

Drawing Valid Inferences

In your own experiences, you probably make inferences automatically. You form first impressions about the people you meet. You might make assumptions about what life is like in a city, a suburb, or a small town. However, once you have made an inference, do you check its accuracy? Is there enough evidence to support the conclusion you have drawn? Have you overlooked any facts? In this section you will read how the American public made false inferences about a radio program.

On Halloween Eve, 1938, the CBS Mercury Theater on Air presented a radio broadcast entitled "War of the Worlds." The script was adapted from an H.G. Wells science fiction novel. The famous actor Orson Welles told the story of an invasion from the planet Mars. Here is an excerpt from the original script:

ANNOUNCER: Ladies and gentlemen, I have a grave announcement to make. Incredible as it may seem, both the observations of science and the evidence of our eyes lead to the inescapable assumption that those strange beings who landed in the Jersey farmlands tonight are the vanguard of an invading army from the planet Mars.

—Excerpted from the original script of "War of the Worlds" by Howard Koch

Because the dramatic interpretation sounded real, thousands of Americans panicked. They were convinced that Martians were actually destroying the country.

These people mistakenly assumed the truth of the broadcast. They feared that their lives were in danger. Yet they didn't check to find out whether their assumptions were based on fact.

How could they have avoided jumping to a hasty conclusion?

1. Listeners heard Orson Welles say, ". . . within two hours three million people moved out of New York." This statement was an important clue. It is impossible for a city to be cleared out so quickly.

2. Reading the newspaper listing of radio programs would have proved that CBS *scheduled* "War of the Worlds" to be broadcast on October 30.

3. By turning the radio dial, the listeners would have discovered that the show was not an authentic broadcast. Had it been authentic, they would have heard this "national crisis" reported on other stations.

4. During intermissions the CBS radio announcer reminded the audience that they were listening to a drama.

What can you learn from this example? One important lesson is that you should understand all the facts before you make an inference.

The same word of advice applies to your reading skills. You need to build *both* literal and inferential understanding. These two skills are closely connected. Discovering the literal meaning of a passage requires you to identify what the author says directly—ideas, factual content, and supporting details. Once you have grasped the stated ideas and facts, you will want to explore what the author says indirectly—the implied or unstated meaning.

In this chapter you will develop the following skills in inferential understanding:

☐ Inferring the unstated main idea

☐ Drawing conclusions from supporting details

☐ Interpreting figurative language

Inferring The Unstated Main Idea

In the last chapter you learned that the main idea expresses the central message of a passage or paragraph. Sometimes authors will suggest the main idea, rather than state it directly. In other words, the main idea is *implied*, and you must *infer* the major point of the reading selection based on the information given.

The following suggestions will help you to infer the unstated main idea:

1. Read the entire passage for its literal meaning. What has the author told you directly?

2. Read between the lines. What do the stated facts and details seem to show? How are they related? Why did the author include these facts and details?

3. Ask yourself, "What is the author suggesting about a person, a place, an event, or a belief?"

Use these guidelines as you read the following passage:

After the game, the team slowly returns to the locker room. There are no television cameramen shooting post-game highlights, no photographers popping flash bulbs, no sportscasters conducting exclusive interviews.

They are all in the opposing team's locker room. The players, too exhausted to shower, sit on wooden benches. They hold their heads down and stare blankly at the floor. No one speaks. The coach bangs his fist against a locker and storms into his office, slamming the door behind him.

Can you infer the main idea of this passage? First, answer these questions:

1. Why do you think the cameramen, the photographers, and the sportscasters are in the opposing team's locker room? _____

    _____

2. Why are the players silent? How do their gestures and reactions reveal their emotions? _____

    _____

3. From the description of the coach's behavior, what can you infer about his feelings? _____

    _____

The author is showing you the team's reaction after losing a game. All the details contribute to the main idea. The author does not directly state, "The team is unhappy about the defeat." Yet you can infer this meaning from your answers to the preceding questions. **1.** The cameramen, photographers, and sportscasters are in the winning team's locker room. **2.** The description of the losing players' silence and gestures suggest that they are depressed. **3.** The description of the coach's behavior suggests that he is upset. By adding these clues together, you were able to make an inference about the main idea.

Inferring the Main Idea from Supporting Details

The next example is the opening paragraph from Langston Hughes's short story, "Thank You M'am." As you read, notice that all the details focus on one event.

She was a large woman with a large purse that had everything in it but a hammer and nails. It had a long strap, and she carried it slung across her shoulder. It was about eleven o'clock at night, dark, and she was walking alone, when a boy ran up behind her and tried to snatch her purse. The strap broke with the sudden single tug the boy gave it from behind. But the boy's weight and the weight of the purse combined caused him to lose his balance. Instead of taking off full blast as he had hoped, the boy fell on his back on the sidewalk and his legs flew up. The large woman simply turned around and kicked him right square in his blue-jeaned sitter. Then she reached down, picked the boy up by his shirt front, and shook him until his teeth rattled.

—Excerpted from "Thank You M'am"
by Langston Hughes

The answers to the following questions will lead you to the main idea:

1. Who are the two people identified in this paragraph?

_____

2. What is the most important object? _____

_____

By combining this information, you can determine the main idea: A woman successfully defends herself against a young purse snatcher. To make this inference, you had to summarize the major descriptive details.

For further practice in inferring the main idea, complete the exercise below.

Exercise 2: Inferring the Unstated Main Idea

Directions: Carefully study the next two passages and answer the multiple-choice questions about the main idea. Be prepared to explain your responses.

Passage 1

Now there were no fish in the river. There were no deep potholes where fish could live. I had not been mistaken as I rode the bus, thinking that the rivers were shallower than I remembered them. The Poor Fork now was not only low; it was apparently the local refuse dump. Tin cans, pop bottles, and discarded automobile tires lined the banks, while the river itself was full of debris which it apparently was too sluggish to move along.

—Excerpted from *Appalachia: A Reminiscence*
by Rebecca Caudill

1. Which of the following statements best summarizes the main idea?

(1)   The river moves slowly.
(2)   The trash in the river is an eyesore.
(3)   People no longer go fishing.
(4)   The river is being destroyed by pollution.
(5)   People should dump their trash in garbage cans.

2. According to the author's observations, what clues in the paragraph support your answer? On the following lines, list the descriptive details that you used as evidence.

_____

_____

_____

_____

Passage 2

A man stood upon a railroad bridge in northern Alabama, looking down into the swift water twenty feet below. The man's hands were tied behind his back, the wrists bound with a cord. A rope closely encircled his neck. It was attached to a stout cross-timber above his head and the slack fell to the level of his knees.

—Excerpted from "An Occurrence at Owl Creek Bridge"
by Ambrose Bierce

3. The purpose of this paragraph is

  (1) to show a man about to be hanged
  (2) to describe the scenery of northern Alabama
  (3) to explain the size of a railroad bridge
  (4) to illustrate the uses of a rope
  (5) to show a man held hostage by terrorists

4. What clues in the paragraph support your answer?

_____

_____

_____

FOR ANSWERS AND EXPLANATIONS, SEE PAGE 271.

Solving a Riddle

As you learned from studying the previous exercises, inferring the main idea is similar to solving a riddle. You discover the major point of a reading selection by adding up certain clues and piecing together bits of information. Your inference is a general statement that correlates the underlying meaning of these details.

Apply this process as you read the following excerpt, a conversation between two fictional characters. What point is General Zaroff, an expert hunter, trying to get across to Rainsford?

The general smiled the quiet smile of one who has faced an obstacle and surmounted it with success. "I had to invent a new animal to hunt," he said.
"A new animal? You're joking."
"Not at all," said the general. "I never joke about hunting. I needed a new animal. I found one. So I bought this island, built this house, and here I do my hunting. The island is perfect for my purposes—there are jungles with a maze of trails in them, hills, swamps—"
"But the animal, General Zaroff?"
"Oh," said the general, "it supplies me with the most exciting hunting in the world. No other hunting compares with it for an instant. Every day I hunt, and I never grow bored now, for I have a quarry with which I can match my wits."
Rainsford's bewilderment showed in his face.

"I wanted the ideal animal to hunt," explained the general.

"So I said: 'What are the attributes of an ideal quarry?' And the answer was, of course: 'It must have courage, cunning, and above all, it must be able to reason.' "

"But no animal can reason," objected Rainsford.

"My dear fellow," said the general, "there is one that can."

"But you can't mean—" gasped Rainsford.

"And why not?"

"I can't believe you are serious, General Zaroff. This is a grisly joke."

"Why should I not be serious? I am speaking of hunting."

"Hunting? Good God, General Zaroff, what you speak of is murder."

—Excerpted from "The Most Dangerous Game"
by Richard Connell

Here is the subject of this dialogue restated as a riddle: What animal is never boring and most exciting to hunt? (You may need to go back and read the passage again carefully.)

Answer: _____

You were correct if you wrote "a human being." Now let's expand this answer into the main idea of the passage: General Zaroff explains to Rainsford that he has found the ideal animal to hunt—a human being. Did you notice that General Zaroff's spoken words create suspense? Rather than making straightforward remarks, he drops hints. Both Rainsford and you, the reader, have to infer his intended meaning.

Writing Exercise

You often form impressions about people from what they say aloud. On a separate sheet of paper, write a short paragraph describing either Zaroff or Rainsford. Use some exact phrases and sentences that the character says and describe what his spoken words suggest about his outlook on life.

ANSWERS WILL VARY.

Drawing Conclusions from Supporting Details

You have already observed how supporting details are clues to discovering the main idea. These details also serve another purpose. Drawing conclusions from supporting details enables you to interpret the passage. Certain phrases and sentences hint at information that is not directly stated. From these specific details, you can make inferences or draw conclusions about a person, a place, or a situation.

What inferences can you make from the next paragraph? Read the selection carefully and then complete the exercises.

> In walks these three girls in nothing but bathing suits. I'm in the third checkout slot, with my back to the door, so I don't see them until they're over by the bread. The one that caught my eye first was the one in the plaid green two-piece. She was a chunky kid, with a good tan and a sweet broad soft-looking can with those two crescents of white just under it, where the sun never seems to hit, at the top of the back of her legs. I stood there with my hand on a box of HiHo crackers trying to remember if I rang it up or not. I ring it up again and the customer starts giving me hell. She's one of those cash register-watchers, a witch about fifty with rouge on her cheekbones and no eyebrows, and I know it made her day to trip me up.

—Excerpted from "A & P" by John Updike

Identify the clues that support each of the following inferences:

1. The story takes place in a supermarket.

   Clues: _____

   _____

2. The weather outside is hot.

   Clues: _____

   _____

3. The person telling the story is a teen-age boy.

   Clues: _____

   _____

4. The boy is distracted by one of the girls.

   Clues: _____

   _____

5. The checkout boy views the customer as an ugly, nasty-looking woman who enjoys complaining.

   Clues: _____

   _____

Here are the supporting details that provide the clues for each of these inferences:

1. References to "checkout slot," "cash register," "HiHo crackers," and "bread" suggest that the story takes place in a supermarket.

2. The girls are wearing bathing suits.

3. His speech and his interest in the girls suggest that he is a teen-age boy.

4. He has observed every detail about the girl's physical appearance. He was paying so much attention to her that he made a mistake ringing up a customer's groceries.

5. By saying the woman is a "witch" and describing her face, the boy implies that she is ugly and nasty. His statement, "I know it made her day to trip me up," suggests that the customer enjoys complaining.

In the preceding example, notice how much information you were able to infer from the supporting details. What if the author had decided to report all this information directly? Read the following version:

> I am a teen-age boy who works as a cashier in a supermarket. One hot day three girls wearing bathing suits walked into the store. I was so distracted by the girl wearing the two-piece that I made a mistake ringing up a customer's groceries. Although the customer started complaining, I didn't really care. She looked and acted like a mean, old witch.

This paragraph is obviously less interesting to read. One reason authors suggest rather than state ideas is to get the reader more interested.

For additional practice in drawing conclusions from supporting details, complete the next exercise.

Exercise 3: Supporting Details

Directions: Read the following passage. Then circle the correct answers in the multiple-choice questions.

> When Blake stepped out of the elevator, he saw her. A few people, mostly men waiting for girls, stood in the lobby watching the elevator doors. She was among them. As he saw her, her face took on a look of such loathing and purpose that he realized she had been waiting for him. He did not approach her. She had no legitimate business with him. They had nothing to say. He turned and walked toward the glass doors at the end of the lobby, feeling that faint guilt and bewilderment we experience when we by-pass some old friend or classmate who seems threadbare, or sick, or miserable in some other way. It was five-eighteen by the clock in the Western Union office. He could catch the express. As he waited his turn at the revolving doors, he saw that it was still raining. It had been raining all day, and he noticed now how much louder the rain made the noises of the street. Outside, he started walking briskly toward

Madison Avenue. Traffic was tied up, and horns were blowing urgently on a crosstown street in the distance. The sidewalk was crowded.

—Excerpted from "The Five-Forty-Eight"
by John Cheever

1. What place is Blake leaving?

    (1) a department store
    (2) an office building
    (3) a train station
    (4) a high-rise apartment
    (5) a movie theater

2. Who could the woman in the lobby be?

    (1) a stranger
    (2) an old classmate
    (3) a casual acquaintance
    (4) Blake's ex-wife
    (5) an elevator operator

3. How does Blake feel about the woman?

    (1) sick
    (2) uneasy
    (3) comfortable
    (4) impatient
    (5) happy

4. The story takes place in

    (1) a city
    (2) a small town
    (3) a suburb
    (4) a foreign country
    (5) a dangerous neighborhood

FOR ANSWERS AND EXPLANATIONS, SEE PAGE 272.

Drawing Conclusions About People and Their Relationships

Authors often write about people and their relationships—either real or imagined. Through descriptive details authors suggest what a person is like. One way of revealing a person's character is to show how someone else feels about that person's behavior. As you read the next paragraph, what can you conclude about the man, the woman, and their feelings toward each other?

Exercise 4: Character Descriptions

Directions: Read the following paragraph. Then complete the exercise by placing a check next to the statements that are valid conclusions based on the passage. You may check more than one.

> At intervals a car would shoot past below and his wife's eyes would swerve suspiciously after the sound of it and then come back to rest on the newspaper full of beans in her lap. One of the things she did not approve of was automobiles. In addition to her other bad qualities, she was forever sniffing up sin. She did not smoke or dip, drink whiskey, use bad language or paint her face, and God knew some paint would have improved it, Parker thought. Her being against color, it was more remarkable that she married him. Sometimes he supposed that she had married him because she meant to save him. At other times he had a suspicion that she actually liked everything she said she didn't like. He could account for her one way or another; it was himself he could not understand.

—Excerpted from "Parker's Back" by Flannery O'Connor

_____ **1.** Parker's wife behaves as though she has strong religious convictions.

_____ **2.** Parker thinks his wife looks pretty without makeup.

_____ **3.** Parker and his wife appear to be a happily married couple.

_____ **4.** Parker thinks his wife may be a hypocrite.

_____ **5.** Parker does not know himself very well.

_____ **6.** Parker tries to avoid sinning.

FOR ANSWERS AND EXPLANATIONS, SEE PAGE 272.

Interpreting Figurative Language

Words can be defined literally: A *graveyard* is a cemetery, a place where dead people are buried. A *bomb* is an exploding weapon that causes destruction. Words can also have figurative meanings: A mail sorter works the *graveyard* shift at the post office. Theater critics say that a certain Broadway musical is a *bomb*.

According to the literal definitions of *graveyard* and *bomb*, the preceding two sentences make no sense. A mail sorter's job is unrelated to cemetery work. A musical is not a destructive weapon. *Graveyard* and *bomb* are used as figurative language—words that mean something other than their literal definitions. Let's translate both sentences into literal language—words that directly express a factual meaning:

1. A mail sorter works from midnight to 8 A.M. at the post office. (*graveyard shift*)

2. Theater critics say that a certain Broadway musical is a complete failure. *(bomb)*

Did you notice that the figurative language is more colorful and vivid than the literal language? This is because figurative language appeals to your imagination—your ability to understand the creative power of words. When you search for the figurative meaning of an expression, be aware of what the words suggest. What imaginative associations can you infer from the figurative meaning?

You use figurative language in your everyday speech. Here is an example:

Statement: "My new car is a lemon."

Literal Meaning: "My new car is a yellow, sour-tasting piece of fruit."

Figurative Meaning: "My new car is constantly breaking down."

Figures of speech often make comparisons—direct or implied—between two different things. Sometimes figurative language intentionally exaggerates or distorts the truth to emphasize a feeling or an idea.

The next two exercises will help you to build your skills in understanding the differences between literal and figurative language.

Exercise 5: Figurative Expressions

Directions: Match each figurative expression in Column A with its meaning in Column B. Write the correct letter in the blank next to each number.

	A		**B**
_____ **1.**	puppy love	a.	an outstanding athlete or performer
_____ **2.**	penny-pincher	b.	celebrate wildly
_____ **3.**	monkey business	c.	an easy target
_____ **4.**	paint the town red	d.	a teen-age romance
_____ **5.**	tear-jerker	e.	votes cast using dead people's names
_____ **6.**	hothead	f.	a sad story or performance that makes you cry
_____ **7.**	sitting duck	g.	a person with a bad temper
_____ **8.**	ghost ballots	h.	a successful song or performance
_____ **9.**	smash hit	i.	a cheap person
_____ **10.**	star	j.	foolish or playful behavior

FOR ANSWERS AND EXPLANATIONS, SEE PAGE 272.

Exercise 6: Distinguishing Between Literal and Figurative Language

Directions: Identify which of the following sentences are meant literally or figuratively. Write *L* in the blank next to the statements using literal language. Write *F* in the blank next to the statements using figurative language.

_____ **1.** On July 20, 1969, two men walked on the moon.

_____ **2.** The prizefighter kissed the canvas.

_____ **3.** I've got the blues.

_____ **4.** The lion tamer cracked his whip.

_____ **5.** A dentist was the first patient to receive an artificial heart.

_____ **6.** The horror movie was a hair-raising experience.

_____ **7.** He soft-soaped his boss.

_____ **8.** The actor Clark Gable was a lady killer.

_____ **9.** The firefighters rescued the children from the burning building.

_____ **10.** The fly was trapped in the spider web.

FOR ANSWERS AND EXPLANATIONS, SEE PAGE 272.

Figurative Language in Literature

Through figurative language, authors invent original ways of describing a subject or expressing emotions. You can experience how authors see and interpret the world by understanding their figurative language.

The figurative language used in poetry, fiction, and drama is more moving than the literal language used in newspaper articles. For example, a part of the weather forecast might say, "mostly cloudy, overcast skies." This is a factual report, directly stated.

In William Shakespeare's play *Romeo and Juliet*, a tragic love story, the playwright describes the same weather conditions in figurative language. After Romeo and Juliet have died, Shakespeare writes at the end of the play:

The sun, for sorrow, will not show its head.

Shakespeare gives the sun human qualities. The sun is unhappy and appears to be mourning the death of Romeo and Juliet. Because of its grief, "the sun will not show its head," or, in other words, will not appear in the sky. What can you infer from Shakespeare's description?

The sky is dark and overcast and the atmosphere is gloomy.

Of course, Shakespeare never told you directly. You interpreted the meaning from the figurative language. Compare Shakespeare's description to the newspaper account of the weather presented earlier. Shakespeare's words create an imaginary picture and express strong feelings. In contrast, you probably did not respond emotionally to the literal statement about the sky.

Let's look at how another author, John McPhee, uses figurative language. In the following excerpt, he describes a basketball player:

> A star is often a point-hungry gunner, whose first instinct when he gets the ball is to fire away, and whose playing creed might be condensed to "When in doubt, shoot." Another, with legs like automobile springs, is part of the group because of an unusual ability to go high for rebounds.

> —Excerpted from *A Sense of Where You Are*
> by John McPhee

In his description, McPhee makes two comparisons:

1. "A *star* is often a point-hungry *gunner*, whose first instinct when he gets the ball is to fire away"

2. "*legs* like *automobile springs*"

What do these comparisons show? The first presents an exaggerated image of a star player shooting baskets on instinct as a gunner shoots at targets on instinct. The second emphasizes the rebounding power of a basketball player's legs. Here are some suggestions for interpreting figurative language:

☐ Identify the comparisons—direct or implied.

☐ Picture in your mind the two images being compared; for example, a basketball player's legs and automobile strings.

☐ Determine the author's purpose in drawing the comparison. What is he trying to show you?

Apply these suggestions in the next exercise.

Exercise 7: Interpreting Comparisons ━━━━

Directions: Carefully read the following excerpts using figurative language. Identify the two things the author is comparing. Then interpret why the author has made the comparison. Study the example before completing the exercise.

Example: "My father is eighty-six years old and in bed. His heart, that bloody motor, is equally old and will not do certain jobs any more. It still floods his head with brainy light. But it won't let his legs carry the weight of his body around the house."

> —From "A Conversation with My Father"
> by Grace Paley

The father's heart is compared with *an old motor*.

Interpretation: (Why the author has made the comparison) *The comparison explains why the father's heart condition has confined him to his bed.*

1. "Earlier in the evening it had rained, and now icicles hung along the station-house eaves like some crystal monster's vicious teeth."
    —Excerpted from "A Tree of Night" by Truman Capote

    _____ is compared with _____.

    Interpretation: _____

    _____

2. "I feel as if I were walking a tight-rope one hundred feet over a circus audience and suddenly the rope is showing signs of breaking. . . ."
    —Excerpted from "In Dreams Begin Responsibilities"
    by Delmore Schwartz

    _____ is compared with _____.

    Interpretation: _____

    _____

3. "The lid of the left eye twitched; it was exactly as though the lid of the eye was a window shade and someone stood inside the doctor's head playing with the cord."
    —Excerpted from _Winesburg, Ohio_ by Sherwood Anderson

    _____ is compared with _____.

    Interpretation: _____

    _____

4. "The heavy noon-day sun hit him directly in the face, beating down on him like a club."
    —Excerpted from _The Day of the Locust_ by Nathanael West

    _____ is compared with _____.

    Interpretation: _____

    _____

5. "Lucy wiped the perspiration soaked wisp of hair back from her face, and gave that last-minute look around the table to see if anything was missing, like a general inspecting troops."
    —Excerpted from _All the King's Men_ by Robert Penn Warren

    _____ is compared with _____.

    Interpretation: _____

    _____

FOR ANSWERS AND EXPLANATIONS, SEE PAGE 272.

Application

On the GED Interpreting Literature and the Arts Test, you will be asked to transfer a concept from a passage to a different situation. This reading skill, called *application*, requires two steps:

1. First, you must thoroughly understand the main idea or supporting details of a passage or an excerpt.

2. Second, you must apply this information to a new context or setting.

Use this approach for inferring applications as you read the following paragraph:

> When you interview for a job you want to make a good first impression. Dressing neatly and professionally shows the interviewer that you take pride in your appearance. Therefore, use good judgment in selecting the clothes you wear on a job interview. Don't wear outfits that are too casual or flashy.

Suppose you were interviewing for an office job at a local business. Which of the following clothes should you choose to wear for the interview?

(1) a suit
(2) blue jeans and a sweater
(3) slacks and a sporty shirt

The answer is (1). You applied the advice on how to dress in the appropriate way for a job interview to a new situation. A suit is "neat and professional." Blue jeans and a sweater or slacks and a sporty shirt are both too "casual."

Another way of applying ideas is to see a concept or a situation in a different historical context. For example, Shakespeare's play *Romeo and Juliet*, written in the sixteenth century, takes place in an Italian city. The story is about two feuding families—the Montagues and the Capulets. Romeo and Juliet, who are on opposite sides of the feud, fall in love with each other. Despite their families' disapproval, they secretly marry. However, Romeo and Juliet's love is not strong enough to overcome the hatred between their families. Their relationship is doomed to end tragically.

The musical *West Side Story* applies the story of Romeo and Juliet to a modern day situation. The story takes place in New York City. Instead of feuding families, *West Side Story* is about two feuding gangs of teenagers—the Sharks and the Jets. Like Romeo and Juliet, Tony and Maria fall in love, although each associates with a rival gang. Caught in the middle of the conflict, they, too, face tragedy in the end.

For practice in inferring the applications from a passage, complete the following exercise.

Exercise 8: Inferring Applications

Directions: Read the following passage. Then answer the questions on page 49 by circling *yes* or *no*.

Vocational schools can offer sound training for young people who are not college bound and for adults interested in changing or expanding their technical or service training.

Education should be purchased as carefully as any other services, and the source of any course of study should be carefully investigated before you invest in it.

Whether it is a course in automobile mechanics, drafting, practical nursing, locksmithing, or any of the range of vocational education areas that interest you, **move carefully**. Find out whether the course you want is available from the public school system—many vocational courses are. Tuition may be minimal and the quality of instruction excellent, and courses may be offered in night school or adult education classes so that students are able to work during the day and continue their education simultaneously.

Check with your high school guidance counselor for information on public vocational schools.

Do your homework **before** you sign up with any private vocational schools. Get answers to these questions:

- Find out how many students were admitted to the school and how many actually graduated.

- Ask for names and addresses of students who graduated in the past six months. Give them a call.

- Is the school licensed by the state? Call [your state's] Department of Education.

- Is the school accredited by an agency recognized by the U.S. Office of Education, or the Council of Postsecondary Accreditation? (Don't assume that accreditation means that the school is good.)

- If you sign an installment contract for payment for the course, who holds the collection contract? Sometimes your contract is sold to a bank or a finance company, which means that if you have questions about the financial arrangements, you may have to deal with a company other than the school.

Move slowly. There is always another time, and another semester. Reputable schools have no reason to use high-pressure salespeople to solicit students. If the school representative says you must sign a contract (which may be labeled **Application for Enrollment or Enrollment Agreement**) to reserve your place in next semester's class—forget it. A reputable school will give you time to check its credentials.

—Excerpted from the *Consumer Resource Book*
by the Better Business Bureau
of Chicago and Northern Illinois, Inc.

Answer the questions below by circling *yes* or *no*. If the situation is an application of the advice given on page 48, circle *yes*. If it contradicts the advice given on page 48, circle *no*.

1. An educational counselor from a trade school tells an applicant, "We place 98 per cent of our graduates in top-paying jobs. They all have rewarding careers with the most successful companies in the city."

    Should the applicant assume that the educational counselor is telling the truth?   *yes* or *no*

2. At High-Tech, Inc., a computer training school, Sam takes a mathematical aptitude exam. According to the school's admissions representative, Sam's remarkably high test score indicates that he has the potential to become a computer programmer with an annual salary of $30,000.

    Should Sam believe that this test accurately measures his ability and predicts his possible yearly income?   *yes* or *no*

3. Theresa telephones the personnel director of Worldwide Bank, which has an impressive reputation. She asks if the bank hires graduates from Randolph Secretarial School. He replies, "Yes. We try to staff our secretarial positions with graduates from Randolph Secretarial School. Overall, these secretaries have excellent skills and easily adapt to a business environment."

    Based on the personnel director's recommendation, should Theresa consider attending this secretarial school?   *yes* or *no*

4. Felicia wants to become a lab technician. A friend of hers, Sandra, attended Medical Careers Institute and dropped out. When Felicia asked Sandra why, Sandra replied, "The teachers give too much homework. I didn't have enough time for my social life."

    Does Felicia have enough information to judge the quality of education at Medical Careers Institute?   *yes* or *no*

5. On a TV commercial, a well-dressed young man says that he graduated from Alexander Technical College. He shows the new stereo and car he just bought because he landed such a great job. He thanks the technical college for his current success.

    Should you assume that any graduate from Alexander Technical College could tell a similar success story?   *yes* or *no*

6. Cindy has just completed her first interview with the Franklin School of Commerce. The interviewer told her, "Our enrollment in the accounting program is limited to fifty students. If I were you, I'd sign the Enrollment Agreement right now. We have room for only four more students. By tomorrow, we'll probably have no openings."

    Should Cindy postpone signing the Enrollment Agreement?   *yes* or *no*

FOR ANSWERS AND EXPLANATIONS, SEE PAGE 272.

Exercise 9: Chapter Review

Directions: Read the following passages and answer the multiple-choice questions. Use the purpose question to focus your reading.

Passage 1

WHAT KIND OF PEOPLE ARE THESE CONSTRUCTION WORKERS?

They drive into town in big cars, and live in furnished rooms and drink whiskey with beer chasers, and chase women they will soon forget. They linger only a little while, only until they have built the bridge; then they are off again to another town, another bridge, linking everything but their lives.

5   They possess none of the foundation of their bridges. They are part circus, part gypsy—graceful in the air, restless on the ground; it is as if the wide-open road below lacks for them the clear direction of an eight-inch beam stretching across the sky six hundred feet above the sea.

When there are no bridges to be built, they will build skyscrapers, or
10   highways, or power dams, or anything that promises a challenge—and over-time. They will go anywhere, will drive a thousand miles all day and night to be part of a new building boom. They find boom towns irresistible. That is why they are called "the boomers."

In appearance, boomers usually are big men, or if not always big, always
15   strong, and their skin is ruddy from all the sun and wind. Some who heat rivets have charred complexions; some who drive rivets are hard of hearing; some who catch rivets in small metal cones have blisters and body burns marking each miss; some who do welding see flashes at night while they sleep. Those who connect steel have deep scars along their shins from climbing columns.
20   Many boomers have mangled hands and fingers sliced off by slipped steel. Most have taken falls and broken a limb or two. All have seen death.

They are cocky men, men of great pride, and at night they brag and build bridges in bars, and sometimes when they are turning to leave, the bartender will yell after them, "Hey, you guys, how's about clearing some steel out of
25   here?"

—Excerpted from "The Bridge" by Gay Talese

1.   The purpose of this passage is to

   (1)   explain why construction work is a rewarding career
   (2)   describe the physical appearance of construction workers
   (3)   illustrate how skyscrapers and bridges are built
   (4)   suggest that construction workers are irresponsible
   (5)   show the personalities of construction workers

2. Why does the author use the phrase "part circus, part gypsy" (lines 5–6)?

   (1) to show why construction workers like to travel
   (2) to compare the similarities of construction workers to bold acrobats and roaming people
   (3) to contrast the differences between construction workers and roving entertainers
   (4) to show that construction workers are men of great pride
   (5) to illustrate construction workers' outdoor activities

3. These construction workers are called "boomers" because

   (1) they are attracted to new building developments
   (2) they have loud and boisterous personalities
   (3) their rivets make an exploding sound
   (4) they earn extra money working overtime
   (5) their voices sound like thunder

4. Which statement best expresses the main idea of the fourth paragraph?

   (1) Welders and riveters are careless in their work.
   (2) Construction workers have strong muscles.
   (3) Construction work is a dangerous job.
   (4) Construction work requires special skills.
   (5) Construction workers are afraid of injuries and death.

5. You can infer from this excerpt that construction workers would be least likely to

   (1) flirt with women they hardly know
   (2) settle down and lead a safe, easygoing life
   (3) perform other kinds of physical labor
   (4) party wildly with friends at a bar
   (5) seek out adventures and thrilling situations

6. If these construction workers had lived in the late nineteenth century, they would probably have

   (1) built railroads
   (2) raised cattle
   (3) planted crops
   (4) sold real estate
   (5) served liquor

Passage 2

WHAT DOES THE BEHAVIOR OF CONNIE AND HER FAMILY REVEAL ABOUT THEIR PERSONALITIES?

Her name was Connie. She was fifteen and had a quick nervous giggling habit of craning her neck to glance into mirrors, or checking other people's faces to make sure her own was all right. Her mother, who noticed everything and knew everything and who hadn't much reason any longer to look at her

5   own face, always scolded Connie about it. "Stop gawking at yourself, who are
you? You think you're so pretty?" she would say. Connie would raise her
eyebrows at these familiar complaints and look right through her mother, into
a shadowy vision of herself as she was right at that moment: she knew she was
pretty and that was everything. Her mother had been pretty once too, if you
10 could believe those old snapshots in the album, but now her looks were gone
and that was why she was always after Connie.

"Why don't you keep your room clean like your sister?" How've you got
your hair fixed—what the hell stinks? Hair spray? You don't see your sister using
that junk."

15 Her sister June was twenty-four and still lived at home. She was a secretary
in the high school Connie attended, and if that wasn't bad enough—with her in
the same building—she was so plain and chunky and steady that Connie had to
hear her praised all the time by her mother and her mother's sisters. June did
this, June did that, she saved money and helped clean the house and cooked
20 and Connie couldn't do a thing, her mind was filled with trashy daydreams.
Their father was away at work most of the time and when he came home he
wanted supper and he read the newspaper at supper and after supper he went
to bed.

—Excerpted from "Where Are You Going, Where Have
You Been?" by Joyce Carol Oates

7. According to this excerpt, what emotion best describes the mother's feelings
toward Connie?

(1) jealousy
(2) embarrassment
(3) admiration
(4) sympathy
(5) concern

8. ". . . she knew she was pretty and that was everything . . ." (lines 8–9).
The author includes this remark to show that Connie

(1) wants to be a fashion model
(2) needs to attract teen-age boys
(3) is conceited about her looks
(4) is going to enter a beauty contest
(5) is afraid her beauty will fade

9. Which of the following statements best describes the mother's opinion of
June?

(1) June should get married.
(2) June should lose weight.
(3) June is kinder than Connie.
(4) June is a capable secretary.
(5) June is her favorite daughter.

10. Why does the author use the phrase "trashy daydreams" (line 20)?

   (1) to compare Connie's daydreams to her messy room
   (2) to contrast Connie's mind with a garbage can
   (3) to imply that the mother doesn't have those kinds of daydreams
   (4) to suggest that Connie's mother thinks Connie's inner thoughts are worthless
   (5) to explain why Connie doesn't enjoy housework

11. From the description of the father (lines 21-23), you can conclude that he

   (1) is irritable from working long hours
   (2) is uninvolved with his family
   (3) takes pride in supporting his family
   (4) likes to read about current events
   (5) enjoys being with his wife and daughters

12. In this passage, Connie's family is described by a fiction writer. Connie's home life could also be analyzed from the point of view of

   (1) a housekeeper
   (2) a family counselor
   (3) a hair stylist
   (4) a scientist
   (5) a historian

Passage 3

WHAT DOES A WRITER EXPERIENCE WHEN HE TELLS A STORY?

Having, from a conversation overheard or in some other way, got the tone of a tale, I was like a woman who has just become impregnated. Something was growing inside me. At night when I lay in bed I could feel the heels of the tale kicking against the walls of my body. Often as I lay thus every word of the tale
5 came to me quite clearly but when I got out of bed to write it down the words would not come.

I had constantly to seek in roads new to me. Other men had felt what I had felt, had seen what I had seen—how had they met the difficulties I faced? My father when he told his tales walked up and down the room before his audience.
10 He pushed out little experimental sentences and watched his audience narrowly. There was a dull-eyed old farmer sitting in a corner of the room. Father had his eyes on the fellow. "I'll get him," he said to himself. He watched the farmer's eyes. When the experimental sentence he had tried did not get anywhere he tried another and kept trying. Beside words he had—to help the
15 telling of his tales—the advantage of being able to act out those parts for which he could find no words. He could frown, shake his fists, smile, let a look of pain or annoyance drift over his face.

These were his advantages that I had to give up if I was to write my tales rather than tell them and how often I had cursed my fate.

—Excerpted from "On Form, Not Plot, in the Short Story"
by Sherwood Anderson

13. In lines 1–6, why does the author compare himself to a pregnant woman?

   (1) to show that he identifies with women writers
   (2) to illustrate that writers have a heavy burden to carry
   (3) to show that a story is a creative process growing inside him
   (4) to imply that he has a large belly
   (5) to show his respect for mothers and their unborn children

14. What statement best summarizes the main idea of the second paragraph?

   (1) The farmers didn't enjoy listening to the stories of the author's father.
   (2) The author's father could use gestures as well as words to capture his audience's attention.
   (3) The author's father experimented with his sentences.
   (4) The author faced many hardships during his lifetime.
   (5) The author's father should have become a professional actor.

15. Which of the following words best describes the author's feelings toward his father?

   (1) respect
   (2) resentment
   (3) boredom
   (4) shame
   (5) sympathy

16. From the final sentence, what can you conclude about the author's attitude toward writing?

   (1) He would rather write speeches than stories.
   (2) He frequently struggles over his decision to become a writer.
   (3) He regards writing as predictable and routine.
   (4) Writing offers little personal satisfaction.
   (5) He believes that writing a story has more advantages than telling it.

17. Which of the following people would most closely identify with the author's occupation?

   (1) a baby doctor
   (2) a farmer
   (3) a typist
   (4) an artist
   (5) a stage-hand

FOR ANSWERS AND EXPLANATIONS, SEE PAGE 273.

3 ANALYZING STYLE AND STRUCTURE

If you listen to the morning news on the radio, you have probably heard the daily traffic report. A newscaster, flying over the city in a helicopter, might broadcast:

> Rush hour traffic is stop and go on all major expressways. Roads are slick from last night's storm. An overturned truck on Highway 42 has caused delays. Motorists are advised to take an alternate route. Travel time from the western suburbs to downtown is about forty-five minutes.

Notice that the reporter examines certain elements, such as accidents, traffic patterns, weather, and road conditions. The traffic reporter is using the reasoning process called *analysis*. She breaks down a situation into its basic parts and then shows how each part relates to the total picture—an overview of traffic.

Similarly, handwriting experts analyze personality traits as revealed by an individual's penmanship. They study the size and shape of the letters and pay close attention to particular strokes.

The illustration on page 56 provides you with several examples of how handwriting experts analyze personality according to the way letters are formed.

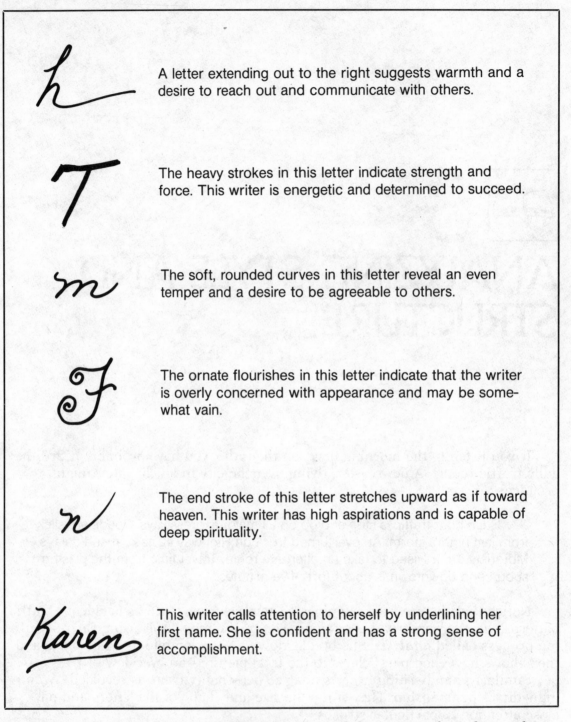

A letter extending out to the right suggests warmth and a desire to reach out and communicate with others.

The heavy strokes in this letter indicate strength and force. This writer is energetic and determined to succeed.

The soft, rounded curves in this letter reveal an even temper and a desire to be agreeable to others.

The ornate flourishes in this letter indicate that the writer is overly concerned with appearance and may be somewhat vain.

The end stroke of this letter stretches upward as if toward heaven. This writer has high aspirations and is capable of deep spirituality.

This writer calls attention to herself by underlining her first name. She is confident and has a strong sense of accomplishment.

Did you notice that the explanation beside each letter is analytical? In other words, certain characteristics of the letter are identified and then associated with specific personality traits—for example, warmth, spirituality, or confidence.

Earlier in this chapter, you observed that analysis studies the relationships of parts to the whole. As a result, you gain a more thorough understanding of the subject or the situation. In reading, analysis requires two steps:

1. Identifying the elements of style and structure in the passage

2. Determining how these elements create an overall effect

You use analysis in your everyday experiences. For instance, one important application of this skill is in looking for a new job. Before you begin planning your job search, you need to determine your qualifications, work habits, and career interests. The "Self-Evaluation Work Sheet" in the following exercise is designed to help you analyze these three areas.

Writing Exercise 1

First, answer the questions in the "Self-Evaluation Work Sheet" below and review your answers. This preliminary analysis should give you a better understanding of yourself and the type of job that would suit you. Next, use this information to write a paragraph in which you summarize your qualifications, work habits, and career interests. Use a separate sheet of paper to write your paragraph.

Self-Evaluation Work Sheet

One important aspect of choosing a position is understanding yourself. Self-evaluation can help you analyze what is important to you in the kind of work you will do and the kind of organization in which you will work.

The following are some of the things you should consider in your own self-evaluation. Your answers should be honest. They are meant to help you and should not represent a "good" or "bad" value judgment.

1. What are the things you do best? Are they related to people, data, things?

   _____ related to _____

   _____ related to _____

   _____ related to _____

2. Do you express yourself well and easily?

   Orally: Yes _____ No _____   In writing: Yes _____ No _____

3. Do you see yourself as a leader of a group or team? Yes _____ No _____

   Do you see yourself as an active participant of a group or team?

   Yes _____ No _____

   Do you prefer to work on your own? Yes _____ No _____

   Do you like supervision? Yes _____ No _____

4. Do you work well under pressure? Yes _____ No _____

   Does pressure cause you anxiety; in fact, is it difficult for you to work well under pressure?

   Yes _____ No _____

5. Do you seek responsibility? Yes _____ No _____

   Do you prefer to follow directions? Yes _____ No _____

6. Do you enjoy new ideas and situations? Yes _____ No _____

   Are you more comfortable with known routines? Yes _____ No _____

7. In your future, which of the following things are most important to you:

   a. Working for a regular salary _____

   b. Working for a commission _____

   c. Working for a combination of both _____

8. Do you want to work a regular schedule (e.g., 9 A.M. to 5 P.M.)?

   Yes _____ No _____

9. Are you willing to travel more than 50 percent of your working time?

   Yes _____ No _____

10. What kind of environment is important to you?

    a. Do you prefer to work indoors? Yes _____ No _____

    b. Do you prefer to work outdoors? Yes _____ No _____

    c. Do you prefer an urban environment (population over a million)?

       Yes _____ No _____

       Population between 100,000 to 900,000? Yes _____ No _____

    d. Do you prefer a rural setting? Yes _____ No _____

11. Do you prefer to work for a large organization? Yes _____ No _____

12. Are you free to move? Yes _____ No _____

    Are there important "others" to be considered? Yes _____ No _____

—From *Business Communications* by Michael E.
Adelstein and W. Keats Sparrow

ANSWERS WILL VARY.

Style

You have probably heard the term *style* used in various contexts. For instance, clothing designers create styles of fashion—distinctive ways of dressing. Designers believe that people's choice of clothes makes a fashion statement—a comment about their personalities and background.

Daisy Miller, the main character in Henry James's novel *Daisy Miller,* dresses according to the style of fashion that was popular in the mid-1870s:

She was dressed in white muslin, with a hundred frills and flounces, and knots of pale colored ribbon. She was bare-headed; but she balanced in her hand a large parasol with a deep border of embroidery . . .

—Excerpted from *Daisy Miller* by Henry James

Based on this description, you can make inferences about the historical setting of the story.

The term style is also used to describe a musician's performance. For example, Ray Charles, a jazz musician, rearranged the musical score of Rodgers and Hammerstein's song "Oh, What a Beautiful Morning," from the Broadway musical *Oklahoma!* Ray Charles's style—the way he performs and sings—contrasts sharply to the style used in the original Broadway musical.

Styles of writing vary as much as styles of fashion and musical performance. Because each author's personality and talents are unique, the style of a written passage is highly individual. How is this individuality achieved? The author's craft—her skills in expressing herself through language—results in a distinctive style. In this section you will learn to analyze two elements that affect an author's style:

1. Diction

2. Tone

Diction

Before an author begins writing, he might ask himself the following questions:

- What is my purpose for writing? To persuade? To inform? To entertain?

- What is my topic?

- Who is my audience?

- What response do I want from my readers?

The answers to these questions affect the author's *diction*—the words he selects to express himself. Diction, or word choice, characterizes an author's writing style.

The following paragraph illustrates different styles of diction. What do you observe about the ways that the scientist, the engineer, the foreman, and the salesman use language? As you read, notice that their statements are related to the function of levers.

Note the many languages within our language. The college freshman learns that "the moment of force about any specified axis is the product of the force and perpendicular distance from the axis to the line of action of the force." Viewing the same physical principle, the engineer says: "To lift a heavy weight with a lever, a man should apply his strength to the end of a long lever arm and work the weight on a short lever arm." Out on the factory floor the foreman shouts, "Shove that brick up snug under the crowbar and get a good purchase; the crate is heavy." The salesman says: "Why let your men kill themselves heaving those boxes all day long? The job's easy with this new long-handled pinch bar. With today's high wages you'll save the cost the first afternoon."

—Excerpted from "Giving Power to Words"
by Philip W. Swain

Let's closely examine these four statements and analyze the writing styles.

Types of Diction

Statement	Analysis
Scientist: "The moment of force about any specified axis is the product of the force and perpendicular distance from the axis to the line of action of the force."	This style is formal. The scientist explains how a lever works according to the principles of physics. She assumes her audience has a scientific background and can understand technical language.
Engineer: "To lift a heavy weight with a lever, a man should apply his strength to the end of a long lever arm and work the weight on a short lever arm."	This style is informal. The engineer uses simpler words to explain how to operate a lever. His message is geared toward a general audience.
Foreman: "Shove that brick up snug under the crowbar and get a good purchase; the crate is heavy."	This style is conversational. The foreman uses words and colorful expressions from everyday speech. The foreman does not scientifically explain that the crowbar is a lever. He directly tells another factory worker how to lift a crate with a crowbar.
Salesman: "Why let your men kill themselves heaving those boxes all day long? The job's easy with this new long-handled pinch bar. With today's high wages you'll save the cost the first afternoon."	This style is also conversational. The salesman's purpose, however, is to persuade factory managers to purchase his product—a crowbar.

You can analyze an author's diction as formal, informal, or conversational. A *formal style* is usually found in scholarly essays, legal documents, and technical articles. The reading level is often very challenging.

An *informal style* generally appears in magazine and newspaper articles. The author's choice of words is directed to the general reading public.

A *conversational style* imitates the way people speak. It may include slang expressions such as "nerd," "out of it," and "strung out."

Fiction writers may choose to tell an entire story in one of these three styles. However, sometimes they combine different kinds of diction. For example, they might write a character description in an informal style and a character's dialogue in a conversational style.

Here is another example that illustrates the three types of writing styles. Notice the different language used in each of the following statements.

Two police officers arrested Mr. Bowman, the motorist, for driving his automobile under the influence of alcohol. His blood alcohol content (BAC), the percentage of alcohol in his blood, was higher than .10. *(formal)*

Two police officers arrested Mr. Bowman for drunken driving. *(informal)*

Two cops threw Bowman into the slammer for driving his car while he was smashed on booze. *(conversational)*

To practice identifying various writing styles, complete the next two exercises.

Exercise 1: Analyzing Writing Style

Directions: What kinds of writing style would you probably find in each of the following examples—*formal, informal,* or *conversational?* Fill in the blank for each example with the appropriate style.

1. A letter to a close friend _____

2. A TV commercial starring football players drinking beer

_____

3. A doctor's medical report analyzing childhood diseases

_____

4. A brochure for parents on taking care of a newborn baby

_____

5. A lawyer's movie contract for a film star _____

6. A newspaper article on drug abuse in professional sports

_____

7. An advice column written by Ann Landers _____

8. A magazine article about Disneyland _____

9. An essay interpreting figurative language _____

10. A script for a cartoon show _____

11. A letter selling a new sports magazine _____

12. A political speech to Midwestern farmers _____

13. A manual on how to use a blender _____

14. A financial report analyzing unemployment trends in major U.S. cities

_____

15. Teenagers' dialogue in a Hollywood movie about runaways

_____

FOR ANSWERS AND EXPLANATIONS, SEE PAGE 273.

Exercise 2: Analyzing Authors' Diction ──────

Directions: Study the diction in the following excerpts. Identify the style as *formal, informal,* or *conversational.*

1. "It was Paul's afternoon to appear before the faculty of the Pittsburgh High School to account for his various misdemeanors. He had been suspended a week ago, and his father had called at the principal's office and confessed his perplexity about his son. Paul entered the faculty room suave and smiling."

    —Excerpted from "Paul's Case" by Willa Cather

    Style _____

2. "You see that cat inside the bar with that long fingernail, don't you? Well, he uses that nail to mark cards with. Every time I get in a game, there is somebody dealing with a long fingernail. It ain't safe!"

    —Excerpted from "Conversation on the Corner" by Langston Hughes

    Style _____

3. "Few evils are less accessible to the force of reason, or more tenacious of life and power, than long-standing prejudice. It is a moral disorder, which creates the conditions necessary to its own existence, and fortifies itself by refusing all contradiction. It paints a hateful picture according to its own diseased imagination, and distorts the features of the fancied original to suit the portrait."

    —Excerpted from "The Color Line" by Frederick Douglass

    Style _____

4. "Jack is wandering around town, not knowing what to do. His girlfriend is babysitting at the Tuckers', and later, when she's got the kids in bed, maybe he'll drop over there. Sometimes he watches TV with her when she's babysitting, it's about the only chance he gets to make out a little since he doesn't own wheels, but they have to be careful because most people don't like their sitters to have their boyfriends over."

    —Excerpted from "The Babysitter" by Robert Coover

    Style _____

5. "The saloon is the most important building in the Western. It is the only place in the story where people can be seen together time after time. It thereby functions as a meetinghouse, social center, church. More important, it is the setting for the climax of the story, the gunfight. No matter where the fight ends, it starts in the saloon."

    —Excerpted from "The Western: The Legend and the Cardboard Hero" by Peter Homans

    Style _____

6. "I stopped at a cafe in Dalhart and ordered a chicken fried steak. Only a rank degenerate would drive 1,500 miles across Texas without eating a chicken fried steak. The cafe was full of boys in football jackets, and the jukebox was playing an odious number called 'Billy Broke My Heart in Walgreen's and I Cried All the Way to Sears.'"

—Excerpted from "Dalhart" by Larry McMurtry

Style _____

7. " 'Yes, it's one mighty fine spring day, but nights still cold.'

" 'Yeh, you're right they are! Had to have a coupla blankets last night, out on the sleeping porch. Say, Sid,' Babbitt turned to Finklestein the buyer, 'got something wanta ask you about. I went out and bought me an electric cigar-lighter for the car, this noon, and—' "

—Excerpted from *Babbitt* by Sinclair Lewis

Style _____

FOR ANSWERS AND EXPLANATIONS, SEE PAGES 273-74.

Figurative Language and Style

In the chapter on inferential understanding, you learned that figures of speech often make direct or implied comparisons between two things. Figurative language suggests a meaning beyond the literal definition of the words.

When you are analyzing the diction of a passage, you should notice if the author uses figurative language. Figurative language characterizes some authors' styles. Through figures of speech, an author can more vividly convey his feelings or viewpoints.

For example, Dr. Martin Luther King uses figurative language to communicate his beliefs. He compares abstract concepts like peace, freedom, and human rights with concrete images. The introductory paragraph to his essay, "The World House," illustrates this technique:

> Some years ago a famous novelist died. Among his papers was found a list of suggested plots for future stories, the most prominently underscored being this one: "A widely separated family inherits a house in which they have to live together." This is the great new problem of mankind. We have inherited a large house, a great "world house" in which we have to live together— black and white, Easterner and Westerner, Gentile and Jew, Catholic and Protestant, Moslem and Hindu—a family unduly separated in ideas, culture and interest, who, because we can never again live apart, must learn somehow to live with each other in peace.
>
> —Excerpted from "The World House"
> by Martin Luther King, Jr.

In this excerpt, Dr. King makes two comparisons:

1. The world is like a house.

2. Mankind is like a family.

Why does he use these comparisons? Write your response on the following lines. He made these comparisons to show that:

_____

_____

_____

Perhaps you said something like this: He made these comparisons to show that people of different cultures, races, and religions must develop peaceful relationships. If you conveyed this idea, you correctly analyzed the purpose of the figurative language.

For further practice in analyzing style for figurative language, complete the next exercise.

Exercise 3: Analyzing Figurative Language

Directions: The following excerpt is from Dr. King's famous speech, "I Have a Dream." Carefully read the speech. Then complete the exercise and answer the multiple-choice questions.

> In a sense we have come to our nation's capital to cash a check. When the architects of our republic wrote the magnificent words of the Constitution and the Declaration of Independence, they were signing a promissory note to which every American was to fall heir. This note was a promise that all men would be
> 5   guaranteed the unalienable rights of life, liberty, and the pursuit of happiness.
>   It is obvious today that America has defaulted on this promissory note insofar as her citizens of color are concerned. Instead of honoring this sacred obligation, America has given the Negro people a bad check, a check which has come back marked "insufficient funds." But we refuse to believe that the bank
> 10 of justice is bankrupt. We refuse to believe that there are insufficient funds in the great vaults of opportunity of this nation. So we have come to cash this check— a check that will give us upon demand the riches of freedom and the security of justice.

> —Excerpted from "I Have A Dream"
> by Martin Luther King, Jr.

1.   List five words in this passage referring to money.

_____   _____

_____   _____

_____

2. The purpose of this passage is to

   (1) persuade the government to give money to minorities
   (2) explain that America denies black people their freedom
   (3) demonstrate how to balance a checkbook
   (4) call for the reform of the federal banking system
   (5) criticize the Declaration of Independence

3. Dr. King compares the denial of civil rights with a bad check. Why is this comparison effective?

   (1) The justice system has financial problems.
   (2) The writers of the Constitution broke their promise.
   (3) Most people realize that a bad check is worthless.
   (4) Life, liberty, and the pursuit of happiness are expensive privileges.
   (5) This nation can't afford to offer equal opportunity to all Americans.

FOR ANSWERS AND EXPLANATIONS, SEE PAGE 274.

Tone

You have probably heard the expression "tone of voice." If you told a friend, "I don't like your tone of voice," you were annoyed by the person's manner of speaking. You were reacting to the sound of the spoken words.

In your daily conversations, you make inferences about people's attitudes based on their speech—their choice of words or the loudness of their voices.

Imagine you are observing the following situation. A customer in a restaurant is dissatisfied with his meal. The steak he ordered is too tough to eat. The way he phrases his complaint to the waiter would reveal his attitude. How would you describe the tone of each of these remarks?

"Would you please return the steak to the kitchen? Tell the chef that this cut of beef is too tough to eat."

"I refuse to pay for this steak dinner! How do you expect me to eat food that I can't chew? Let me see the restaurant manager. Now!"

"What animal did this steak come from? Only a power saw could cut through this meat!"

Let's analyze the tone expressed in each complaint.

The first statement sounds courteous. The word "please" shows politeness.

The second statement reveals the customer's anger. He refuses to pay for his meal and demands to see the restaurant manager.

The third statement is sarcastic. By making a nasty joke about the food, the customer indirectly conveys his feelings. He does not expect the waiter to interpret the words literally.

A person's tone of voice may be described in several ways, and below are some examples. Add some of your own examples in the spaces provided.

friendly   phony   serious
sincere   sad   happy
understanding   polite   violent

_____   _____   _____

_____   _____   _____

Writing Exercise 2

Listen to a TV show or recall a recent conversation with a friend. Pay close attention to the person's tone of voice. On a separate sheet of paper, record three statements that you heard and indicate the attitude conveyed through the person's tone of voice.

ANSWERS WILL VARY.

Tone and Writing Style

Like tone of voice in speech, tone in writing expresses an attitude. *Tone* refers to the emotions revealed by an author's writing style. The author's tone also affects the way you respond to a reading selection.

When you analyze a passage for tone, you should ask yourself the following questions:

☐ After reading the passage, what is my overall reaction?

☐ What topic is the author discussing?

☐ How does the author feel about the topic?

☐ What language or descriptive details in the passage reveal the author's attitude?

Consider these questions as you read the newspaper article in the next example.

> For more than half an hour 38 respectable, law-abiding citizens in Queens watched a killer stalk and stab a woman in three separate attacks in Kew Gardens.
>
> Twice the sound of their voices and the sudden glow of their bedroom lights interrupted him and frightened him off. Each time he returned, sought her out and stabbed her again. Not one person telephoned the police during the assault; one witness called after the woman was dead.
>
> That was two weeks ago today. But Assistant Chief Inspector Frederick M. Lussen, in charge of the borough's detectives and a veteran of 25 years of homicide investigations, is still shocked.
>
> He can give a matter-of-fact recitation of many murders. But the Kew Gardens slaying baffles him—not because it is a murder, but because the "good people" failed to call the police.
>
> "As we have reconstructed the crime," he said, "the assailant had three chances to kill this woman during a 35-minute period. He returned twice to

complete the job. If we had been called when he first attacked, the woman might not be dead now."

—Excerpted from "37 Who Saw Murder Didn't Call the
Police" by Martin Gansberg

What was your initial response to the account of the crime? Like the inspector, were you also shocked that thirty-seven "good people" witnessed a stabbing and didn't call the police? Although the journalist does not directly tell you his feelings, you can infer his attitude toward the news story. What phrases from the article reveal the journalist's critical attitude toward the witnesses? Write your responses on the following lines.

_____

_____

_____

Did your answers include some of the following phrases?

☐ "respectable, law-abiding citizens"

☐ "good people"

☐ "not one person telephoned the police"

If so, you inferred the critical tone of the article from the journalist's choice of words.

In the next exercise, you will apply your skills in analyzing tone.

Exercise 4: Analyzing Tone

Directions: Study each of the following excerpts. Then circle the word on the right that best describes the tone.

1. "I am the whistler. And I know many things, for I
   walk by night. I know many strange tales hidden in
   the hearts of men and women who have stepped in
   the shadows. Yes . . . I know the nameless terrors of
   which they dare not speak."
      —Excerpted from the radio show "The Shadow"

   threatening
   silly
   joyful
   rude

2. "Fifteen. What a weird age to be male. Most of us
   have forgotten about it, or have idealized it. But
   when you are fifteen . . . well, things tend to be less
   than perfect.
      "You can't drive. You are only a freshman in
   high school. The girls your age look older than you
   and go out with upperclassmen who have cars. You
   probably don't shave. You have nothing to do on
   weekends.
      —Excerpted from "Fifteen" by Bob Greene

   serious
   nasty
   funny
   grim

3. "About five o'clock our procession of three cars   somber
    reached the cemetery and stopped in a thick drizzle   disrespectful
    beside the gate—first a motor hearse, horribly black   insincere
    and wet, then Mr. Gatz and the minister and I in the   peaceful
    limousine, and a little later four or five servants and
    the postman from West Egg, in Gatsby's station
    wagon, all wet to the skin."
                        —Excerpted from *The Great Gatsby*
                            by F. Scott Fitzgerald

4. These devils will afflict the damned in two ways, by   sarcastic
    their presence and by their reproaches. We can have   mysterious
    no idea how horrible these devils are. Saint   friendly
    Catherine of Siena once saw a devil and she has   scary
    written that, rather than look again for one single
    instant on such a frightful monster, she would
    prefer to walk until the end of her life along a track
    of red coals.
                        —Excerpted from *A Portrait of the Artist*
                            as a Young Man by James Joyce

FOR ANSWERS AND EXPLANATIONS, SEE PAGE 274.

Structure

Study the four designs in the accompanying illustration. Which designs are arranged in an organized pattern?

DESIGN 1   DESIGN 2

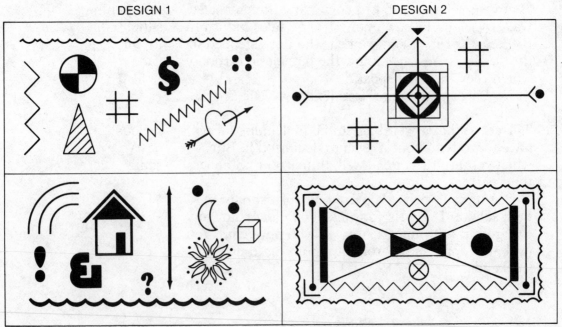

DESIGN 3   DESIGN 4

If you said Design 2 and Design 4, you were correct. The marks are grouped together to form an organized pattern. Therefore, you can see a particular structure in the design.

Similarly, authors structure their writing to make their ideas clear to the reader. *Structure* refers to the methods authors use to organize their message.

Depending on the author's topic and purpose, he devises a plan to order his information. In the following excerpt, a journalist discusses the problem of reporting the assassination of President John F. Kennedy:

> At first no one knew what happened, or how, or where, much less why. Gradually, bits and pieces began to fall together and within two hours a reasonably coherent version of the story began to be possible. Even now, however, I know no reporter who was there who has a clear and orderly picture of that surrealistic afternoon; it is still a matter of bits and pieces thrown hastily into something like a whole.

> —Excerpted from "The Assassination" by Tom Wicker

According to this paragraph, a reporter's job was to make sense of an event that seemed disordered and confused. To accomplish this task, he used the process of analysis. He had to assemble "bits and pieces" to form a "whole"—a complete version of the story that the American public would understand.

The following newspaper account by the same author presents a "clear and orderly picture" of that story:

> DALLAS, Nov. 22—President John Fitzgerald Kennedy was shot and killed by an assassin today.
>
> He died of a wound in the brain caused by a rifle bullet that was fired at him as he was riding through downtown Dallas in a motorcade.
>
> Vice President Lyndon Baines Johnson, who was riding in the third car behind Mr. Kennedy's, was sworn in as the 36th President of the United States 99 minutes after Mr. Kennedy's death.
>
> Mr. Johnson is 55 years old; Mr. Kennedy was 46.
>
> Shortly after the assassination, Lee H. Oswald, who once defected to the Soviet Union and who has been active in the Fair Play for Cuba Committee, was arrested by the Dallas police. Tonight he was accused of the killing.

> —Excerpted from "Kennedy is Killed by Sniper as He
> Rides in Car in Dallas" by Tom Wicker

You probably found this article easy to understand because the reporter structured the information. The first sentence introduces the main idea—the assassination of President Kennedy. The remaining sentences summarize the most important facts relating to this event.

The next section of this chapter will help you to analyze the structure of passages. You will learn

☐ The ways an author arranges information

☐ How the arrangement or organization reveals the author's purpose

You will study four methods of organization:

☐ Time order

☐ Classification

☐ Comparison and contrast

☐ Cause and effect

Time Order

To prepare a frozen TV dinner, you follow the instructions on the package:

1. Preheat oven to 375 degrees.

2. Remove foil wrapping from tray.

3. Cook for 35–40 minutes.

These step-by-step directions illustrate a method of organization called ***time order***. If the author's purpose is to explain a process or an event, he will often use this structure. He arranges the information according to a sequence—a related series of actions.

For example, Ernest Hemingway, like many other fiction writers, uses time order in describing how an incident occurs:

> Nick laid the bottle full of jumping grasshoppers against a pine trunk. Rapidly he mixed some buckwheat flour with water and stirred it smooth, one cup of flour, one cup of water. He put a handful of coffee in the pot and dipped a lump of grease out of a can and slid it sputtering across the hot skillet. On the smoking skillet he poured smoothly the buckwheat batter. It spread like lava, the grease spitting sharply. Around the edges the buckwheat cake began to firm, then brown, then crisp. The surface was bubbling slowly to porousness. Nick pushed under the browned undersurface with a fresh pine chip. He shook the skillet sideways and the cake was loose on the surface. I won't try to flop it, he thought. He slid the chip of clean wood all the way under the cake, and flopped it over onto its face. It sputtered in the pan.
>
> When it was cooked Nick regreased the skillet. He used all the batter. It made another big flapjack and one smaller one.
>
> —Excerpted from "Big Two-Hearted River"
> by Ernest Hemingway

In the preceding passage, Hemingway shows you how Nick, a camper, cooks breakfast. Did you clearly understand the stages in this process? Did you notice that each action and movement happens in an ordered sequence? If you answered *yes* to these questions, you correctly analyzed the structure of this excerpt.

In the next exercise, you will apply what you have just learned about analyzing time order.

Exercise 5: Analyzing Time Order

Directions: The following passage describes how a young man shines his customer's shoes. As you read, notice the order in which he explains this process. Then complete the exercise.

When I got a customer, we both played our roles. The customer, tall and aloof, smiled, "Gimme a shine, kid," and I replied, "*Sí, señor*, sir, I'll give you one that you'll have to put sunglasses on to eat the bright down."

My knees grinding against the gritty sidewalk, I adopted a serious, businesslike air. Carefully, but confidently, I snaked out my rags, polish, and brushes. I gave my cool breeze customer the treatment. I rolled his pants cuff up—"That'll keep shoe polish off"—straightened his socks, patted his shoe, assured him he was in good hands, and loosened and retied his shoes. Then I wiped my nose with a delicate finger, picked up my shoe brush, and scrunched away the first hard crust of dirt. I opened my bottle of black shoe cleaner—dab, rub in, wipe off, pat the shoe down. Then I opened my can of polish—dab on with three fingers, pat-a-pid, pat-a-pid. He's not looking—spit on the shoe, more polish, let it dry, tap the bottom of his sole, smile up at Mr. Big Tip (you hope), "Next, sir."

I repeated the process on the other shoe, then picked up my brush and rubbed the bristles very hard against the palm of my hand, scientific-like, to warm the brush hairs up so they would melt the black shoe wax and give a cool unlumpy shine. I peeked out of the corner of my eye to see if Mr. Big Tip was watching my modern shoeshine methods. The bum *was* looking. I hadn't touched his shoe, forcing him to look.

The shoe began to gleam dully—more spit, more polish, more brush, little more spit, little more polish, and a lotta rag. I repeated on the other shoe. As Mr. Big Tip started digging in his pocket, I prepared for the climax of my performance. Just as he finished saying, "Damn nice shine, kid," I said, "Oh, I ain't finished, sir. I got a special service," and I plunged my wax-covered fingers into a dark corner of my shoe box and brought out a bottle of "Special shoe lanolin cream for better preservation of leather."

I applied a dab, a tiny dab, pausing long enough to say very confidently, "You can't put on too much or it'll spoil the shine. It gotta be just right." Then I grabbed the shoe rag firmly, like a maestro with a baton, and hummed a rhythm with it, slapping out a beat on the shoes. A final swish here and there, and *mira!*—finished. Sweating from the effort of my creation, I slowly rose from my knees, bent from the strain, my hand casually extended, palm flat up, and murmured, "Fifteen cents, sir," with a look that said, "But it's worth much more, don't you think?" Mr. Big Tip dropped a quarter and a nickel into the offering plate, and I said, "Thanks a mil, sir," thinking, *Take it cool*, as I cast a watchful eye at his retreating back.

—Excerpted from *Down These Mean Streets*
by Piri Thomas

In the following list are the steps the young man uses in shining shoes. However, the steps are arranged in a jumbled order. Rearrange the steps in the order that they appear in the passage. Number the steps 1 through 9 to show the correct sequence.

_____ Dabs some polish on the shoe

_____ Rubs in the cleaner and wipes it off

_____ Brushes the shoes until they're shiny

_____ Takes out the rags, polish, and brushes

_____ Applies lanolin cream to preserve the shoe leather

_____ Opens the bottle of black shoe cleaner

_____ Opens the can of polish

_____ Repeats the process on the other shoe

_____ Lets the shoe dry

FOR ANSWERS AND EXPLANATIONS, SEE PAGE 274.

Writing Exercise 3

On a separate sheet of paper, explain a simple step-by-step process that you perform frequently—for example, a job responsibility, a household chore, a sport, or a hobby. Identify the topic, and then list the steps in their proper sequence.

ANSWERS WILL VARY.

Classification

When you go to a new shopping mall, you probably check the store directory. The directory lists the stores under titles describing types of merchandise. For example:

Men's Apparel
Women's Apparel
Men's and Women's Apparel
Children's Apparel
Shoes
Jewelry
Books and Cards
Plants and Flowers
Food Specialties and Candies
Home Furnishings and Accessories
Music, Records, and Home Entertainment
Restaurants

As you know, these categories help you to plan your shopping. Sorting things, people, or ideas into categories is called *classification*. The following chart on the zodiac uses this method of organization. Notice that the information is grouped into four categories: sun sign, dates, symbol, and element.

The Zodiac

Sun Sign	Dates	Symbol	Element
Aries	March 21–April 20	Ram	Fire
Taurus	April 21–May 20	Bull	Earth
Gemini	May 21–June 20	Twins	Air
Cancer	June 21–July 22	Crab	Water
Leo	July 23–August 22	Lion	Fire
Virgo	August 23–September 22	Virgin	Earth
Libra	September 23–October 22	Scales	Air
Scorpio	October 23–November 22	Scorpion	Water
Sagittarius	November 23–December 21	Archer	Fire
Capricorn	December 22–January 20	Goat	Earth
Aquarius	January 21–February 19	Water-bearer	Air
Pisces	February 20–March 20	Fish	Water

Based on this chart, rearrange the information on the zodiac according to these categories:

Signs Related to Fire
_____
_____
_____

Signs Related to Earth
_____
_____
_____

Signs Related to Air
_____
_____
_____

Signs Related to Water
_____
_____
_____

Did you correctly classify the sun signs? Here are the answers:

- fire signs: Aries, Leo, Sagittarius
- earth signs: Taurus, Virgo, Capricorn
- air signs: Gemini, Libra, Aquarius
- water signs: Cancer, Scorpio, Pisces

Writing Exercise 4

Take an informal poll of at least three friends or family members. Ask each person the following questions:

☐ What is your astrological sign?

☐ Do you believe that your astrological sign influences your personality? Why or why not?

☐ How often do you read your horoscope?

Write up the results of your poll in paragraph form.

ANSWERS WILL VARY.

Authors use classification to structure their writing when they analyze a topic according to categories. For instance, a music critic analyzing popular music might divide the topic into the following categories: (1) blues, (2) jazz, (3) rock 'n' roll, and (4) country western. A literary scholar classifies Shakespeare's plays as comedies, tragedies, and histories.

Exercise 6: Analyzing Categories

Directions: As you read the following passage, notice the categories of information. Then complete the exercise.

The kind of vehicle you drive reveals your personality, say behavior experts.

"Surveys have shown a direct relationship between automobiles and personality," said California psychologist Dr. Stephen Brown.

Here are the personality traits revealed by different kinds of "wheels," according to Dr. Brown and New York psychiatrist Dr. Emory Breitner.

Subcompact: These drivers like to be in control, and it's easy to be in control of a tiny subcompact. They're frugal, pragmatic people who are in a hurry. Subcompact owners don't want to be bogged down by a big car—with payments to match.

Mid-size or Compact: Reserved and conservative, these drivers rarely make moves without considerable thought. They're sensitive and emotional—but never foolish. They don't gamble, they check things out, work hard and are honest to a fault. These drivers like to blend in, not make waves.

Full-size: The drivers of these giants like to do everything in a big way. They're ambitious, desire money and material goods—and are literally driven to success.

They like big homes—and if they throw a party, they want it to be an all-out affair with people singing, eating and having a ball. They aim for important jobs, and can't stand a cramped office or a tiny car that cramps their style.

Station Wagon: Family comes first for these people. They're good neighbors, very friendly, enjoy children and animals, and will always try to help you out if you have a problem. Image isn't important. They just want to use their station wagon to enjoy life.

Jeep: These drivers are trailblazers who love adventure. They enjoy striking out on their own, and don't mind questioning authority. They're practical, energetic survivors who like to win under tough conditions, and work best when they can make their own rules.

Convertible: The top's up one day, and down the next. These drivers are exactly like their car—changing from day to day. Convertible owners are impulsive, quick-witted and restless. But they're excellent in communicating ideas and love to shine on short-term projects—jobs where they can see instant results. They love art, music and creative activities.

Pickup Truck: These people are ready to tackle any job. They have a determined, fighting spirit, and a do-it-yourself attitude that makes them self-sufficient. They're forceful, opinionated, and like to pitch right in and get a job done.

—Excerpted from "Type of Vehicle You Drive Reveals Your Personality" by Byron Lutz

Column 1 lists categories of cars. Column 2 lists personality traits. Match the personality trait associated with the type of car by writing the correct letter in front of each number.

Column 1	Column 2
_____ **1.** Subcompact	a. is restless and changeable
_____ **2.** Mid-size or compact	b. desires money and success
_____ **3.** Full-size	c. completes a job and is self-sufficient
_____ **4.** Station wagon	d. likes to control situations
_____ **5.** Jeep	e. loves adventure
_____ **6.** Convertible	f. is reserved and sensitive
_____ **7.** Pickup truck	g. values family

FOR ANSWERS AND EXPLANATIONS, SEE PAGE 274.

Comparison and Contrast

Suppose you wanted to move into a new apartment. After looking at several apartments, you found two that you liked. Before you chose which apartment to rent, you would probably evaluate certain features of each apartment:

Features	Apartment #1	Apartment #2
Monthly rent	$390.00	$410.00
Location and neighborhood	Fair	Good
Amount of space	5 rooms/1 bedroom	4 rooms/1 bedroom
Condition of appliances	Reconditioned	New
Maintenance	Good	Fair

Comparing and contrasting Apartment #1 with Apartment #2 helps you to make your final decision. This reasoning process can show you why you prefer either the first or the second apartment.

Authors use **comparison and contrast** as a method of organization when their purpose is

1. to judge two different things, or

2. to illustrate the similarities and differences between two topics

For example, a sports writer would predict the likely winner of the World Series by comparing and contrasting the two baseball teams. A movie critic might analyze the similarities and differences between Alice Walker's novel *The Color Purple* and the film version.

In the following writing exercise, you will structure your information using the comparison-and-contrast method. Then in Exercise 7 you will analyze the structure of a passage that compares and contrasts two topics.

Writing Exercise 5

Compare and contrast yourself with a close friend. How are your backgrounds, personalities, and physical appearance similar? How are they different? List some of these similarities and differences on a separate sheet of paper.

ANSWERS WILL VARY.

Exercise 7: Comparisons and Contrasts

Directions: In the following passage, an imaginary psychologist named Dr. Applebaum discusses his opinion of television shows. Read the excerpt carefully and complete the exercises.

"Now," said Applebaum, "have you ever said to a taxi driver, 'Follow that car and don't lose him'?"

"Not really."

"Well, if you had, the driver would have told you to blow it out your ear. No taxi driver is in a mood to follow another car because that means he's going to get involved. But on TV every cabdriver looks as if he'd like nothing better to do than to drive 90 miles an hour through a rain-swept street trying to keep up with a carful of hoods. And the worst thing is that the kids believe it."

"What else have you discovered?"

"Kids have a perverted sense of what emergency wards of hospitals are really like. On TV shows they take a kid to an emergency ward and four doctors come rushing down to bandage his leg. In a real life situation the kid would be sitting on the bench for two hours before he even saw an intern. On TV there always happens to be a hospital bed available when a kid needs it. What the kids in this country don't know is that sometimes you have to wait three days to get a hospital bed and then you have to put a cash deposit of $500 down before they give it to you."

—Excerpted from "Unreality of TV" by Art Buchwald

1. The purpose of this passage is to compare and contrast

    _____ with _____.

2. In paragraph 3, _____ is compared and contrasted with

    _____.

3. In paragraph 5, _____ is compared and contrasted with

    _____.

4. According to this excerpt, what can you conclude about Dr. Applebaum's opinion of television shows?

    _____

    _____

FOR ANSWERS AND EXPLANATIONS, SEE PAGE 274.

Cause and Effect

People who are confronted with a new or demanding situation often experience stress—a feeling of being under pressure or strain. Listed here are situations that cause stress:

Common Causes of Stress

marriage	divorce or separation
job promotion	losing a job
moving into a new home	becoming a parent
illness	changing careers
death of a loved one	returning to school

People who find themselves in one of these situations may experience some of the following symptoms:

Typical Effects of Stress

depression	fatigue
irritability	indigestion
inability to concentrate	nightmares
loss of appetite or overeating	increased smoking
inability to sleep	increased drinking

You can determine the connection between stressful situations and their possible consequences by using a method of analysis called *cause and effect*. For example, suppose you just became a parent. Since the birth of your baby, you notice that you tire easily but have problems falling asleep. By analyzing the cause-and-effect relationship, you can understand your reaction to your new role of mother or father.

The following diagram illustrates a stress-producing situation (becoming a parent) which results in two effects (fatigue and inability to sleep).

Becoming a parent *(cause)* ———→ fatigue *(effect)*
———→ inability to sleep *(effect)*

From your own experience, identify a stress-producing situation. How did this situation affect you emotionally or physically? On the lines in the next diagram, write the cause and one or two effects.

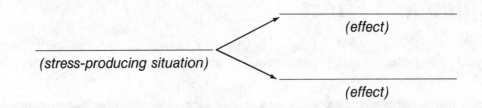

_____ *(effect)*

(stress-producing situation)

_____ *(effect)*

When an author analyzes the causes and effects of a topic, she answers two questions:

1. Why does a situation occur? *(causes)*

2. What are the results or reactions? *(effects)*

For instance, in the essay "Who's Afraid of Math and Why?" Sheila Tobias divides her topic into reasons and results. She explains why some individuals have problems learning math and how this affects their academic performance and career choices.

Sometimes authors focus on either the causes or the effects. For example, you might read a magazine article that discusses how divorce affects men and women (effects). In contrast, another article may analyze the reasons why marriages end in divorce (causes).

Analyzing Cause-and-Effect Relationships

In the following dialogue from D. H. Lawrence's short story, "The Rocking-Horse Winner," the mother explains a cause-and-effect relationship to her son:

"Oh!" said the boy. "Then what is luck, mother?"
"It's what causes you to have money. If you're lucky you have money. That's why it's better to be born lucky than rich. If you're rich, you may lose your money. But if you're lucky, you will always get more money."

—Excerpted from "The Rocking-Horse Winner"
by D. H. Lawrence

Can you identify the cause-and-effect relationship?

The cause, _____, results in _____.

If you said that *luck* (the cause) results in *money* (the effect), you were right.

For practice in analyzing the cause and effect of an event read this excerpt from the folk ballad, "Frankie and Johnny." (Frankie is the woman's name.)

> Frankie went down to the hotel, looked in the window so high;
> There she saw her lovin' Johnny makin' love to Nellie Bly.
> He was her man, but he was doin' her wrong.
>
> Frankie threw back her kimono, took out that old forty-four.
> Root-a-toot-toot three times she shot, right through the hotel door.
> She was after her man who was doin' her wrong.
>
> Johnny grabbed off his Stetson, cried, "O Lord, Frankie, don't shoot!"
> But Frankie put her finger on the trigger, and the gun went root-a-toot-toot.
> He was her man, but she shot him down.

Now answer the following questions:

1. What crime did Frankie commit? _____

    _____

2. What was her motive for committing the crime? _____

    _____

Here are the correct responses: **1.** Frankie shot her boyfriend Johnny *(effect)*. **2.** She shot him because he was cheating on her. She caught him "makin' love" to another woman, Nellie Bly *(cause)*.

For additional practice in analyzing cause-and-effect relationships, complete the next exercise.

Exercise 8: Cause-and-Effect Relationships ━━━━━

Directions: In the following excerpt, Huck Finn describes the way he reacts to a certain situation. As you read the passage, identify the cause-and-effect relationship. Then answer the multiple-choice questions.

> Then away out in the woods I heard that kind of a sound that a ghost makes when it wants to tell about something that's on its mind and can't make itself understood, and so can't rest easy in its grave, and has to go about that way every night grieving. I got so downhearted and scared I did wish I had some company. Pretty soon a spider went crawling up my shoulder, and I flipped it off and it lit in the candle; and before I could budge it was all shriveled up. I didn't need anybody to tell me that that was an awful bad sign and would fetch me some bad luck, so I was scared and most shook the clothes off of me. I got up and turned around in my tracks three times and crossed my breast every

time; and then I tied up a little lock of my hair with a thread to keep witches away. But I hadn't no confidence. You do that when you've lost a horseshoe that you've found, instead of nailing it up over the door, but I hadn't ever heard anybody say it was any way to keep off bad luck when you'd killed a spider.

—Excerpted from *Huckleberry Finn* by Mark Twain

1. According to Huck Finn, which of the following actions causes bad luck?

    (1) nailing a horseshoe
    (2) lighting a candle
    (3) hearing ghostly sounds
    (4) killing a spider
    (5) keeping witches away

2. Which of the following words best describes Huck's immediate reaction to the sign of bad luck?

    (1) confident
    (2) calm
    (3) miserable
    (4) scared
    (5) irritable

FOR ANSWERS AND EXPLANATIONS, SEE PAGE 274.

★ **GED PRACTICE**★

Exercise 9: Chapter Review

Directions: Read the following passages and answer the multiple choice questions. Use the purpose question to focus your reading.

Passage 1

HOW SHOULD PEOPLE SEEK REVENGE ON A MACHINE?

The guy in front of me put his dime in the coffee machine. The cup dropped, the machine whirred, but nothing came out.

He muttered, then started to walk away looking dejected and embarrassed. That's the way many people react when a machine doesn't come through: as if
5 they have been outwitted. They feel foolish.

"Aren't you going to do anything about it?" I asked.

"What's there to do?"

What a question. If he had gone in a bar and ordered a beer, and if the bartender had taken his money but not given him a beer, he'd do something.
10 He'd yell or fight or call the police.

But he let a machine cow him.

"Kick it," I said.

"What good will that do?" he said.

"You'll feel better," I said.

15 He came back and got in position to kick it, but I stopped him.

"Not like that. You are going to kick it with your toe, but you can hurt yourself that way. Do it this way."

I stepped back and showed him the best way. You use the bottom of your foot, as if you're kicking in a bedroom door.

20 I stepped aside, and he tried it. The first time he used the ball of his foot. It was a weak effort.

"Use more of the heel," I suggested.

That did it. He gave it two good ones and the machine bounced. He has big feet.

25 "With feet like that," I told him, "you could knock over a sandwich machine."

He stepped back looking much more self-confident.

Somebody else who had been in line said: "I prefer pounding on it. I'll show you."

30 Leaning on it with his left hand, he put his forehead close to the machine, as if in deep despair. Then he pounded with his clenched fist.

"Never use the knuckles," he said, "because that hurts. Use the bottom of the fist, the way you'd pound on the table."

"Why just one fist?" someone else said. "I always use two."

35 He demonstrated, standing close to the machine, baring his teeth, and pounding with both fists, as if trying to break down a bedroom door with his hands.

Just then, another guy with a dime stepped up. Seeing us pounding on the machine, he asked: "Is it out of coffee?"

40 We told him it had shorted on a cup.

He hesitated, then said: "Sometimes it only skips one, then it works OK."

"It's your money," I told him.

He put in his dime, the cup dropped, the machine whirred, and nothing came out.

45 All he said was "Hmm," and started to walk away.

"Why don't you kick it?" I said.

He grimaced. "It's only a dime."

—Excerpted from "How to Kick a Machine"
by Mike Royko

1. The author's attitude toward the coffee machine is

    (1) neutral
    (2) fearful
    (3) angry
    (4) foolish
    (5) embarrassed

2. The writing style used in this passage would also be effective in

    (1) a presidential campaign speech
    (2) an advertisement for health insurance
    (3) a magazine article on city colleges
    (4) a job application letter
    (5) a script for a TV comedy series

3. In lines 15–21, the author's purpose is

    (1) to explain a process
    (2) to analyze causes and effects
    (3) to classify information
    (4) to contrast different events
    (5) to compare people to machines

4. Which of the following techniques does the author use to show people's reactions to the coffee machine?

    (1) summaries of complaint letters
    (2) conversations between two or more people
    (3) newspaper reports about vending machines
    (4) interviews with bartenders
    (5) a national survey of dissatisfied customers

Passage 2

HOW DOES THE AUTHOR ANALYZE TEENAGERS?

In Brooklyn you fall into one of two categories when you start growing up. The names for the categories may be different in other cities, but the categories are the same. First, there's the minority of the minority, the "ducks," or suckers. These are the kids who go to school every day. They even want to go to
5   college. Imagine that! School after high school! They don't smoke cheeb (marijuana) and they get zooted (intoxicated) after only one can of beer. They're wasting their lives for a dream that won't come true.

The ducks are usually the ones getting beat up on by the majority group— the "hard rocks." If you're a real hard rock you have no worries, no cares.
10 Getting high is as easy as breathing. You just rip off some duck. You don't bother going to school; it's not necessary. You just live with your mom until you get a job—that should be any time a job comes looking for you. Why should you bother to go look for it? Even your parents can't find work.

I guess the barrier between the ducks and the hard rocks is the barrier of
15 despair. The ducks still have hope, while the hard rocks are frustrated. They're caught in the deadly, dead-end environment and can't see a way out. Life becomes the fast life—or incredibly boring—and death becomes the death that you see and get used to every day. They don't want to hear any more promises. They believe that's just the white man's way of keeping them under control.

—Excerpted from "Ducks vs. Hard Rocks"
by Deairich Hunter

5. The author's main purpose in the passage is to

    (1) list the causes of juvenile delinquency
    (2) analyze the effects of urban crime
    (3) describe the physical appearance of city kids
    (4) compare and contrast two types of teenagers
    (5) explain the importance of a high school diploma

6. The author's attitude toward the hard rocks is

   (1) comical
   (2) overemotional
   (3) critical
   (4) unbiased
   (5) approving

7. In the passage, the author uses language from

   (1) police reports
   (2) his Brooklyn neighborhood
   (3) psychology textbooks
   (4) crime movies
   (5) newspaper articles

Passage 3

WHAT DOES THE STORYTELLER SAY ABOUT HIS CRIME?

True!—nervous—very, very dreadfully nervous I had been and am! but why
will you say that I am mad? The disease had sharpened my senses—not
destroyed—not dulled them. Above all was the sense of hearing acute. I heard
all things in the heaven and in the earth. I heard many things in hell. How, then,
5 am I mad? Hearken! and observe how healthily—how calmly I can tell you the
whole story.

It is impossible to tell how first the idea entered my brain; but once
conceived, it haunted me day and night. Object there was none. Passion there
was none. I loved the old man. He had never wronged me. He had never given
10 me insult. For his gold I had no desire. I think it was his eye! Yes, it was this! One
of his eyes resembled that of a vulture—a pale blue eye, with a film over it.
Whenever it fell upon me, my blood ran cold; and so by degrees—very
gradually—I made up my mind to take the life of the old man, and thus rid
myself of the eye forever.

15 Now this is the point. You fancy me mad. Madmen know nothing. But you
should have seen *me*. You should have seen how wisely I proceeded—with
what caution—with what foresight—with what dissimulation I went to work!

I was never kinder to the old man than during the whole week before I killed
him. And every night, about midnight, I turned the latch of his door and opened
20 it— oh so gently! And then, when I had made an opening sufficient for my head,
I put in a dark lantern, all closed, closed, so that no light shone out, and then I
thrust in my head. Oh, you would have laughed to see how cunningly I thrust
it in! I moved it slowly—very, very slowly, so that I might not disturb the old
man's sleep. It took me an hour to place my whole head within the opening so
25 far that I could see him as he lay upon his bed. Ha!—would a madman have
been so wise as this? And then, when my head was well in the room, I undid the
lantern cautiously—oh, so cautiously—cautiously (for the hinges creaked)—
and I undid it just so much that a single thin ray fell upon the vulture eye.

—Excerpted from "The Tell-Tale Heart"
by Edgar Allan Poe

8. Throughout the entire passage, the storyteller's language and manner of speaking reveal that he is

   (1) a loyal, considerate friend
   (2) a calm, gentle person
   (3) a vicious, blood-thirsty killer
   (4) disturbed by serious mental problems
   (5) insensitive to soft noises

9. The tone of the storyteller's account is

   (1) suspenseful
   (2) sympathetic
   (3) polite
   (4) nasty
   (5) dishonest

10. The details in the fourth paragraph are arranged to show

   (1) the motives for committing the crime
   (2) the similarities between the old man and his eye
   (3) the effects of crime upon society
   (4) the different types of murder weapons
   (5) the sequence of events preceding the crime

FOR ANSWERS AND EXPLANATIONS, SEE PAGE 274.

4 NONFICTION PROSE

On the GED Interpreting Literature and the Arts Test, you will be asked to read and interpret passages from *nonfiction prose*. The topics of nonfiction prose include real people, places, events, and social issues. Prose fiction, on the other hand, deals with imaginary people, events, and places that are invented by the author. The purpose of nonfiction reading selections is to present factual information or to express a viewpoint. Examples of nonfiction prose include newspaper and magazine articles, essays, speeches, biographies, and books about true experiences.

Reading Skills for Understanding Nonfiction Prose

When you study nonfiction prose, you apply all the reading skills discussed in the first three chapters of this book:

1. Understanding the literal meaning
   ☐ Identifying the directly stated main idea
   ☐ Recognizing supporting details—examples, facts, descriptions, and reasons

2. Making inferences
   ☐ Locating clues that suggest the main idea
   ☐ Drawing conclusions from supporting details
   ☐ Interpreting figurative language
   ☐ Applying information to a specific context

3. Analyzing style and structure
   ☐ Examining the effects of the language used in a passage
   ☐ Determining how and why an author organizes information

The exercises in this chapter will provide you with extensive practice in applying these reading skills. Each exercise contains a purpose question like those you'll find on the GED Interpreting Literature and the Arts Test. Use the purpose question to focus your reading.

The following reading selections are grouped according to the topics they explore—the world of work, sports and entertainment, and social issues. There are also some additional selections to give you more practice in interpreting nonfiction prose.

The World of Work

The following three excerpts explore the relationship between people and their jobs. They range from telling the experiences of an unemployed steelworker and a homemaker to informing job seekers about questions an employer legally can ask during a job interview.

Exercise 1: An Unemployed Steelworker

Directions: Carefully read the passage and answer the questions.

HOW DOES A STEELWORKER FEEL ABOUT LAYOFFS?

Jimmy Runyan is twenty-seven, he works (worked) at Wheeling Steel's Yorkville, Ohio, mill, and he says he's been laid off maybe fifty times. That, no doubt, is an exaggeration, but after a while you get too numb to count. The layoffs started in 1982, when the company began to ask the union for
5 concessions. "It was a couple weeks on and a couple weeks off," Runyan recalls. "You kind of got used to it. Sometimes you could do an interplant, go to the mill in Benwood, West Virginia, and work there. But this last time, they just shut Benwood down. Forever. That's when I figured it was going to be different. But you don't want to accept it. My wife, Joyce, is a nurse. We don't have kids.
10 We could go somewhere—maybe Canada—but it's hard. I can't explain it. You feel paralyzed."

He sat at home. He listened to records. The phone would ring—always bad news, people wanting money. "It's embarrassing, but what can I say to them? I'd get off the phone real depressed and have nothing but the four walls for

15 company—and the soaps. I get *real* depressed sometimes; not suicidal, more like wanting to take it out on someone else."

He'd take it out on the pavement, walking. He tried to think about the future, which wasn't easy. He thought a lot about the past, the decision he'd made at age seventeen to work in the mill instead of going to computer school. The mill

20 was offering about ten dollars an hour, which seemed a fortune. But he didn't take it just to blow it; he had plans. He was going to save the money and buy a music store. Now that dream was gone with his savings.

The dream hadn't seemed so important when he was working. The big thing then was the union, the Steelworkers. Jimmy had calm eyes and a hot

25 temper, great tools for a union man. He was a shop steward when he was twenty-three—he's treasurer of his local now— and it felt more like family than anything he'd ever known. The bond became deeper as times got harder and the union was blamed for all the bad things happening. "Like it was us that destroyed the steel industry and not greed," he says.

—Excerpted from "Pride Locked Out" by Joe Klein

1. How old is Jimmy Runyan? _____

2. Where did he work? _____

3. How does Jimmy Runyan feel about being unemployed?

    (1) suicidal
    (2) depressed
    (3) relieved
    (4) calm
    (5) numb

4. How old was he when he decided to work at the mill? _____

5. Initially, what did Jimmy Runyan dream of doing with the money he saved? _____

6. The passage focuses on

    (1) the personal crisis of Jimmy Runyan
    (2) the role of the labor union
    (3) the causes of the layoffs in the steel industry
    (4) the effects of unemployment on the nation's economy
    (5) the greediness of the steel industry

7. The phrase "great tools for a union man" in line 25 refers to

    (1) power-driven machinery
    (2) manipulated steelworkers
    (3) simple gadgets
    (4) personality traits
    (5) foolish employers

8. Why is the steelworkers' labor union compared with a family (lines 26–27)?

   (1) The union members fight like brothers and sisters.
   (2) Many of Jimmy Runyan's relatives belong to the union.
   (3) Deep-rooted relationships exist among union members.
   (4) The union members are married to their jobs.
   (5) The union's conflict with the steel industry resembles sons rebelling against their father.

9. Which one of the following methods does the author use in discussing unemployment in the steel industry?

   (1) an economic analysis of the problem
   (2) a steelworker's first-hand account
   (3) interviews with steel industry leaders
   (4) reports about labor negotiations
   (5) descriptions of shut-down steel mills

10. Which of the following words best describes the author's attitude toward his topic?

   (1) amused
   (2) hostile
   (3) indifferent
   (4) concerned
   (5) overemotional

11. The style of language used in this article would also be appropriate for

   (1) a biography
   (2) a political speech
   (3) a legal document
   (4) a scientific investigation
   (5) a psychology textbook

FOR ANSWERS AND EXPLANATIONS, SEE PAGE 275.

Exercise 2: A Homemaker's Experience

Directions: Carefully read the passage and answer the questions.

HOW DOES A HOMEMAKER FEEL ABOUT HER RESPONSIBILITIES?

I start my day here at five o'clock. I get up and prepare all the children's clothes. If there's shoes to shine, I do it in the morning. About seven o'clock I bathe the children. I leave my baby with the baby sitter and I go to work at the settlement house. I work until twelve o'clock. Sometimes I'll work longer if I
5   have to go to welfare and get a check for somebody. When I get back, I try to make hot food for the kids to eat. In the afternoon it's pretty well on my own. I scrub and can and cook and do whatever I have to do.

Welfare makes you feel like you're nothing. Like you're laying back and not doing anything and it's falling in your lap. But you must understand, mothers,

10 too, work. My house is clean. I've been scrubbing since this morning. You could
check my clothes, all washed and ironed. I'm home and I'm working. I am a
working mother.

A job that a woman in a house is doing is a tedious job—especially if you
want to do it right. If you do it slipshod, then it's not so bad. I'm pretty much of
15 a perfectionist. I tell my kids, hang a towel. I don't want it thrown away. That is
very hard. It's a constant game of picking up this, picking up that. And putting
this away, so the house'll be clean.

Some men work eight hours a day. There are mothers that work eleven,
twelve hours a day. We get up at night, a baby vomits, you have to be calling the
20 doctor, you have to be changing the baby. When do you get a break, really? You
don't. This is an all-around job, day and night. Why do they say it's charity?
We're working for our money. I am working for this check. It is not charity. We
are giving some kind of home to these children.

—Excerpted from *Working* by Studs Terkel

1. According to the passage, a homemaker's job is

   (1) boring
   (2) easy
   (3) meaningless
   (4) unrewarding
   (5) demanding

2. In the passage above, Jesusita Novarro, a homemaker, describes her work.
On the following lines, write three of Jesusita's household chores.

_____

_____

_____

3. How does being on welfare make Jesusita feel?

   (1) hard-working and responsible
   (2) lazy and worthless
   (3) ambitious and independent
   (4) embarrassed and ashamed
   (5) insecure and anxious

FOR ANSWERS AND EXPLANATIONS, SEE PAGE 275.

 Writing Exercise 1

Is a homemaker's work as difficult as a regular nine-to-five job? On a separate sheet of paper, state the reasons that support your answer.

ANSWERS WILL VARY.

Exercise 3: Advice to Job Seekers

Directions: Carefully read the passage and answer the questions.

WHAT JOB INTERVIEW QUESTIONS ARE CONSIDERED ILLEGAL?

Interviewers may ask you if you were ever convicted of a crime. They cannot ask if you were arrested or accused. They may inquire into your use of drugs and alcohol. They cannot ask about anything related to national origin, race, or religion. They cannot get such information through devious channels by asking questions about your relatives' citizenship or about what your name was before you changed it. Women cannot be asked for their maiden name.

Women, particularly, must understand that they cannot be asked questions about their marital status, like, "Will your relationship with men interfere with the job?" "Are you free to travel?" and "Do you have periodic health problems?" For example, employers cannot ask if a woman's family commitments (children) would prevent her from traveling. If the job requires travel, they can specify this requirement and permit a person to withdraw the application if necessary.

Questions about sexual preference (homosexuality) are not illegal, although some local jurisdictions have ruled them out.

Employers can ask questions about your character and interests.

Illegal questions place you in a peculiar position. If you refuse to answer, the interviewer may see you as resistant or uncooperative. Because it is very hard to prove discrimination, you need to have a personal policy on what you will do if you are asked a question that you need not answer. Merely complying often places you in a compromising position. Before you go to the interview, decide whether you will simply answer if asked or whether you will make a statement about why you choose not to answer. If you take the latter course, the simplest way to handle it is to say, "I would prefer not to answer that question because it is ruled out under the Equal Employment Opportunity Act." Don't confront the interviewer or appear argumentative.

—Excerpted from *Communicating in Organizations*
by Gerald M. Phillips

1. Based on the passage above, label each of the following job interview questions *legal* or *illegal*.

    (1) Were you ever convicted of a crime? _____

    (2) Were you ever arrested for shoplifting? _____

    (3) How much liquor do you drink a week? _____

    (4) Are you Italian? _____

    (5) When do you and your husband expect to start a family?

    _____

    (6) What are your religious beliefs? _____

    (7) In previous jobs, how did you get along with your co-workers?

    _____

    (8) What personal traits will help you to succeed in this position?

    _____

(9) Will your obligation to raise your children detract from your commitment to perform your job? _____

(10) Have you ever smoked marijuana? _____

2. During a job interview, Miriam Lorca, a single parent with two preschool children, is asked the following questions: "How do you intend to take care of your children if you're working from nine to five? Are you going to hire a baby-sitter or send them to a day-care center?"

Based on the passage, how should Miriam respond to this? Write your answer on the following lines.

_____

_____

FOR ANSWERS AND EXPLANATIONS, SEE PAGE 275.

Sports and Entertainment

The next four excerpts address issues relating to how people spend their free time. The selections cover a variety of topics, ranging from the disadvantages of glorifying athletics to the benefits of playing video games and watching soap operas.

Exercise 4: A Tennis Pro's Opinion

Directions: Carefully read the passage and answer the questions.

WHAT IS A PROFESSIONAL ATHLETE'S ATTITUDE TOWARD EDUCATION?

Somehow, parents must instill a desire for learning alongside the desire to be Walt Frazier. Why not start by sending black professional athletes into high schools to explain the facts of life?

5 I have often addressed high school audiences and my message is always the same: "For every hour you spend on the athletic field, spend two in the library. Even if you make it as a pro athlete, your career will be over by the time you are 35. You will need that diploma."

Have these pro athletes explain what happens if you break a leg, get a sore arm, have one bad year or don't make the cut for five or six tournaments.
10 Explain to them the star system, wherein for every star earning millions there are six or seven others making $15,000 or $20,000 or $30,000. Invite a benchwarmer or a guy who didn't make it. Ask him if he sleeps every night. Ask him whether he was graduated. Ask him what he would do if he became disabled tomorrow. Ask him where his old high school athletic buddies are.

—Excerpted from "A Black Athlete Looks at Education"
by Arthur Ashe

1. Which of the following statements best summarizes the most important message expressed in the passage?

   (1) Parents should encourage their children to learn.
   (2) The careers of most professional athletes end at age thirty-five.
   (3) Physical disabilities can ruin a professional athlete's career.
   (4) All aspiring athletes should realize the value of a high school diploma.
   (5) Only a minority of professional athletes earn amazingly high salaries.

2. According to the author's viewpoint, which of the following conclusions can you draw about the passage? If a statement supports the author's viewpoint, write *valid*. If the statement does not reflect the author's viewpoint, write *invalid*.

   (1) Most professional athletes are stupid. _____

   (2) Many high school students are shortsighted about the realities of professional sports. _____

   (3) Many high school athletes underestimate the importance of education. _____

   (4) Athletic superstars are paid too much money. _____

   (5) Some professional athletes don't sleep at night because they are studying. _____

FOR ANSWERS AND EXPLANATIONS, SEE PAGE 275.

Exercise 5: Children and Sports

Directions: Carefully read the passage and answer the questions.

WHAT HAPPENS WHEN CHILDREN PARTICIPATE IN SPORTS?

It's the worry of every parent with a child involved in sports. The call from the coach. The ride to the hospital. The cry of an injured son or daughter.

It's not just the boys who are competing in organized sports these days, and it's not just the outstanding athletes. With 20 million boys and girls
5 participating in community sports, injuries are a justifiable concern among parents, coaches and the medical community.

"The recent trend toward competitive sports participation by younger age groups," said Dr. George Shybut, codirector of Northwestern's Center for Sports Medicine, "has made us just start to realize the problems of the younger
10 athletes. An example is distance running. It used to be unheard of for children under 12 to be competing in long distance runs."

Not anymore. The youngest entrant in April's 26-mile Lake County Marathon was 7 years old.

As physicians begin to put children under the sports medicine microscope,
15 they are seeing new types of injuries among preadolescents, in numbers that have become the subject of much debate. And as they try to guide parents and

children in safe directions, they are questioning the appropriateness of sports for young children.

20   Dr. Lyle Micheli, director of sports medicine at Boston's Children's Hospital, is one of the most vocal spokesmen addressing the dangers of youth sports.

"We're seeing an absolute epidemic of injured kids," Micheli said. "I couldn't say one sport is worse than another. It depends more on how the sport is done—how much yardage the child is doing, and how he's being coached."

—Excerpted from "Too Young for Sports?"
by Jody Homer

1. Which of the following statements best summarizes the main idea of the passage?

    (1) Children should be banned from participating in all competitive sports.
    (2) Children under twelve are competing in long-distance runs.
    (3) Boys are more prone to sports injuries than girls.
    (4) Parents, coaches, and doctors are justifiably concerned about children's sports injuries.
    (5) Coaches are responsible for preventing children's sports injuries.

2. What evidence does the author use to support his ideas?

    (1) letters from concerned parents
    (2) quotations from doctors
    (3) interviews with coaches
    (4) facts from a sports encyclopedia
    (5) reactions of injured children

3. Which of the following statements best explains the meaning of "physicians begin to put children under the sports medicine microscope" (line 14)?

    (1) Doctors are using microscopes in their medical research.
    (2) Doctors have invented a microscope for examining children's sports injuries.
    (3) Microscopes magnify images of broken bones and torn muscles.
    (4) Sports injuries aren't visible to the naked eye.
    (5) Doctors are closely examining the causes of children's sports injuries.

FOR ANSWERS AND EXPLANATIONS, SEE PAGE 275.

Exercise 6: Games and Education

Directions: Carefully read the passage and answer the questions.

WHAT PURPOSE DO GAMES SERVE?
Programmed to Play

A teenager stands transfixed before a video machine. His pockets bulge with quarters, and his dinner—a room-temperature slice of pizza—sits forgotten on a paper plate. Asked what he is doing, he responds, "Nothing, just playing." His mother feels differently: "He's wasting his time," she says. "That's what he's
5   doing."

They're both wrong. The teenager is learning—and learning well.

Games are one of the most ancient and time-honored methods of educating. They are the ideal learning technology, for they have received the seal of approval of natural selection.

10 Consider the animal kingdom. Watch as two lion cubs playfully wrestle with each other in games designed to teach them the skills of survival, the craft of hunting. Watch as a house cat stalks a crumpled ball of cellophane or a dog grabs a shoe and gives it a violent, death-dealing shake. Imagine how much human children are learning as they match wits over a chess board or butt
15 heads on a football field.

In light of this, the question "Can games have educational value?" becomes absurd. It is not games but schools that are the newfangled notion, the untested fad, the violators of tradition.

Video games are fun precisely because they are so powerfully educational.
20 The learning experience from an arcade screen is direct, immediate and compelling. We play over and over because we can see our improvement with each game, because we can see that we are learning. The fact that what we learn has nothing to do with real life in no way diminishes our pleasure; we pursue learning not for practical reasons but for pure recreation.

25 Increasingly, however, games are being designed that allow players to translate what they see on a video screen into useful information about the world around them. One new game appears, at first glance, to be geared toward nothing more than amusement and action, but, in fact, is intended to provide subtle instruction in the complexities of Boolean logic. Another, called Energy
30 Czar, teaches players about the barter and trade-offs involved in contemporary energy negotiations. Even the Army is now using video technology to train soldiers in skills as diverse as equipment repair and gunnery.

Obviously, games alone are not enough. Always, teachers will be needed for guidance, for the human interaction so vital to education. Games are tools,
35 nothing more. But someday, with video systems properly integrated into the educational system, students may frolic through multiplication tables and algebra, through adverbs and prepositions, as gaily as lion cubs wrestling with each other on the plains of the Serengeti.

—by Chris Crawford*

1. What is the main question that the essay addresses?

  (1)   Do animals learn survival skills by playing games?
  (2)   Is video technology effective in training soldiers?
  (3)   Do teachers play a vital role in the learning process?
  (4)   Can games have educational value?
  (5)   Are teenagers spending too much time at the video arcades?

2. What does the game called Energy Czar teach? _____

_____

3. According to the concluding paragraph, someday video systems may teach students

   (1) animal behavior
   (2) math and grammar
   (3) human interaction
   (4) wrestling
   (5) geography

4. Which of the following would the author find most educationally useful?

   (1) memorizing grammar rules
   (2) watching TV's "Dynasty"
   (3) joining the Army
   (4) watching a Rolling Stones video
   (5) playing Scrabble

FOR ANSWERS AND EXPLANATIONS, SEE PAGES 275-76.

Writing Exercise 2

What games do you remember playing as a child? Choose one game that you played often. On a separate sheet of paper, describe the game. Explain why you enjoyed it. Then describe the skills or knowledge you gained from playing that game.

ANSWERS WILL VARY.

Exercise 7: Soap Operas

Directions: Carefully read the passage and answer the questions.

HOW DO SOAP OPERAS AFFECT TV VIEWERS?
Soap Operas: A Healthy Habit, After All?

Ever feel guilty about watching your favorite day-or-night soaps when "you really should be doing something worthwhile"? Consider this: psychologists say that watching soaps can benefit many people, provide a method of relaxation, a release from daily stresses, even a cure for loneliness. Some
5 psychotherapists even "prescribe" watching soaps to patients whose particular situation is being confronted by a show's characters. "It gives the person another way of thinking about the problem; and, in most cases, the more alternatives one has for solutions, the easier the problem will be to solve," said Mary Cassata, Ph.D., associate professor of communications at the State
10 University of New York at Buffalo.

"One of the reasons that soaps involve viewers so much is that the characters become a surrogate set of acquaintances," said Kenneth W. Haun, Ph.D., professor of psychology at Monmouth College in New Jersey, who teaches a course on soap operas. "A hundred years ago, you would have
15 tuned into your neighbors for gossip; but in today's more fragmented and alienated society, we can't do that as easily."

Unlike people, your soap opera "friends" can travel with you wherever there's a television set; and if you miss being with them one day or week, you can always catch up with them the next. This isn't to say that soap opera
20 characters should take the place of a person's real friends, but knowing they're there can be a comfort. Said Dr. Haun, "College students who are away from home for the first time report that one of the reasons they enjoy watching the soaps is that the characters are like friends from home. It makes them feel less lonely, less homesick."

25 Dr. Haun told of a New Jersey hospital in which nurses who check-in pregnant mothers ask the women if they have a favorite soap opera. If so, they try to match the woman with a roommate who watches the same show. "Usually the women stay in the hospital for days in a room with only one T.V.; and, normally, they don't talk very much. But if they watch the same soap opera,
30 they have a whole circle of friends in common."

Dr. Haun's research shows that soap opera audiences are generally about 65 percent female, 35 percent male, though the number of men viewers is steadily climbing as is the number of viewers under thirty years old. "Also, there doesn't seem to be any relationship between socio-economic levels, occupa-
35 tions, or education among those who watch soaps," said Dr. Haun. "I know bank presidents who are hooked."

"People will watch soaps for years and remember the most minute details," said Dr. Cassata. "That's because the viewers are made part of the show; they're told secrets; they know what a character is thinking; they know what a certain
40 look means. And today, the characters have become so complex, it's hard to tell the good guy from the bad guy; but that's often the way life is."

—by Laura Flynn McCarthy

1. According to the first paragraph of the passage, what are three benefits of watching soap operas?

   (1) _____

   (2) _____

   (3) _____

2. Why do college students who are away from home watch soap operas?

   (1)   to avoid doing homework
   (2)   to feel less homesick
   (3)   to develop their imaginations
   (4)   to avoid making new friends
   (5)   to escape into a fantasy world

3. With which of the following statements would the author agree?

   (1)   People who watch soap operas should feel guilty.
   (2)   Watching soap operas causes quarreling among pregnant women.
   (3)   Soap opera characters are better friends than real people are.
   (4)   Soap operas are bad because they encourage gossip.
   (5)   Soap operas are therapeutic to those who watch them.

4. Based on the passage on pages 95–96, label each of the following state-
    ments as either *true* or *false*.

    (1) Most people who watch soap operas are uneducated housewives.
    _____

    (2) Today's soap operas strictly categorize characters into two distinct
    types—"the good guys" and "the bad guys."_____

    (3) According to Mary Cassata, Ph.D., a soap opera character's way of
    solving a problem can be helpful to a member of the audience who is
    experiencing a similar problem. _____

    (4) The number of soap opera watchers under thirty is steadily
    decreasing. _____

5. Why does the author quote a psychology professor and a communications
    professor?

    (1) to demonstrate the author's high level of education
    (2) to support the author's opinion with experts' observations
    (3) to prove that the author communicates well
    (4) to show that only troubled people watch soap operas
    (5) to show that the author is a good listener

    FOR ANSWERS AND EXPLANATIONS, SEE PAGE 276.

Social Issues

The problem of missing children and the treatment of Vietnam veterans are
the subjects of the next two excerpts. They touch on issues that recently have
confronted American society.

Exercise 8: Missing Children

Directions: Carefully read the passage and answer the questions.

HOW HAS AMERICA REACTED TO THE PROBLEM OF MISSING CHILDREN?

Roger Pearson, a Detroit area teacher was walking his dog when he saw a
small boy fall off his bike. Pearson stopped to help him up, but the boy became
terrified and ran away and hid. "He was so scared of me," Pearson said, "he
didn't even take his bike with him."

5   Nancy Zimmerman of Washington, D.C. drives three miles out of her way
to shop at a store that puts her groceries in plain bags. She also buys milk in
plastic, gallon containers because the paper half gallons she used to buy all
bear the pictures of missing children. "Every morning when they eat breakfast,

my kids don't need to see pictures of children who have been separated from
10   their parents," she says. "Children feel powerless enough as it is."

America suddenly seems full of missing children. Their faces are everywhere, on grocery store bags, on TV specials, on huge corporate-sponsored
banners in children's clothing stores. Book and toy store shelves are flooded
with books and games that warn children against the "stranger danger."
15   Companies selling personal alarms, insurance policies and dental identity disks
have sprung up overnight. Safety programs have proliferated in schools
promoting the "yell and tell" message. Shopping centers host fingerprinting
campaigns.

Surely one missing child is too many, but experts who work in the field of
20   missing, sexually abused and runaway children say the avalanche of publicity
has grossly distorted the situation. Indeed, many feel that by overstating the
problem we are poisoning relations between children and adults and creating a
national paranoia that may permanently damage the psyches of our children.

—Excerpted from "Are We Filling Our Children with
Fear?" by Gini Hartzmark

1. Who is Roger Pearson? _____

2. Why does Nancy Zimmerman buy milk in plastic containers instead of paper
cartons?

    (1) Plastic is a stronger material.
    (2) Milk in plastic containers is cheaper.
    (3) Milk spoils more quickly in paper cartons.
    (4) Her grocery store doesn't sell milk in paper cartons.
    (5) Pictures of missing children don't appear on plastic cartons.

3. What conclusion does the author reach about the topic?

    (1) Because the issue of missing children is not a serious problem, publicity
        is unnecessary.
    (2) Too much publicity about the problem of missing children is damaging
        to children's mental health and their relationships with adults.
    (3) Many missing children are runaways, not kidnap victims.
    (4) Fingerprinting children makes them feel like criminals.
    (5) School safety programs effectively teach children how to avoid
        strangers.

FOR ANSWERS AND EXPLANATIONS, SEE PAGE 276.

 Writing Exercise 3

In the preceding passage you read about some tactics being used to address
the problem of missing children. Do you believe that these tactics help to resolve
the problem or do they worsen the situation? On a separate sheet of paper,
choose two of the following tactics. Then state and support your opinion on
the effectiveness of each.

1. Fingerprinting children
2. School safety programs
3. Children's pictures on milk cartons and grocery store bags
4. Television specials
5. Banners in children's stores
6. Books and games about "stranger danger"

ANSWERS WILL VARY.

Exercise 9: Treatment of Vietnam Veterans

Directions: Carefully read the passage and answer the questions.

HOW DID CHICAGO HONOR VIETNAM VETERANS?

Chicago tried to mend its fences with America's Vietnam veterans this weekend. It opened its heart and cheered them on, shook their hands, embraced them on the streets, showered them with ticker tape, bought them a beer, threw them a party in Grant Park two nights in a row and offered them
5   their city for the weekend.

An overwhelming 200,000 marchers including Vietnam veterans from across America responded to the invitation—at least 100 percent more than had been expected by the parade committee. It was one of the largest parades in Chicago history.

10   "You realize how much these men needed this when you see how many men turned up," said a woman in one of the two reviewing stands near City Hall. "Look at this. There are waves and waves of them as far as you can see. This parade goes on and on. They really needed it. Look at their faces. Just look at them."

15   "Thank you," yelled Chicagoans to the veterans and their families as they passed by. "Thank you. Thank you, Chicago," the veterans yelled back.

It was, perhaps, one of the most intimate parades Chicago has ever thrown for anyone. The veterans walked arm and arm with one another, held hands or reached out in the crowd to kiss a woman, hug a man or give a "high five" hand
20   slap to an amused but willing police officer. Parade onlookers, often fickle in Chicago, never thinned in ranks during the 4½-hour parade.

"Our unit was walking behind a woman who lost her son in Vietnam and the lady was carrying his picture," said Steve Boyer, who was a medic in Vietnam. "Everyone on the street, when they saw her and that picture, started crying.
25   Why? I guess they know they treated us bad when we came home."

The attitude of the police was more than congenial. No veteran who might be suspected of hiding a beer in his fatigue jacket pocket as he marched down LaSalle Street was pulled from the ranks.

"Man, this is their parade, and this is their day," said Larry Heise, Deering
30   District tactical officer, who was wearing his Vietnam campaign ribbons on his Chicago Police Department uniform. "Nobody greeted them at the airport, but Chicago is greeting them now. They can do what they want today. My handcuffs are staying on my belt."

A sign carried by one small military unit fit the mood of the parade and of
35   the entire weekend. It read: "There Are No Strangers Here. Only Friends We
Haven't Met."

—Excerpted from "Soldiers and a City March to the
Same Tune" by Anne Keegan

1. Why did a Chicago police officer, who was also a Vietnam veteran, say, "My
   handcuffs are staying on my belt" (lines 32–33)?

   (1)   He wants to impress the crowd with his authority.
   (2)   He doesn't intend to arrest any Vietnam veterans.
   (3)   He wants to show the crowd that he was a former prisoner of war.
   (4)   He is not on duty for the parade.
   (5)   He is prepared to restrain lawbreakers.

2. The word *intimate* in line 17 means

   (1)   important
   (2)   crowded
   (3)   military
   (4)   nonviolent
   (5)   personal

3. The phrase "mend its fences" in line 1 means

   (1)   build barriers
   (2)   improve relationships
   (3)   repair walls
   (4)   heal war injuries
   (5)   separate people

4. In the final paragraph, why does the author describe the sign carried by one
   of the military units?

   (1)   to reveal the mood of the parade
   (2)   to show the soldier's patriotism
   (3)   to explain the soldiers' attitude toward combat
   (4)   to analyze feelings about an unpopular war
   (5)   to make the reader feel guilty

5. Which of the following statements summarizes the most important message
   of the passage?

   (1)   Military parades are exciting to watch.
   (2)   Painful wartime memories should be quickly forgotten.
   (3)   Soldiers who fight in a war deserve public recognition.
   (4)   Veterans often glorify their war experiences.
   (5)   The American public didn't support U.S. involvement in Vietnam.

FOR ANSWERS AND EXPLANATIONS, SEE PAGE 276.

More on Nonfiction Prose

The following excerpts give you more practice in understanding nonfiction prose. The first selection deals with the capture of legendary criminal John Dillinger. The second is a description of an Oklahoma scene.

Exercise 10: John Dillinger's Violent End

Directions: Carefully read the passage and answer the questions.

HOW WAS A FAMOUS CRIMINAL SHOT?

John Dillinger, ace bad man of the world, got his last night—two slugs through his heart and one through his head. He was tough and he was shrewd, but wasn't as tough and shrewd as the Federals, who never close a case until the end. It took twenty-seven of them to end Dillinger's career, and their

5   strength came out of his weakness—a woman.

Dillinger was put on the spot by a tip-off to the local bureau of the Department of Justice. It was a feminine voice that Melvin H. Purvis, head of the Chicago office, heard. He had waited long for it.

It was Sunday, but Uncle Sam doesn't observe any NRA* and works seven

10   days a week.

The voice told him that Dillinger would be at a little third-run movie house, the Biograph, last night— that he went there every night and usually got there about 7:30. It was almost 7:30 then. Purvis sent out a call for all men within reach and hustled all men on hand with him. They waited more than an hour. They

15   knew from the informer that he must come out, turn left, turn again into a dark alley where he parked his Ford-8 coupé.

Purvis himself stood at the main exit. He had men on foot and in parked inconspicuous cars strung on both sides of the alley. He was to give the signal. He had ascertained about when the feature film, *Manhattan Melodrama*, would

20   end. Tensely eying his wrist watch he stood. Then the crowd that always streams out when the main picture finishes came. Purvis had seen Dillinger when he was brought through from Arizona to Crown Point, Indiana, and his heart pounded as he saw again the face that has been studied by countless millions on the front pages of the world.

25   Purvis gave the signal. Dillinger did not see him. Public Enemy No. 1 lit a cigarette, strolled a few feet to the alley with the mass of middle-class citizens going in that direction, then wheeled left.

A Federal man, revolver in hand, stepped from behind a telegraph pole at the mouth of the passage. "Hello, John," he said, almost whispered, his voice

30   husky with the intensity of the classic melodrama. Dillinger went with lightning right hand for his gun, a .38 Colt automatic. He drew it from his trousers pocket.

But, from behind, another government agent pressed the muzzle of his service revolver against Dillinger's back and fired twice. Both bullets went through the bandit's heart.

*National Recovery Administration (NRA), a New Deal agency that, among other functions, regulated the hours of work in industry.

35   He staggered, his weapon clattered to the asphalt paving, and as he went three more shots flashed. One bullet hit the back of his head, downward, as he was falling, and came out under his eye.

Police cleared the way for the police car which was there in a few minutes. The police were there not because they were in on the capture, but because the

40   sight of so many mysterious men around the theater had scared the manager into thinking he was about to be stuck up and he had called the nearest station.

—Excerpted from "Dillinger 'Gets His' " by Jack Lait

1. The shooting occurred in

   (1) Arizona
   (2) Chicago
   (3) Indiana
   (4) New York
   (5) Washington, D.C.

2. *Manhattan Melodrama* is the title of

   (1) a play
   (2) a short story
   (3) a soap opera
   (4) a classical symphony
   (5) a movie

3. The author's style of language can be compared with

   (1) a police report
   (2) a criminal law textbook
   (3) a gangster novel
   (4) a medical diagnosis
   (5) a horror movie script

4. The following events are arranged in jumbled order. Rearrange the events in the order in which they happen in the passage. Number the sentences 1 through 6 to show the correct sequence.

_____ Purvis gave the signal to his men.

_____ Dillinger drew his gun on a Federal man.

_____ Purvis and his men were stationed around the Biograph theater.

_____ A police car arrived shortly after the shooting.

_____ Another government agent shot Dillinger in the back.

_____ A woman informer tipped off Purvis.

FOR ANSWERS AND EXPLANATIONS, SEE PAGE 276.

Exercise 11: A View of Oklahoma

Directions: Carefully read the passage and answer the questions.

WHAT DOES A PLAIN LOOK LIKE?

A single knoll rises out of the plain in Oklahoma, north and west of the Wichita range. For my people, the Kiowas, it is an old landmark, and they gave it the name Rainy Mountain. The hardest weather in the world is there. Winter brings blizzards, hot tornadic winds arise in the spring, and in the summer the
5 prairie is an anvil's edge. The grass turns brittle and brown, and it cracks beneath your feet. There are green belts along the rivers and creeks, linear groves of hickory and pecan, willow and witch hazel. At a distance in July or August the steaming foliage seems almost to writhe in fire. Great green and yellow grasshoppers are everywhere in the tall grass, popping up like corn to
10 sting the flesh, and tortoises crawl about on the red earth, going nowhere in the plenty of time. Loneliness is an aspect of the land. All things in the plain are isolate; there is no confusion of objects in the eye, but *one* hill or *one* tree or *one* man. To look upon that landscape in the early morning with the sun at your back, is to lose the sense of proportion. Your imagination comes to life, and this,
15 you think, is where Creation was begun.

—Excerpted from "The Way to Rainy Mountain"
by N. Scott Momaday

1. What is the name of the author's Indian tribe? _____

2. On the following lines, write a descriptive phrase from the passage that appeals to each of the following senses:

Sight:_____

Hearing:_____

Touch:_____

3. Why does the author state "the steaming foliage seems almost to writhe in fire" (line 8)?

(1) to emphasize the intense summer heat
(2) to suggest that forest fires are commonplace
(3) to describe the fiery sunset
(4) to explain the effects of daylight on plant growth
(5) to show that Native Americans worship the sun

4. The author's description of the plain can be compared with

(1) a weather report
(2) a map of Oklahoma
(3) a passage from the Bible
(4) a landscape painting
(5) a real estate brochure

5. You can infer that the word *knoll* (line 1) means

   (1) a hill
   (2) a landmark
   (3) a blizzard
   (4) a tornado
   (5) a prairie

FOR ANSWERS AND EXPLANATIONS, SEE PAGES 276-77.

★ **GED PRACTICE** ★

Exercise 12: Chapter Review

Directions: Read the following passages and answer the multiple-choice questions. Use each purpose question to focus your reading.

Passage 1

HOW DOES A POLICE ARTIST PERFORM HIS JOB?

Initially, Mr. Hagenlocher tries to put witnesses at ease so they trust him, rather than barging up and identifying himself as a police officer. When questioning someone, the artist tries to exact as much detail as possible about the suspect, though he can get by on remarkably few facts. As a rule, he looks
5 for five features: shape of face, hair, eyes, ears, and mouth. Distinguishing scars, birthmarks, beards, and mustaches are an artist's dream for producing a useful sketch, but they don't often crop up.

Mr. Hagenlocher always carts along 150 to 200 of the 900,000 mug shots the police force keeps. Witnesses are asked to leaf through these to try to find
10 a similar face, and then subtle changes can be made in the sketch. "You could use just one photo and work from that," Mr. Hagenlocher says. "Using that as a base, you have the witness compare the hair—is it longer or shorter?—the mouth—is it thinner or wider?—and so forth. But that's harder and takes more time. It's usually much quicker to show him a lot of photos and have them pick
15 the one that's close."

"But I remember one time," the artist goes on, "when a girl flipped through a mess of photos and finally picked one. 'That looks exactly like him,' she said, 'except the hair was longer, the mouth was wider, the eyes were further apart, the nose was smaller, and the face was rounder.' She was a big help."
20 Besides the five basic features, Mr. Hagenlocher also questions witnesses about a suspect's apparent nationality and the nature of the language he used. This can be of subtle assistance in sketching the suspect, but it can also sometimes link several sketches together. For instance, if over a short period of time three suspects are described as soft-spoken, in addition to having other
25 similar traits, then chances are they are the same person. It is also a good idea to ask a witness if a suspect resembled a famous person. Suspects have been compared to Marlon Brando, Rod Steiger, Winston Churchill, Nelson Eddy, Jack Palance, Jackie Gleason, Mick Jagger and a Greek god.

After Mr. Hagenlocher completes a sketch, he shows it to the witness or
30 witnesses for their reaction. Usually, there will be lots of minor, and sometimes
not too minor, changes to be made. When it's finished, the sketch isn't intended
to approach the polished form of a portrait. "We're just trying to narrow down
the possibilities," Mr. Hagenlocher says. "If you've just got a big nose and a thin
mouth to go with, then at least you've ruled out all the people with small noses
35 and thick mouths. There are still millions of people still in the running, but
millions have also been eliminated."

—Excerpted from "Portraits of a Cop" by N. R. Kleinfield

1. The major purpose of the entire passage is to

   (1) analyze witnesses' observations
   (2) explain the process of sketching a suspect
   (3) classify different types of suspects
   (4) compare drawing to photography
   (5) describe how witnesses remember faces

2. When Mr. Hagenlocher first meets witnesses, what does he do?

   (1) He badgers them with questions.
   (2) He emphasizes that he is a police officer.
   (3) He mistrusts their descriptions.
   (4) He makes them feel comfortable.
   (5) He evaluates their intelligence.

3. Why do witnesses examine mug shots?

   (1) to determine whether the suspect is a former convicted criminal
   (2) to find faces similar to the suspect's
   (3) to test their photographic memories
   (4) to study criminal-looking faces
   (5) to observe how criminals pose for photographs

4. Which of the following questions would Mr. Hagenlocher *not* ask a witness?

   (1) Does the suspect resemble a famous person?
   (2) What is the suspect's apparent nationality?
   (3) How does the suspect use language?
   (4) Was the suspect armed?
   (5) Does the suspect have a distinguishing birthmark?

5. Which of the following techniques does the author use to develop the topic?

   (1) the court testimony of witnesses
   (2) interviews with arrested suspects
   (3) a description of a notorious suspect
   (4) excerpts from an official police report
   (5) quotations from Mr. Hagenlocher

6. Which of the following people could most closely identify with Mr. Hagenlocher's work?

   (1) a photographer
   (2) a plastic surgeon
   (3) a portrait painter
   (4) a film director
   (5) a sculptor

Passage 2

WHAT DOES PRESIDENT KENNEDY EXPECT FROM THE AMERICAN PEOPLE?

In your hands, my fellow citizens, more than mine, will rest the final success or failure of our course. Since this country was founded, each generation of Americans has been summoned to give testimony to its national loyalty. The graves of young Americans who answered the call to service surround the
5 globe.

Now the trumpet summons us again—not as a call to bear arms, though arms we need—not as a call to battle, though embattled we are—but a call to bear the burden of a long twilight struggle, year in and year out, "rejoicing in hope, patient in tribulation"—a struggle against the common enemies of man:
10 Tyranny, poverty, disease and war itself.

Can we forge against these enemies a grand and global alliance, North and South, East and West, that can assure a more fruitful life for all mankind? Will you join in that historic effort?

In the long history of the world, only a few generations have been granted
15 the role of defending freedom in its hour of maximum danger.

I do not shrink from this responsibility—I welcome it. I do not believe that any of us would exchange places with any other people or any other generation. The energy, the faith, the devotion, which we bring to this endeavor will light our country and all who serve it—and the glow from that fire can truly
20 light the world.

And so, my fellow Americans: Ask not what your country can do for you— ask what you can do for your country.

My fellow citizens of the world: Ask not what America will do for you, but what together we can do for the freedom of man.

25 Finally, whether you are citizens of America or citizens of the world, ask of us here the same high standards of strength and sacrifice which we ask of you. With a good conscience our only sure reward, with history the final judge of our deeds, let us go forth to lead the land we love, asking His blessing and His help, but knowing that here on earth God's work must truly be our own.

—Excerpted from "Inaugural Address"
by John F. Kennedy

7. What is the main idea of the passage?

    (1) War and poverty are America's worst enemies.
    (2) The American people are responsible for the fate of the nation.
    (3) Americans are selfishly preoccupied with their individual problems.
    (4) Military strength is necessary in the struggle for freedom.
    (5) Only the president of the United States can solve the country's problems.

8. The phrase "graves of young Americans" (line 4) refers to

    (1) soldiers who died for their country
    (2) poverty-stricken citizens who died of hunger
    (3) citizens who were killed by foreign terrorists
    (4) teenagers who were victims of deadly diseases
    (5) citizens who were killed in civil rights demonstrations

9. John F. Kennedy states that during the course of American history, each generation has demonstrated its

    (1) freedom of speech
    (2) fear of illness
    (3) financial success
    (4) national loyalty
    (5) hatred toward foreign countries

10. The tone of the speech is intended to be

    (1) frightening
    (2) overemotional
    (3) inspiring
    (4) tragic
    (5) argumentative

11. According to this passage, what is John F. Kennedy's attitude toward the presidency?

    (1) He is overwhelmed by the enormous responsibilities.
    (2) He enthusiastically accepts the challenges of leadership.
    (3) He is greedy with power and wants total control of the government.
    (4) He welcomes the opportunity to build the military.
    (5) He looks forward to shaping economic policies.

12. The writing style of the concluding sentence resembles the language used in

    (1) a newscaster's report
    (2) a lawyer's appeal
    (3) a preacher's sermon
    (4) a historian's analysis
    (5) a magazine advertisement

Passage 3

HOW DID MALCOLM X IMPROVE HIMSELF DURING HIS PRISON TERM?

The Norfolk Prison Colony's library was in the school building. A variety of classes was taught there by instructors who came from such places as Harvard and Boston universities. The weekly debates between inmate teams were also held in the school building. You would be astonished to know how worked up
5   convict debaters and audiences would get over subjects like "Should Babies Be Fed Milk?"

Available on the prison library's shelves were books on just about every general subject. Much of the big private collection that Parkhurst had willed to the prison was still in crates and boxes in the back of the library—thousands of
10   old books. Some of them looked ancient: covers faded, old-time parchment-looking binding. Parkhurst, I've mentioned, seemed to have been principally interested in history and religion. He had the money and the special interest to have a lot of books that you wouldn't have in general circulation. Any college library would have been lucky to get that collection.

15   As you can imagine, especially in a prison where there was heavy emphasis on rehabilitation, an inmate was smiled upon if he demonstrated an unusually intense interest in books. There was a sizable number of well-read inmates, especially the popular debaters. Some were said by many to be practically walking encyclopedias. They were almost celebrities. No university would ask
20   any student to devour literature as I did when this new world opened to me, of being able to read and *understand*.

I read more in my room than in the library itself. An inmate who was known to read a lot could check out more than the permitted maximum number of books. I preferred reading in the total isolation of my own room.

25   When I had progressed to really serious reading, every night at about ten P.M. I would be outraged with the "lights out." It always seemed to catch me right in the middle of something engrossing.

Fortunately, right outside my door was a corridor light that cast a glow into my room. The glow was enough to read by, once my eyes adjusted to it. So
30   when "lights out" came, I would sit on the floor where I could continue reading in that glow.

—Excerpted from *The Autobiography of Malcolm X*
by Malcolm X and Alex Haley

13. Who taught the academic classes at the prison?

   (1) prison guards
   (2) librarians
   (3) college-educated convicts
   (4) professional debaters
   (5) university instructors

14. What was the prison officials' reaction to inmates who were interested in books?

    (1) suspicious
    (2) critical
    (3) indifferent
    (4) approving
    (5) surprised

15. Why does Malcolm X refer to certain inmates as "walking encyclopedias" (line 19)?

    (1) They were responsible for carrying books.
    (2) They used to sell encyclopedias door to door.
    (3) They were well-informed on a variety of topics.
    (4) They paced around the library while they read.
    (5) They liked to exercise their minds.

16. Why was Malcolm X annoyed with the "lights out" rule at 10 P.M.?

    (1) He was afraid of the dark.
    (2) He had difficulties falling asleep.
    (3) His reading was interrupted.
    (4) He was outraged with unfair prison regulations.
    (5) He disliked childish treatment.

17. What is the major point that Malcolm X expresses in the passage?

    (1) his respect for his fellow inmates
    (2) his enthusiasm for reading and learning
    (3) his support of rehabilitating convicts
    (4) his attitude toward the prison system
    (5) his interest in books about history and religion

18. If Malcolm X were alive today, which of the following statements would he most likely support?

    (1) Classroom instruction is not effective.
    (2) Debates often result in arguments.
    (3) People have the ability to educate themselves.
    (4) Prison libraries are poorly stocked.
    (5) University students know less than self-taught convicts.

FOR ANSWERS AND EXPLANATIONS, SEE PAGE 277.

5
PROSE FICTION

Fiction writers invent a self-contained world where imaginary events unfold and create characters who play a role in these events. On the GED Interpreting Literature and the Arts Test, you will read excerpts from two types of fiction—the novel and the short story. The novel is a book-length story, a fully developed portrayal of people, situations, and places. Because it is more concise, the short story usually focuses on one major event or a series of closely related incidents.

In this chapter, you will study the following elements of fictional prose:

☐ Setting

☐ Plot

☐ Point of view

☐ Characterization

☐ Figurative language

☐ Theme

By understanding these elements, you will build your skills in analyzing and interpreting fiction.

Setting

Fiction writers stage the action of their stories by establishing *setting*—the place, the time, and the atmosphere in which dramatic situations occur.

The **place** roots the action to a specific location or geographical area. For example, the following list identifies some of the places described in short stories and novels:

a bingo parlor	a jungle island off the Brazilian coast
a supermarket	a small town in Ohio
a roadside diner	a Southern plantation
a courtroom	a city in Ireland

The **time** frames the action of the story by explaining when the events happened—the time of day, the season, or the historical period. Ralph Ellison's short story "King of the Bingo Game" takes place in the evening. John Updike's short story "A & P" occurs during the summer. F. Scott Fitzgerald's novel *The Great Gatsby* is set in the 1920s.

The **atmosphere** conveys the emotions associated with the story's physical environment. Descriptions of specific places often create the atmosphere. An intimate, candle-lit restaurant may evoke romantic feelings. The emotions associated with funeral parlors are grief and loss.

Apply your understanding of the terms place, time, and atmosphere as you read the following paragraph:

> It was raining that morning, and still very dark. When the boy reached the streetcar café he had almost finished his route and he went in for a cup of coffee. The place was an all-night café owned by a bitter and stingy man called Leo. After the raw, empty street the café seemed friendly and bright: along the counter there were a couple of soldiers, three spinners from the cotton mill, and in a corner a man who sat hunched over with his nose and half his face down in a beer mug.

> —Excerpted from "A Tree. A Rock. A Cloud"
> by Carson McCullers

In the following spaces, identify the three elements of setting:

Place: _____

Time of day: _____

Atmosphere of the place: _____

If you wrote that the scene occurs in the morning at a streetcar cafe, you correctly named the time and the place. The phrase "bright and friendly" describes the atmosphere of the cafe.

In the preceding excerpt, you see a young boy, Leo the owner, and some customers. The fictional setting provides the background in which characters enact the events of the story.

How Authors Establish Setting

As you noticed in the excerpt from "A Tree. A Rock. A Cloud," the author tells you the place, the time, and the atmosphere. Sometimes authors directly state these elements of setting. Here are some examples:

Place

We went to a nightclub on a short, dark street, downtown.

—Excerpted from "Sonny's Blues" by James Baldwin

The village of Loma is built, as its name implies, on a low round hill that rises like an island out of the flat mouth of the Salinas Valley in central California.

—Excerpted from "Johnny Bear" by John Steinbeck

Murphy slams the phone down and bounds back upstairs to his room in the YMCA to sit alone. . . .

—Excerpted from "Murphy's Xmas" by Mark Costello

The military School of St. Severin. The gymnasium. The class in their white cotton shirts stand in two rows under the big gas lights.

—Excerpted from "Gym Period" by Rainer Maria Rilke

Time

I sit in the sun drinking gin. It is ten in the morning.

—Excerpted from "The Fourth Alarm" by John Cheever

It was the second day of Easter week.

—Excerpted from "The Peasant Marey"
by Fyodor Dostoevsky

The morning of June 27th was clear and sunny, with the fresh warmth of a full-summer day. . . .

—Excerpted from "The Lottery" by Shirley Jackson

It was December—a bright frozen day in the early morning.

—Excerpted from "A Worn Path" by Eudora Welty

Atmosphere

Hadleyburg was the most honest and upright town in all the region round about it.

—Excerpted from "The Man that Corrupted Hadleyburg"
by Mark Twain

The room in which I found myself was very large and lofty. . . . I felt that I breathed an atmosphere of sorrow. An air of stern, deep, and irredeemable gloom hung over and pervaded all.

—Excerpted from "The Fall of the House of Usher"
by Edgar Allan Poe

Inferring Place and Time

When authors do not name the place or time, you will have to infer this information from the descriptive details. Can you infer where the action in the following paragraph occurs?

The pass was high and wide and he jumped for it, feeling it slap flatly against his hands, as he shook his hips to throw off the halfback who was driving at him. The center floated by, his hands desperately brushing Darling's knee as Darling picked his feet up high and delicately ran over a blocker and an opposing linesman in a jumble on the ground near the scrimmage line.

—Excerpted from "The Eighty Yard Run" by Irwin Shaw

If you said "a football field," you were correct. What are some of the clues that support this inference? Write the words or phrases on the following lines:

_____   _____

_____   _____

"Pass," "halfback," "blocker," and "scrimmage line" all refer to football. Therefore, you can conclude that the men are playing this sport on a football field.

In the next example, the author does not announce to the reader the era in which the story is set. However, you can infer the historical period from the description of the main character, a man who is hanged for treason.

Peyton Farquhar was a well-to-do planter, of an old and highly respectable Alabama family. Being a slave owner and like other slave owners a politician he was naturally an original secessionist and ardently devoted to the Southern cause.

—Excerpted from "An Occurrence at Owl Creek Bridge"
by Ambrose Bierce

What clues from the character description suggest that the story happens during the Civil War? On the following lines, write two phrases that support this inference about setting:

_____

_____

As you probably noted, Peyton Farquhar is a "slave owner" who is "devoted to the Southern cause," which included preserving the institution of slavery. During the Civil War, the Emancipation Proclamation abolished slavery.

Inferring Atmosphere

As mentioned earlier in this section, atmosphere refers to the emotional qualities associated with a place. Authors usually suggest the atmosphere by describing the physical appearance of the place or by showing how characters react to their environment.

The following paragraph describes an abandoned house. Notice the feelings conveyed by the descriptive language.

> On a night the wind loosened a shingle and flipped it to the ground. The next wind pried into the hole where the shingle had been, lifted off three, and the next, a dozen. The midday sun burned through the hole and threw a glaring spot on the floor. The wild cats crept in from the fields at night, but they did not mew at the doorstep any more. They moved like shadows of a cloud across the moon, into the rooms to hunt the mice. And on windy nights the doors banged, and the ragged curtains fluttered in the broken windows.

> —Excerpted from *The Grapes of Wrath*
> by John Steinbeck

This excerpt illustrates how the sun and the wind are gradually destroying the empty house. What is your impression of the atmosphere? Desolate? Bleak? Dreary? These are some of the words that capture the overall feeling of this place. John Steinbeck, the author, conveys the atmosphere through images relating to sights and sounds. Reread his concluding sentence. Try to imagine seeing and hearing "doors banging on a windy night" and "ragged curtains fluttering in broken windows."

For additional practice in inferring atmosphere, complete the next exercise.

Exercise 1: Inferring Atmosphere

Directions: Read the following passage and answer the questions.

> And so the house came to be haunted by the unspoken phrase: There must be more money! There must be more money! The children could hear it all the time, though nobody said it aloud. They heard it at Christmas, when the expensive and splendid toys filled the nursery. Behind the shining modern rocking-horse, behind the smart doll's house, a voice would start whispering: "There must be more money! There must be more money!" And the children would stop playing, to listen for a moment. They would look into each other's eyes, to see if they had all heard. And each one saw in the eyes of the other two that they too had heard. "There must be more money! There must be more money!"
>
> It came whispering from the springs of the still-swaying rocking-horse, and even the horse, bending his wooden, champing head, heard it. The big doll, sitting so pink and smirking in her new pram, could hear it quite plainly, and seemed to be smirking all the more self-consciously because of it. The foolish puppy, too, that took the place of the teddy-bear, he was looking so extraordinarily foolish for no other reason but that he heard the secret whisper all over the house: "There must be more money!"

Yet nobody ever said it aloud. The whisper was everywhere, and therefore no one spoke it. Just as no one ever says: "We are breathing!" in spite of the fact that breath is coming and going all the time.

—Excerpted from "The Rocking-Horse Winner"
by D. H. Lawrence

1. What is the unspoken phrase that haunts the house?

_____

2. Who can hear the secret whisper?

_____ _____

_____ _____

3. Which word best describes the atmosphere of this house?

   (1) childish
   (2) ordinary
   (3) supernatural
   (4) splendid
   (5) foolish

FOR ANSWERS AND EXPLANATIONS, SEE PAGE 277.

For a review in understanding setting, complete the next exercise.

Exercise 2: Understanding Setting

Directions: As you read the passage below, pay close attention to the details that establish setting. Then complete the exercise.

It was freezing cold, with a fog that caught your breath. Two large searchlights were crisscrossing over the compound from the watchtowers at the far corners. The lights on the perimeter and the lights inside the camp were on full force. There were so many of them that they blotted out the stars.

With their felt boots crunching on the snow, prisoners were rushing past on their business—to the latrines, to the supply rooms, to the package room, or to the kitchen to get their groats cooked. Their shoulders were hunched and their coats buttoned up, and they all felt cold, not so much because of the freezing weather as because they knew they'd have to be out in it all day. But the Tartar in his old overcoat with shabby blue tabs walked steadily on and the cold didn't seem to bother him at all.

They went past the high wooden fence around the punishment block (the stone prison inside the camp), past the barbed-wire fence that guarded the bakery from the prisoners, past the corner of the HQ where a length of frost-covered rail was fastened to a post with heavy wire, and past another post where—in a sheltered spot to keep the readings from being too low—the thermometer hung, caked over with ice. Shukhov gave a hopeful sidelong glance at the milk-white tube. If it went down to forty-two below zero they weren't supposed to be marched out to work. But today the thermometer wasn't pushing forty or anything like it.

—Excerpted from *One Day in the Life of Ivan Denisovich* by Alexander Solzhenitsyn

1. The story most likely takes place in

    (1) a military academy
    (2) an army post
    (3) a prison camp
    (4) a combat zone
    (5) a reform school

2. The atmosphere depicted in this passage is

    (1) violent
    (2) suspenseful
    (3) dull
    (4) hopeful
    (5) oppressive

3. List four phrases referring to the weather. _____

    _____

    _____

    _____

FOR ANSWERS AND EXPLANATIONS, SEE PAGE 278.

Writing Exercise 1

Where would you like to be at this moment? At the beach? In the mountains? With friends and family? On a separate sheet of paper, write one paragraph describing the setting and atmosphere of the scene you envision. Experiment with the techniques that other authors have used in this chapter.

ANSWERS WILL VARY.

Plot

The **plot** of the story refers to the action—the sequence of events. As author John Steinbeck comments, writers structure these events in an orderly sequence: "Of course, a writer rearranges life, shortens the intervals, sharpens events, and devises beginnings, middles, and ends." In other words, writers present an organized version of experiences that may occur in real life.

In fiction, the action progresses toward a believable conclusion. Individual incidents or episodes are connected logically. For example, the events may unfold in a series of cause-and-effect relationships. When you are reading a fictional passage, you should ask yourself why an event happened, what the outcome was, and what happens next.

Summarizing the action of a scene will also help you to see how plot details are related. Can you identify the main incident described in the following excerpt?

> The dogs were cast, still on leash. They struck immediately. The trail was good, easily followed because of the dew. The fugitive had apparently made no effort whatever to hide it. They could even see the prints of his knees and hands where he had knelt to drink from a spring. "I never yet knew a murderer that had more sense than that about the folks that would chase him," the deputy said. "But this durn fool dont even suspect that we might use dogs."
>
> "We been putting dogs on him once a day ever since Sunday," the sheriff said. "And we aint caught him yet."
>
> "Them were cold trails. We aint had a good hot trail until today. But he's made his mistake at last. We'll get him today. Before noon, maybe."
>
> "I'll wait and see, I reckon," the sheriff said.
>
> "You'll see," the deputy said. "This trail is running straight as a railroad. I could follow it, myself almost. Look here. You can even see his footprints. The durn fool aint even got enough sense to get into the road, in the dust, where other folks have walked and where the dogs cant scent him. Them dogs will find the end of them footprints before ten o'clock."
>
> Which the dogs did. Presently the trail bent sharply at right angles. They followed it and came onto a road, which they followed behind the lowheaded and eager dogs who, after a short distance, swung to the roadside where a path came down from a cotton house in a nearby field. They began to bay, milling, tugging, their voices loud, mellow, ringing; whining and surging with excitement. "Why, the durn fool!" the deputy said. "He set down here and rested: here's his footmarks: them same rubber heels. He aint a mile ahead right now! Come on, boys!" They went on, the leashes taut, the dogs baying, the men moving now at a trot.
>
> —Excerpted from *Light in August* by William Faulkner

Which statement best summarizes the action of this passage?

(1) A murderer runs away from the law.
(2) A fugitive outsmarts the sheriff and his deputy.
(3) A sheriff, a deputy, and his dogs try to track down a murderer.
(4) A sheriff and his deputy disagree on plans for a manhunt.
(5) The dogs are useless in capturing the fugitive.

Answer (3) is the right response. The entire scene traces the sheriff, the deputy, and the dogs' pursuit of the murderer. Let's examine why the other responses are wrong. Answer (1) describes the reason for the manhunt, but does not summarize the action. Answers (2) and (5) are possible outcomes, but they are not the main action in the passage. Answer (4) describes a specific moment from the scene.

As you read the passage, did you also notice that the setting changes? The author reveals this shift in location by showing where the sheriff and his deputy have found the fugitive's handprints and footmarks. Study the passage again. On the following lines, describe the locations where the passage begins and ends:

1. _____

2. _____

The two locations are **1.** an area near a spring and **2.** a path coming down from a cotton house in a nearby field.

Conflict in Plot

Newspaper headlines often report conflicts—clashes between opposing forces:

Hurricane Off Florida Coastline Forces Residents to Evacuate
Professional Athlete Struggles to Overcome Drug Problems
Citizens Stage Protest Against Nuclear Weapons and the Arms Race
Two Men Arrested in Barroom Brawl
Negotiations Continue Between Striking Teachers and Board of Education
Movie Star Tells About Battle to Recover from Stroke
Terrorists Hold Five Americans Hostage

As these headlines illustrate, conflict is a part of everyday life. People find themselves at odds with their environment, society, or other individuals. They also confront personal problems that result in inner conflicts. These kinds of real-life conflicts also occur in fictional plots.

The events of a story often arise when characters defy society or other individuals, cope with dangerous surroundings, or struggle with their own emotions. These conflicts create moments of tension in the plot.

The following excerpt from Richard Wright's novel *Native Son* shows Bigger, the main character, in a tense situation. As you read the passage, notice the detailed account of the conflict.

"There he is!" the mother screamed again.

A huge black rat squealed and leaped at Bigger's trouser-leg and snagged it in his teeth, hanging on.

"Goddamn!" Bigger whispered fiercely, whirling and kicking out his leg with all the strength of his body. The force of his movement shook the rat loose and it sailed through the air and struck a wall. Instantly, it rolled over and leaped again. Bigger dodged and the rat landed against a table leg. With clenched teeth, Bigger held the skillet; he was afraid to hurl it, fearing that he might miss. The rat squeaked and turned and ran in a narrow circle, looking for a place to hide; it leaped again past Bigger and scurried on dry rasping feet to one side of the box and then to the other, searching for the hole. Then it turned and reared upon its hind legs.

"Hit 'im, Bigger!" Buddy shouted.

"Kill 'im!" the woman screamed.

The rat's belly pulsed with fear. Bigger advanced a step and the rat emitted a long thin song of defiance, its black beady eyes glittering, its tiny forefeet pawing the air restlessly. Bigger swung the skillet; it skidded over the floor, missing the rat, and clattered to a stop against a wall.

"Goddamn!"

The rat leaped. Bigger sprang to one side. The rat stopped under a chair and let out a furious screak. Bigger moved slowly backward toward the door.

"Gimme that skillet, Buddy," he asked quietly, not taking his eyes from the rat.

Buddy extended his hand. Bigger caught the skillet and lifted it high in the air. The rat scuttled across the floor and stopped again at the box and searched quickly for the hole; then it reared once more and bared long yellow fangs, piping shrilly, belly quivering.

Bigger aimed and let the skillet fly with a heavy grunt. There was a shattering of wood as the box caved in. The woman screamed and hid her face in her hands. Bigger tiptoed forward and peered.

"I got 'im," he muttered, his clenched teeth bared in a smile. "By God, I got 'im."

—Excerpted from *Native Son* by Richard Wright

Can you analyze the conflict revealed in this scene? On the following lines, state the conflict and explain how it was resolved.

The conflict is between _____ and the _____.

The conflict was resolved when _____

_____.

You responded correctly if you said that the conflict was between Bigger and the rat. Bigger resolved the conflict by killing the rat with a skillet.

For further practice in analyzing conflict, complete the next exercise.

Exercise 3: Analyzing Conflict

Directions: "The Bench" is a short story set in South Africa, where apartheid, the official policy of racial segregation, is strictly enforced. The laws under apartheid deny blacks certain human rights. As you read the following excerpt from "The Bench," be aware of how the setting influences Karlie and his actions. Then complete the exercise.

> Here was his challenge! *The bench.* The railway bench with "Europeans Only" neatly painted on it in white. For one moment it symbolized all the misery of the plural South African society.
>
> Here was his challenge to the rights of a man. Here it stood. A perfectly ordinary wooden railway bench, like thousands of others in South Africa. His challenge. That bench now had concentrated in it all the evils of a system he could not understand and he felt a victim of. It was the obstacle between himself and humanity. If he sat on it, he was a man. If he was afraid he denied himself membership as a human being in a human society. He almost had visions of righting this pernicious system, if he only sat down on that bench. Here was his chance. He, Karlie, would challenge.
>
> He seemed perfectly calm when he sat down on the bench, but inside his heart was thumping wildly. Two conflicting ideas now throbbed through him. The one said, "I have no right to sit on this bench." The other was the voice of a new religion and said, "Why have I no right to sit on this bench?" The one voice spoke of the past, of the servile position he had occupied on the farm, of his father, and his father's father who were born black, lived like blacks, and died like mules. The other voice spoke of new horizons and said, "Karlie, you are a man."

—Excerpted from "The Bench" by Richard Rive

1. What action does Karlie take to challenge the system of racial injustice in South Africa?

     _____

     _____

2. In the third paragraph, Karlie struggles with two conflicting ideas. Identify those opposing ideas on the following lines.

     _____

     _____

     _____

3. Which of the following words best describes Karlie's behavior?

     (1) calm
     (2) courageous
     (3) reckless
     (4) silly
     (5) cowardly

4. If Karlie were living in the United States today, he would probably support

    (1) people opposed to school busing
    (2) stronger law enforcement
    (3) financial aid to foreign countries
    (4) discrimination against protesters
    (5) the civil rights movement

FOR ANSWERS AND EXPLANATIONS, SEE PAGE 278.

Writing Exercise 2

On a separate sheet of paper, write about a conflict from your own experience. Some suggested topics include (1) a conflict with another person—a relative, a friend, a boss, an enemy, etc., (2) an inner conflict about making a decision—getting married, returning to school, breaking a rule, etc. Organize your paragraphs by answering each of these questions:

Paragraph 1: What were the two opposing sides of the conflict?

Paragraph 2: What caused the conflict?

Paragraph 3: What tense moments did the conflict create?

ANSWERS WILL VARY.

Point of View

When you read a story, through whose eyes do you see the setting, the plot, and the characters? The person telling the story is the ***narrator***. That person determines the way that you see people, actions, and situations. This is called the narrator's ***point of view***.

Generally, you learn about what happens in a story from one of two types of narrators:

- the author acting as narrator

- a character acting as narrator

Author as Narrator

One type of narrator is the author acting as an all-knowing reporter who explains what happens from her own perspective. Because this type of narrator is not a character participating in the action, she recounts the story from a distance. She relates the characters' experiences and may tell you about their thoughts and feelings, as if she could read their minds.

This method of narration or storytelling is used in many types of fiction. As you read the following excerpt from the fairy tale "Hansel and Gretel," notice whose voice is conveying information about the characters, their circumstances, and their environment.

> Close to a large forest there lived a woodcutter with his wife and his two children. The boy was called Hansel and the girl Gretel. They were always very poor and had very little to live on. And at one time when there was famine in the land, he could no longer procure daily bread.
>
> One night when he lay in bed worrying over his troubles, he sighed and said to his wife, "What is to become of us? How are we to feed our poor children when we have nothing for ourselves?"
>
> "I'll tell you what, husband," answered the woman. "Tomorrow morning we will take the children out quite early into the thickest part of the forest. We will light a fire and give each of them a piece of bread. Then we will go to our work and leave them alone. They won't be able to find their way back, and so we shall be rid of them."
>
> "Nay, wife," said the man, "we won't do that. I could never find it in my heart to leave my children alone in the forest. Wild animals would soon tear them to pieces."
>
> "What a fool you are!" she said. "Then we must all four die of hunger. You may as well plane the boards for our coffins at once."
>
> She gave him no peace till he consented. "But I grieve over the poor children all the same," said the man.
>
> —Excerpted from "Hansel and Gretel"
> by the Brothers Grimm

In the preceding passage, who tells you about a poverty-stricken family living in a "large forest"?

(1) the woodcutter
(2) the woodcutter's wife
(3) Hansel
(4) Gretel
(5) an unnamed narrator

Answer (5) is the correct response. The narrator is not identified. You do not sense the narrator's actual presence in the story. Instead, you are aware of a voice describing the situation. The authors, the Brothers Grimm, act as a single storyteller who tells you about the family's financial problems and the parents' plan to abandon the son and the daughter.

This method of narration or storytelling is also used in *The Godfather*, a novel about the underworld of organized crime:

> On the day after the murder of Sollozzo and Captain McCluskey, the police captains and lieutenants in every station house in New York City sent out the word: there would be no more gambling, no more prostitution, no more deals of any kind until the murderer of Captain McCluskey was caught. Massive raids began all over the city. All unlawful business activities came to a standstill.
>
> —Excerpted from *The Godfather* by Mario Puzo

As you read the paragraph, did you notice that you discovered the police officers' reactions to two murders from an unidentified narrator's point of view?

Character as Narrator

An author may also invent a character to tell the story. The character participates in the action, and you witness the events through his eyes. In this method of narration, the story sounds like a first-hand report.

For example, in Mark Twain's novel *Huckleberry Finn*, Huck Finn, the central character, is the narrator. The novel begins with Huck introducing himself to you, the reader:

> You don't know about me without you have read a book by the name of *The Adventures of Tom Sawyer*; but that ain't no matter. That book was made by Mark Twain, and he told the truth, mainly. There was things which he stretched, but mainly he told the truth.
>
> —Excerpted from *Huckleberry Finn* by Mark Twain

In his own language, Huck relates the experiences that follow. You personally observe the way in which Huck, a teen-age boy, views his surroundings and other characters.

Writing Exercise 3

Reread the excerpt from *The Godfather* on page 122. As you already know, an outside narrator reports these events. Imagine you are a police captain. Using the pronoun "I," announce to your precinct your plans to crack down on gangster activities. You can invent plot details not included in the original excerpt. Write your plans on a separate sheet of paper.

ANSWERS WILL VARY.

Characterization

In this section on characterization, you will apply your understanding of point of view. You get to know fictional characters, like real people, by their actions, relationships, conversations, and environment. When you read fiction, you find out this information from either the author's viewpoint or a character's viewpoint.

How do you form impressions about the people you meet? In the list that follows, check the numbered items that show how you judge others:

_____	**1.** physical appearance		_____	**6.** conversations
_____	**2.** age		_____	**7.** other people's opinions
_____	**3.** clothing		_____	**8.** past experiences
_____	**4.** possessions		_____	**9.** family life
_____	**5.** actions		_____	**10.** neighborhood

Add your own:

11. _____

12. _____

13. _____

14. _____

15. _____

You become acquainted with fictional characters in a similar way. The methods an author uses in presenting characters to the reader are called *characterization*. The author uses various techniques to portray the human qualities— physical appearance, personality traits, actions—of imaginary individuals.

When reading a short story or a novel, pay close attention to the following means of revealing character:

☐ The author's comments

☐ Another character's comments

☐ Dialogue

☐ Scenes depicting characters in action

Author's Comments

One way of learning about a character is from the author's point of view. The author, acting as the person telling the story, may show you how a character looks. He may also provide you with background information or summarize moments from the character's past.

In the following excerpt, what does the author tell you about Mr. and Mrs. Mooney and their relationship?

Mrs. Mooney was a butcher's daughter. She was a woman who was quite able to keep things to herself: a determined woman. She had married her father's foreman and opened a butcher's shop near Spring Gardens. But as soon as his father-in-law was dead Mr. Mooney began to go to the devil. He drank, plundered the till, ran headlong into debt. It was no use making him take the pledge: he was sure to break out again a few days after. By fighting his wife in the presence of customers and by buying bad meat he ruined his business. One night he went for his wife with the cleaver and she had to sleep in a neighbour's house.

After that they lived apart. She went to the priest and got a separation from him with care of the children.

—Excerpted from "The Boarding House" by James Joyce

Now answer the following questions about the characters:

1. What two personality traits of Mrs. Mooney are described in the passage?

    _____   _____

2. How did Mr. Mooney's behavior change after his father-in-law's death?

    _____

    _____

3. How did Mr. Mooney ruin his business? _____

    _____

    _____

4. Why did Mrs. Mooney seek a separation from her husband?

    _____

Here are the correct responses:
1. private and determined
2. He drank and went into debt.
3. He fought his wife in front of customers and bought bad meat.
4. Mr. Mooney went after her with a meat cleaver.

Did you notice that you derived information about the characters, their behavior, and their relationship from the author's statements? From these literal or direct statements, you can make additional inferences about Mr. and Mrs. Mooney. For instance, because Mr. Mooney went after his wife with a meat cleaver, you can infer that he is capable of physical violence. Since Mrs. Mooney requested a separation from her priest, you can assume that she is Catholic. Once you understand what the author directly tells you, you will be better prepared to draw your own conclusions about the characters.

In the next exercise, you again will learn about a character from the author's point of view.

Exercise 4: Interpreting Character—Author's Point of View

Directions: As you study the following passage, identify the facts relating to the character's life. Then complete the exercises.

He had been as Tony a kid of many dreams and schemes, especially getting out of this tenement-crowded, kid-squawking neighborhood, with its lousy poverty, but everything had fouled up against him before he could. When he was sixteen he quit the vocational school where they were making him into a shoemaker, and began to hang out with the gray-hatted, thick-soled-shoe boys, who had the spare time and the mazuma and showed it in fat wonderful rolls down in the cellar clubs to all who would look, and everybody did, popeyed. They were the ones who had bought the silver caffe espresso urn and later the television, and they arranged the pizza parties and had the girls down; but it was getting in with them and their cars, leading to the holdup of a liquor store, that had started all the present trouble. Lucky for him the coal-and-ice man who was their landlord knew the leader in the district, and they arranged something so nobody bothered him after that. Then before he knew what was going on—he had been frightened sick by the whole mess—there was his father cooking up a deal with Rosa Agnello's old man that Tony would marry her and the father-in-law would, out of his savings, open a candy store for him to make an honest living. He wouldn't spit on a candy store, and Rosa was too plain and lank a chick for his personal taste, so he beat it off to Texas and bummed around in too much space, and when he came back everybody said it was for Rosa and the candy store, and it was all arranged again and he, without saying no, was in it.

—Excerpted from "The Prison" by Bernard Malamud

Part I: Factual Statements About Characterization

1. Where did Tony grow up? _____

   _____

2. How old was Tony when he quit vocational school? _____

3. Who were his friends? _____

   _____

4. How did Tony break the law? _____

   _____

5. What arrangement did Tony's father make with Rosa Agnello's father?

   _____

   _____

Part II: Making Inferences About Characterization

6. Which of the following words best describes Tony's life before his marriage?

    (1) frightening
    (2) carefree
    (3) honest
    (4) troubled
    (5) wonderful

7. From this passage, you can infer that

    (1) Tony was a victim of his environment
    (2) Tony was eager to get married
    (3) Tony had ambitions of managing a candy store
    (4) Tony was interested in learning a trade
    (5) Tony had little imagination

FOR ANSWERS AND EXPLANATIONS, SEE PAGE 278.

Character's Comments

A character narrating a story frequently comments about the other characters. This type of narrator often has direct contact with these characters, and you see them from his point of view. Through his impressions and his personal relationships, you learn about both the narrator's personality and the characters he knows.

This method of revealing character is used in Tillie Olsen's short story "I Stand Here Ironing." A mother, the narrator of the story, recalls the hardships of raising her daughter alone during the 1930s and '40s. Like most single parents, she is torn between two conflicting responsibilities—holding down a job and taking care of her child. In the following excerpt, notice what the mother says about herself, her daughter, and their relationship:

> I will never total it all. I will never come in to say: She was a child seldom smiled at. Her father left her before she was a year old. I had to work her first six years when there was work, or I sent her home and to his relatives. There were years she had care she hated. She was dark and thin and foreign-looking in a world where the prestige went to blondeness and curly hair and dimples, she was slow where glibness was prized. She was a child of anxious, not proud, love. We were poor and could not afford for her the soil of easy growth. I was a young mother, I was a distracted mother.
>
> —Excerpted from "I Stand Here Ironing" by Tillie Olsen

From the mother's point of view, you catch a glimpse of the daughter's physical appearance—"dark and thin and foreign-looking." The mother also tells you about the conditions affecting her daughter's upbringing. Summarize these circumstances on the lines on page 128:

Your statements should have included the following information about the daughter:

1. Her father abandoned her before she was a year old.

2. She was frequently separated from her mother.

3. She had a deprived childhood.

In the last sentence of the excerpt, the mother admits some of her own shortcomings as a parent: "I was a young mother, I was a distracted mother."

Writing Exercise 4

Based upon what the mother says about herself and her daughter, what is your impression of these two characters? On a separate sheet of paper, write a brief paragraph describing your feelings about the mother and the daughter.

ANSWERS WILL VARY.

In the next exercise, you will read a passage from F. Scott Fitzgerald's novel *The Great Gatsby*. Nick Carraway, the character who narrates the story, describes Tom Buchanan, his old college friend.

Exercise 5: Interpreting Character: Another Character's Point of View

Directions: As you study the passage, notice how Nick Carraway describes Tom Buchanan's physical appearance. Then complete the exercise.

> The front was broken by a line of French windows, glowing now with reflected gold and wide open to the warm windy afternoon, and Tom Buchanan in riding clothes was standing with his legs apart on the front porch.
>
> He had changed since his New Haven years. Now he was a sturdy straw-haired man of thirty with a rather hard mouth and a supercilious manner. Two shining arrogant eyes had established dominance over his face and gave him the appearance of always leaning aggressively forward. Not even the effeminate swank of his riding clothes could hide the enormous power of that body—he seemed to fill those glistening boots until he strained the top lacing, and you could see a great pack of muscle shifting when his shoulder moved under his thin coat. It was a body capable of enormous leverage—a cruel body.

—Excerpted from *The Great Gatsby*
by F. Scott Fitzgerald

1. What is Tom wearing? _____

2. Identify these facts about Tom:

   Age: _____

   Hair color: _____

3. Nick uses emotional words to describe Tom's facial features and build. Write the word next to the physical trait it describes.

   "_____" mouth

   "_____" eyes

   "_____" body

4. List the words or phrases that suggest Tom's strength and force.

   _____   _____

   _____   _____

5. According to this excerpt, you can infer that Nick's attitude toward Tom is

   (1) cautious
   (2) critical
   (3) sympathetic
   (4) unbiased
   (5) respectful

FOR ANSWERS AND EXPLANATIONS, SEE PAGE 278.

Dialogue

Dialogue is a conversation between characters. You hear the characters' speech—the actual words they use to express their thoughts, feelings, and attitudes. Characters reveal their personalities when they communicate aloud.

An author encloses the character's exact spoken words in quotation marks. This punctuation signals to you, the reader, that a character is talking. When the conversation switches to another speaker, the author begins a new paragraph. Words not enclosed in quotation marks identify the speaker, comment on the character, or present additional plot details.

This format indicating dialogue is used in the following passage, an excerpt from a 1920s gangster novel.

> The men looked uneasily at Arnie. Little by little they were losing their nerve.
> "Speak up," said Pepi, "where you guys from?"
> "We're from Detroit," said one of the men.
> "Where the hell's that?" Joe Sansone inquired. "I never heard of it."
> "Say," said Pepi, "don't you know that tough guys like you oughtn't to be running around loose. No sir. You're liable to get arrested for firing a rod in the city limits."

"Listen," said one of the men from Detroit, "what you guys got against us? We ain't done nothing. We just got in."

They were thoroughly intimidated.

—Excerpted from *Little Caesar* by R. W. Burnett

Exercise 6: Speakers in Dialogue

Directions: The following list contains lines of dialogue from the preceding passage. Name the character who says each of the following quotations:

1. "Speak up, where you guys from?" _____

2. "We're from Detroit." _____

3. "Where the hell's that? I never heard of it." _____

4. "Say, don't you know that tough guys like you oughtn't to be running around loose. No sir. You're liable to get arrested for firing a rod in the city limits."

   _____

5. "Listen, what you guys got against us? We ain't done nothing. We just got in." _____

FOR ANSWERS AND EXPLANATIONS, SEE PAGE 278.

Reading Dialogue

The gangsters' conversation in the previous example illustrates a method of characterization. Their rough language shows how hoodlums relate to one another.

When you read dialogue, ask yourself the following questions:

☐ What is the topic of conversation?

☐ What is the literal meaning of the speaker's statements?

☐ Does the speaker's tone of voice emphasize or change the literal meaning of the spoken words?

☐ What is the relationship between the character's dialogue and his personality and background?

☐ What do other characters say in response to the first speaker? Based on these responses, can you make inferences about the relationships of the characters involved in the conversation?

You will find these questions useful in interpreting and analyzing fictional conversations.

In the next example, a woman seeks the advice of Sherlock Holmes, a fictional detective. From the following dialogue, what do you learn about Sherlock Holmes and his client?

"Good-morning, madam," said Holmes, cheerily. "My name is Sherlock Holmes. This is my intimate friend and associate, Dr. Watson, before whom you can speak as freely as before myself. Ha! I am glad to see that Mrs. Hudson has had the good sense to light the fire. Pray draw up to it, and I shall order you a cup of hot coffee, for I observe that you are shivering."

"It is not cold which makes me shiver," said the woman, in a low voice, changing her seat as requested.

"What, then?"

"It is fear, Mr. Holmes. It is terror." She raised her veil as she spoke, and we could see that she was indeed in a pitiable state of agitation, her face all drawn and gray, with restless, frightened eyes, like those of some hunted animal. Her features and figure were those of a woman of thirty, but her hair was shot with premature gray, and her expression was weary and haggard. Sherlock Holmes ran her over with one of his quick, all-comprehensive glances.

"You must not fear," said he, soothingly, bending forward and patting her forearm. "We shall soon set matters right, I have no doubt."

—Excerpted from "The Speckled Band"
by Sir Arthur Conan Doyle

First, let's examine how Sherlock Holmes's brief conversation with the woman reveals some of his personality traits. In the following chart, notice the correlation between Holmes's spoken words and inferences about his character:

Dialogue	Personality Traits
"I shall order you a cup of hot coffee, for I observe that you are shivering."	Considerate and observant
"We shall soon set matters right, I have no doubt."	Helpful and self-confident

Second, the woman directly tells Sherlock Holmes why she is shivering: "It is fear, Mr. Holmes. It is terror." Therefore, you know her emotional condition and probably wonder about her predicament.

In the passage, the sentences not enclosed in quotation marks are the comments of Dr. Watson, Sherlock Holmes's associate, who is telling the story. From his point of view, you see the woman's physical appearance. He also describes both the woman's and Sherlock Holmes's facial expressions and gestures.

For further practice in understanding how dialogue reveals character, complete the next exercise.

Exercise 7: Interpreting Dialogue

Directions: In the following passage, two brothers are talking to each other. To guide your reading, be aware of the following format for indicating dialogue. After you read the passage, answer the questions.

☐ The words "I asked" or "I said" signal that the older brother is speaking.

☐ The words "he said" signal that Sonny, the younger brother, is speaking.

☐ When the conversation switches to another speaker, the author begins a new paragraph.

☐ Sentences not enclosed in quotation marks are the comments of the older brother, from whose point of view the story is told.

"What do you want to do?" I asked him.

"I'm going to be a musician," he said.

For he had graduated, in the time I had been away, from dancing to the juke box to finding out who was playing what, and what they were doing with it, and
5 he had bought himself a set of drums.

"You mean, you want to be a drummer?" I somehow had the feeling that being a drummer might be all right for other people but not for my brother Sonny.

"I don't think," he said, looking at me very gravely, "that I'll ever be a good
10 drummer. But I think I can play a piano."

I frowned. I'd never played the role of the older brother quite so seriously before, had scarcely ever, in fact, *asked* Sonny a damn thing. I sensed myself in the presence of something I didn't really know how to handle, didn't understand. So I made my frown a little deeper as I asked: "What kind of
15 musician do you want to be?"

He grinned. "How many kinds do you think there are?"

"Be *serious*," I said.

He laughed, throwing his head back, and then looked at me. "I *am* serious."

"Well, then, for Christ's sake, stop kidding around and answer a serious
20 question. I mean, do you want to be a concert pianist, you want to play classical music and all that, or—or what?" Long before I finished he was laughing again. "For Christ's *sake*, Sonny!"

He sobered, but with difficulty. "I'm sorry. But you sound so—*scared*!" and he was off again.
25 "Well, you may think it's funny now, baby, but it's not going to be so funny when you have to make your living at it, let me tell you *that*." I was furious because I knew he was laughing at me and I didn't know why.

"No," he said, very sober now, and afraid, perhaps, that he'd hurt me, "I don't want to be a classical pianist. That isn't what interests me. I mean"—he
30 paused, looking hard at me, as though his eyes would help me to understand, and then gestured helplessly, as though perhaps his hand would help—"I mean, I'll have a lot of studying to do, and I'll have to study *everything*, but, I mean, I want to play with—jazz musicians." He stopped. "I want to play jazz," he said.

Well, the word had never before sounded as heavy, as real, as it sounded
35 that afternoon in Sonny's mouth. I just looked at him and I was probably frowning a real frown by this time. I simply couldn't see why on earth he'd want

to spend his time hanging around nightclubs, clowning around on bandstands, while people pushed each other around a dance floor. It seemed—beneath him, somehow. I had never thought about it before, had never been forced to, but I
40 suppose I had always put jazz musicians in a class with what Daddy called "good-time people."

—Excerpted from "Sonny's Blues" by James Baldwin

1. The overall topic of conversation in this passage is

    (1) famous jazz musicians
    (2) people who enjoy nightclubs
    (3) Sonny's choice of careers
    (4) the older brother's appreciation of classical pianists
    (5) high-paying jobs

2. In lines 25–27, what is the older brother's tone of voice?

    (1) angry
    (2) understanding
    (3) polite
    (4) depressed
    (5) suspicious

3. In lines 31–33, what is Sonny's tone of voice?

    (1) childish
    (2) sarcastic
    (3) rude
    (4) sincere
    (5) bitter

4. The following list of inferences is about Sonny, his older brother, and their relationship. If an inference can be made based on the passage, write *valid* on the line. If the passage does not support an inference, write *invalid*.

    (1) There is tension between the two brothers. _____

    (2) Sonny's brother doesn't respect jazz musicians. _____

    (3) Sonny's brother doesn't believe that Sonny is musically talented.

      _____

    (4) Sonny wants to study music at a fine arts college. _____

    (5) Sonny and his brother understand each other. _____

    (6) Sonny doesn't take life seriously. _____

    (7) The older brother is protective of Sonny. _____

    (8) Sonny wants to make his own decisions. _____

FOR ANSWERS AND EXPLANATIONS, SEE PAGE 278.

Scenes Depicting Characters in Action

Characters act out the events of the plot. The actions they take in the story reveal traits of their personality. For example, Sherlock Holmes consistently shows ingenuity, courage, intelligence, and remarkable powers of observation whenever he solves a crime. Huck Finn establishes his own code of morality when he decides not to turn in his friend Jim, a slave. This action reveals that Huck's loyalty to a friend means more to him than breaking the law.

Showing a character in action is another method of characterization. You judge the character by what he does. Is the character drawn to threatening or safe situations? In a crisis, does the character behave responsibly or irresponsibly? What are the character's motives for his involvement in the story's events? Selfishness? Adventure? Concern for others? You discover the answers to these questions by observing the character's behavior.

In John Cheever's short story "The Housebreaker of Shady Hill," Johnny Hake, the central character, finds himself in a predicament. Johnny, a 36-year-old businessman living in a wealthy suburb, doesn't tell his wife Christina that they're broke. What steps does Johnny take to get money? In the next exercise, you'll find out how Johnny solves his financial problems.

Exercise 8: Observing a Character

Directions: In the next passage, Johnny Hake relates an experience from his point of view. As you read the excerpt, notice how the character and the event are closely linked. Then complete the questions about characterization and plot.

I tossed my cigarette into the toilet (ping) and straightened my back, but the pain in my chest was only sharper, and I was convinced that the corruption had begun. I had friends who would think of me kindly, I knew, and Christina and the children would surely keep alive an affectionate memory. But then I thought about money again, and the Warburtons, and my rubber checks approaching the clearinghouse, and it seemed to me that money had it all over love. I had yearned for some women—turned green, in fact—but it seemed to me that I had never yearned for anyone the way I yearned that night for money. I went to the closet in our bedroom and put on some old blue sneakers and a pair of pants and a dark pullover. Then I went downstairs and out of the house. The moon had set, and there were not many stars, but the air above the trees and hedges was full of dim light. I went around the Trenholmes' garden then, gumshoeing over the grass, and down the lawn to the Warburtons' house. I listened for sounds from the open windows, and all I heard was the ticking of a clock. I went up the front steps and opened the screen door and started across the floor from the old Ritz. In the dim night light that came in at the windows, the house looked like a shell, a nautilus, shaped to contain itself.

I heard the noise of a dog's license tag, and Sheila's old cocker came trotting down the hall. I rubbed him behind the ears, and then he went back to wherever his bed was, grunted and fell asleep. I knew the plan of the Warburtons' house as well as I knew the plan of my own. The staircase was carpeted, but I first put my foot on one of the treads to see if it creaked. Then I started up the stairs. All the bedroom doors stood open, and from Carl and

Sheila's bedroom, where I had often left my coat at big cocktail parties, I could hear the sound of deep breathing. I stood in the doorway for a second to take my bearings. In the dimness I could see the bed, and a pair of pants and a jacket hung over the back of a chair. Moving swiftly, I stepped into the room and took a big billfold from the inside pocket of the coat and started back to the hall. The violence of my emotions may have made me clumsy, because Sheila woke. I heard her say, "Did you hear that noise, darling?" "S'wind," he mumbled, and then they were quiet again. I was safe in the hall—safe from everything but myself. I seemed to be having a nervous breakdown out there. All my saliva was gone, the lubricants seemed to drain out of my heart, and whatever the juices were that kept my legs upright were going. It was only by holding onto the wall that I could make any progress at all. I clung to the banister on my way down the stairs, and staggered out of the house.

Back in my own dark kitchen, I drank three or four glasses of water. I must have stood by the kitchen sink for a half hour or longer before I thought of looking in Carl's wallet. I went into the cellarway and shut the cellar door before I turned the light on. There was a little over nine hundred dollars. I turned the light off and went back into the dark kitchen. Oh, I never knew that a man could be so miserable and that the mind could open up so many chambers and fill them with self-reproach.

—Excerpted from "The Housebreaker of Shady Hill"
by John Cheever

Part I: A Character's Role in the Plot

In the passage, Johnny Hake tells you a moment-by-moment account of his actions. These actions are listed here in jumbled order. Number the statements 1 through 7 according to the sequence reported by Johnny.

_____ Stepped swiftly into the bedroom

_____ Took a big billfold from inside the pocket of the coat

_____ Found a little over $900 in Carl's wallet

_____ Went down the lawn to the Warburtons' house

_____ Went into the cellarway and shut the cellar door

_____ Left his own house

_____ Returned to his own dark kitchen

Part II: Characterization

The following statements describe Johnny Hake's character. Label each statement either *true* or *false*.

1. Johnny believes that love is more important than money. _____

2. Johnny is a loner who doesn't have any friends. _____

3. Johnny feels that what he has done is corrupt and disgraceful.

_____

4. Johnny is concerned about how his wife Christina and his children will remember him. _____

5. Johnny thinks that robbing his neighbor is a thrilling experience. _____

6. Johnny is greedy and can't wait to count the stolen money. _____

7. Johnny is an inexperienced thief. _____

8. Financial pressures cause Johnny to behave like a criminal. _____

FOR ANSWERS AND EXPLANATIONS, SEE PAGE 278.

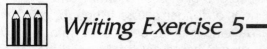 *Writing Exercise 5*

In this exercise, you will apply the techniques that professional authors use in portraying a character. On a separate sheet of paper, write about a person you know as though he or she were a character in a story. You want your reader to "see" this person. The following topics will help you to organize your information:

☐ Character

☐ Physical appearance

☐ Background

☐ Personality strengths

☐ Personality weaknesses

Then, write a short dialogue involving your character and another person. The words enclosed in quotation marks should imitate the way these people really talk.

ANSWERS WILL VARY.

Figurative Language*

In the chapters on inferential understanding and analysis, you learned that **figurative language** suggests a meaning beyond the literal definition of the words. Through figurative language, authors invent original ways of describing a subject or expressing feelings. In fictional prose, descriptions using figurative language are more vivid and emotionally powerful than descriptions using literal language.

*For a review of figurative language, read pages 42–46 and 63–65.

Let's review the differences between literal and figurative language. The following sentences are excerpted from Toni Morrison's novel *The Bluest Eye*. Write *L* in the blank next to the statements using literal language. Write *F* next to the statements using figurative language.

1. "The air seemed to strangle him, hold him back." (p. 124) _____ .

2. "Soon, like bright bits of glass, the events of that afternoon cut into him." (p. 124) _____

3. "Rosemary Villanucci, our next-door friend who lives above her father's cafe, sits in a 1939 Buick eating bread and butter." (p. 12) _____

4. "The rags have fallen from the window crack, and the air is cold." (p. 14) _____ .

5. "The big, the special, the loving gift was always a big, blue-eyed Baby Doll." (p. 19) _____

6. "And the years folded up like pocket handkerchiefs." (p. 159) _____

7. "Meridian. The sound of it opens the windows of a room like the first four notes of a hymn." (p. 167) _____

8. "And these houses loomed like hothouse sunflowers among the rows of weeds that were the rented houses." (p. 18) _____

9. "In Kentucky they lived in a real town, ten to fifteen houses on a single street, with water piped right into the kitchen." (p. 89) _____

10. "Each pale yellow wrapper has a picture on it." (p. 43) _____

Sentences 3, 4, 5, 9, and 10 use literal language. Sentences 1, 2, 6, 7, and 8 use figurative language.

In sentences 2, 6, 7, and 8, the phrase that states the comparison is introduced by the word *like*. A direct comparison, using the words *like* or *as*, is a figure of speech called a **simile**. For example, Toni Morrison directly compares the passing of years with folded handkerchiefs in this sentence: "And the years folded up *like* pocket handkerchiefs."

A **metaphor** is an implied comparison that states that something *is* something else. The words *like* and *as* are not used in a metaphor. If Toni Morrison had stated, "The passing years have become folded handkerchiefs," she would be making the comparison with a metaphor.

The chapter on poetry will discuss types of figurative language in more detail. On the GED Literature and the Arts Test you will be asked to read figures of speech and interpret their meaning. You will not have to define what kind of language is used.

Interpreting Figurative Language

After you recognize that a fiction writer is using figurative language, how do you infer the meaning? Here are some suggestions for interpreting figurative language:

- [ ] Identify the comparisons—direct or implied—between two different things.

- [ ] Picture in your mind the two images being compared.

- [ ] Determine the author's purpose in drawing the comparison. What is she trying to show?

Apply these steps as you read the following sentence:

> Now he faced the raging crowd with defiance, its screams penetrating his eardrums like trumpets shrieking from a juke-box.

> —Excerpted from "King of the Bingo Game"
> by Ralph Ellison

What two things is the author comparing?

_____ are compared with _____

What does the comparison show?

_____

You correctly identified the comparison if you said that the crowd's screams are compared with trumpets shrieking from a jukebox. This figure of speech emphasizes the shrill, ear-piercing sound coming from the crowd.

For further practice in interpreting figurative language complete the next two exercises.

Exercise 9: Interpreting Comparisons

Directions: Carefully read the following sentences from Flannery O'Connor's short novel *Wise Blood.* Identify the two things the author is comparing. Then interpret why the author has made the comparison.

1. "Nearer, the plowed fields curved and faded and the few hogs nosing in the furrows looked like large spotted stones."

   _____ are compared with _____

   Interpretation: _____

   _____

2. "He moved like a crow, darting from table to table."

   _____ is compared with _____

   Interpretation: _____

   _____

3. "Her mouth was open and her eyes glittered on him like two chips of green bottle glass."

_____ are compared with _____

Interpretation: _____

_____

4. "Mrs. Watts' grin was as curved and sharp as the blade of a sickle."

_____ is compared with _____

Interpretation: _____

_____

5. "It began to drizzle rain and he turned on the windshield wipers; they made a great clatter like two idiots clapping in church."

_____ are compared with _____

Interpretation: _____

_____

FOR ANSWERS AND EXPLANATIONS, SEE PAGE 279.

Exercise 10: Figurative Language

Directions: Read the following passage from Charles Dickens's novel _Hard Times_, in which he describes a city named Coketown. Pay close attention to the descriptive language, particularly figures of speech. Then answer the questions.

It was a town of red brick, or brick that would have been red if the smoke and ashes had allowed it; but as matters stood it was a town of unnatural red and black like the painted face of a savage.

It was a town of machinery and tall chimneys, out of which interminable serpents of smoke trailed themselves for ever and ever, and never got uncoiled.

It had a black canal in it, and a river that ran purple with ill-smelling dye, and vast piles of building full of windows where there was a rattling and a trembling all day long, and where the piston of the steam-engine worked monotonously up and down like the head of an elephant in a state of melancholy madness.

—Excerpted from _Hard Times_ by Charles Dickens

1. In lines 2–3, the author compares the town's red-and-black brick to a savage's painted face to suggest that

    (1) savages live in the city
    (2) the town is overrun with violence
    (3) the buildings need repainting
    (4) the town appears wild and uncivilized
    (5) painting faces is socially unacceptable

2. The phrase "serpents of smoke" (line 5) is used to create an impression of

    (1) evil
    (2) prosperity
    (3) slyness
    (4) selfishness
    (5) deceit

3. Why does the author compare the motions of a piston, an engine part, to an elephant's head?

    (1) to analyze how machines affect animal behavior
    (2) to suggest that elephants should replace machines
    (3) to give the reader an image of the steam engine's motion
    (4) to show that machines are more durable than animals
    (5) to explain what a steam engine does

4. From the descriptive details in this passage, you can conclude that Coketown is

    (1) a fast-paced, modern city
    (2) an ugly, industrial city
    (3) a smog-free, unpolluted city
    (4) a thriving, wealthy city
    (5) a quiet, peaceful city

5. From the passage, identify a phrase that describes a sound.

_____

6. Identify a phrase that describes an odor.

_____

FOR ANSWERS AND EXPLANATIONS, SEE PAGE 279.

Theme

The *theme* is a general statement that explains the underlying meaning of the story. In fables, like the following one, the author summarizes the significance of the plot.

The Shepherd Boy and the Wolf
A shepherd boy who tended his sheep grew lonely. Thinking to have some fun and pass the time he cried out, "Wolf! Wolf!"

His neighbors rushed over to help him, but of course there was no wolf. He merely laughed at them for coming. Three times he raised a false cry of *Wolf*. Three times the neighbors came running.

At last a wolf really did come. The shepherd boy cried out in terror, "Wolf! Wolf! The wolf is killing the sheep."

No one came or paid any attention to his cries. The wolf, having nothing to fear, proceeded to destroy the entire flock.

The Point—No one believes a liar—even when he speaks the truth.

—An Aesop's Fable in *Myths and Folklore*
by Henry I. Christ

The point or theme of the fable, "No one believes a liar—even when he speaks the truth," is revealed by the characters and their actions. Three times the shepherd boy jokingly cries "Wolf!" to fool his neighbors. His neighbors ignore the real plea for help because they assume that the boy is lying. The theme of "The Shepherd Boy and the Wolf" is a moral judgment about human behavior. Did you notice that you can apply this moral to situations outside the story? You may have heard parents telling their children, "Don't be like the boy who cried, 'Wolf!' "

Themes in short stories and novels express beliefs and opinions about life. The central message reflects the author's attitudes toward political or social issues and his perceptions about human nature and relationships.

The story itself is a concrete portrayal of people enacting events in a particular environment. For example, Ernest Hemingway's novel *The Old Man and the Sea* details the struggles of an old Cuban fisherman named Santiago. The novel is a fictional account of this true story.

An old man fishing alone in a skiff out of Cabanas hooked a great marlin that, on the heavy sashcord line, pulled the skiff far out to sea. Two days later the old man was picked up by fishermen sixty miles to the eastward, the head and forward part of the marlin lashed alongside. What was left of the fish, less than half, weighed eight hundred pounds. The old man had stayed with him a day, a night, a day, and another night while the fish swam deep and pulled the boat. When he had come up, the old man had pulled the boat up on him and harpooned him. Lashed alongside, the sharks had hit him and the old man had fought them out alone in the Gulf Stream in a skiff, clubbing them, stabbing at them, lunging at them with an oar until he was exhausted and the sharks had eaten all that they could hold. He was crying in the boat when the fishermen picked him up, half crazy from his loss, and the sharks were still circling the boat.

—Excerpted from "On the Blue Water: A Gulf Stream Letter"
by Ernest Hemingway

The significance of this event is one of the major themes in *The Old Man and the Sea*.

In the novel, Santiago has caught a big fish. As he returns to shore, a shark attacks his prize catch and devours it. The following passage describes Santiago's reaction to this incident. Study the excerpt carefully. Then underline the two sentences that state an important theme—Santiago's insight about his situation.

"He took about forty pounds," the old man said aloud. He took my harpoon too and all the rope, he thought, and now my fish bleeds again and there will be others.

He did not like to look at the fish anymore since he had been mutilated. When the fish had been hit it was as though he himself were hit.

But I killed the shark that hit my fish, he thought. And he was the biggest *dentuso* that I have ever seen. And God knows I have seen big ones.

It was too good to last, he thought. I wish it had been a dream now and that I had never hooked the fish and was alone in bed on the newspapers.

"But man is not made for defeat," he said. "A man can be destroyed but not defeated." I am sorry that I killed the fish though, he thought. Now the bad time is coming and I do not even have the harpoon. The *dentuso* is cruel and able and strong and intelligent. But I was more intelligent than he was. Perhaps not, he thought. Perhaps I was only better armed.

—Excerpted from *The Old Man and the Sea*
by Ernest Hemingway

Did you underline the following statement? *"But man is not made for defeat," he said. "A man can be destroyed but not defeated."* If so, you correctly identified one of the novel's major themes. Santiago's comment is a personal statement about the meaning of his own disappointing experience, as well as life's disappointments in general. Through the character of Santiago, Hemingway presents a theme that applies to people everywhere; the strength of the human spirit enables an individual to cope with misfortune. A devastating incident ultimately does not ruin a person; he is a survivor.

Writing Exercise 6

In a paragraph, describe an experience in which someone overcomes a personal failure. Use a separate sheet of paper for your description.

ANSWERS WILL VARY.

Inferring Theme

As you discovered in the preceding example, a character's comments may reveal the theme. Authors seldom state the major theme directly. Therefore, you will have to infer the story's meaning by interpreting the significance of the fictional elements—setting, plot, point of view, characterization, and figurative language. As you read a passage, pay close attention to how these fictional elements suggest the theme:

☐ The influence of the setting upon the characters and their actions

☐ The significance of important events

☐ The characters' comments and observations about life and human behavior

□   The author's comments and observations about life and human behavior

□   The language the author uses to tell the story

For further practice in interpreting theme, complete the following exercise.

Exercise 11: Interpreting Theme

Directions: The following excerpt describes a conflict between Manuel Gutierrez, a migrant farm worker, and Roberto Morales, his boss. As you study the passage, notice the fictional elements that reveal the theme. Then answer the multiple-choice questions.

Whenever Roberto Morales spoke, Manuel had to force himself not to answer. He had to keep his temper from flaring.

"Now," announced Morales at last, in his friendliest tone. "Now. I must take two cents from every bucket. I am sorry. There was a miscalculation. Every-
5   body understands. Everybody?" He slid his eyes around smiling, palms up.

The tired, exhausted pickers gasped as one.

Yes. Everyone understood. Freezing in place. After all that hard work.

"Any questions, men?"

Still grinning, knowing, everyone realizing that he had the upper hand, that
10   that would mean a loss of two or three dollars out of each picker's pay that day, a huge windfall for Morales.

"You promised to take nothing!" Manuel heard himself saying. Everyone turned in astonishment to stare at Manuel.

"I said two cents, hombre. You got a problem or what?"
15   "You promised."

The two men, centered in a huge ring of red-ringed eyes, glared at each other. Reaching for each other's jugular. The other exhausted animals studied the tableau through widening eyes. It was so unequal. Morales remained calm, confident, studying Manuel. As though memorizing his features. He had the
20   whole advantage. Then, with his last remaining energy, Manuel lifted his foot and clumsily tipped over his own last bucket of cots. They rolled away in all directions around everyone's feet.

Roberto Morales' eyes blazed. His fists clenched. "You pick them up, Gutierrez."
25   So. He knew his name. After all. For answer, Manuel kicked over another bucket, and again the fruit rolled away in all directions.

Then an astonishing thing happened.

All the other pickers moved toward their own buckets still standing beside them on the ground awaiting the truck gatherer, and took an ominous position
30   over them, straddling their feet over them. Without looking around, without taking his eyes off Manuel, Roberto Morales said sharply, "All right. All right, men, I shall take nothing this time."

Manuel felt a thrill of power course through his nerves.

He had never won anything before. He would have to pay for this, for his
35   defiance, somehow, again, later. But he had shown defiance. He had salvaged his money savagely and he had earned respect from his fellow slaves. The

gringo . . . would never know of this little incident, and would probably be surprised, and perhaps even a little mortified, for a few minutes. But they wouldn't give a damn. It was bread, pan y tortillas out of his children's mouths.

40 But they still wouldn't give a single damn. Manuel had wrenched Morales' greedy fingers away and removed a fat slug of a purse from his sticky grasp. And in his slow way, in his stupid, accidental, dangerous way, Manuel had made an extravagant discovery, as Don Gaspar had also made two centuries before, in almost exactly the same spot. And that was—that a man counted for

45 something. For men, Manuel dimly suspected, are built for something more important and less trifling than the mere gathering of prunes and apricots, hour upon hour, decade upon decade, insensibly, mechanically, antlike. Men are built to experience a certain sense of honor and pride.

Or else they are dead before they die.

—Excerpted from *The Plum, Plum Pickers*
by Raymond Barrio

1. Why does Roberto Morales ask all the fruit pickers to pay him two cents?

    (1) The men owe him the money.
    (2) He unintentionally cheated the men.
    (3) He is greedy and wants to increase his profits.
    (4) He is collecting money to buy new equipment.
    (5) He is in debt and needs the extra cash.

2. In line 18, why does the author describe the other migrant farm workers as "exhausted animals"?

    (1) to suggest that they act like caged beasts in a zoo
    (2) to reveal their stupidity and inability to speak
    (3) to show that their hard work robs them of their humanity
    (4) to illustate that animals perform some jobs better than men
    (5) to suggest their wild and violent personalities

3. What action does Manuel Gutierrez take to defy Roberto Morales?

    (1) He kicks over two buckets of fruit.
    (2) He talks the other men into challenging Roberto.
    (3) He gets into a fistfight with Roberto.
    (4) He resigns from his job.
    (5) He asks for a raise in his salary.

4. Which of the following words best describes the fruit pickers' attitude toward Roberto Morales after Manuel Gutierrez challenges him?

    (1) indifference
    (2) amazement
    (3) pity
    (4) disbelief
    (5) contempt

5. Which of the following statements summarizes the major theme of the entire passage?

(1) Hard labor turns people into machine-like creatures.
(2) Work gives people's lives a sense of purpose.
(3) Angry outbursts are unproductive.
(4) Every person is important and deserves respect.
(5) Picking fruit is a frustrating job.

FOR ANSWERS AND EXPLANATIONS, SEE PAGE 279.

Exercise 12: Reading a Short Story

This selection is a complete short story that is longer than the reading selections on the GED Interpreting Literature and the Arts Test. It is included here to give you an opportunity to see how writers use all the elements of fiction that you have studied.

Directions: In the following short story, Walter Mitty, the main character, has five fantasies. He pretends that he is a make-believe person. Except for the fantasies in the first and last paragraph, the passages in which Walter Mitty fantasizes are set off at the beginning and end by three dots called an ellipsis (. . .). These events occur in his imagination. The other paragraphs tell what really is happening in the story. Carefully read the short story and answer the questions.

The Secret Life of Walter Mitty

"We're going through!" The Commander's voice was like thin ice breaking. He wore his full-dress uniform, with the heavily braided white cap pulled down rakishly over one cold gray eye. "We can't make it, sir. It's spoiling for a hurricane, if you ask me." "I'm not asking you, Lieutenant Berg," said the Commander. "Throw on the power lights! Rev her up to 8,500! We're going through!" The pounding of the cylinders increased: ta-pocketa-pocketa-pocketa-*pocketa-pocketa*. The Commander stared at the ice forming on the pilot window. He walked over and twisted a row of complicated dials. "Switch on No. 8 auxiliary!" he shouted. "Switch on No. 8 auxiliary!" repeated Lieutenant Berg. "Full strength in No. 3 turret!" The crew, bending to their various tasks in the huge, hurtling eight-engined Navy hydroplane, looked at each other and grinned. "The Old Man'll get us through," they said to one another. "The Old Man ain't afraid of Hell!" . . .

"Not so fast! You're driving too fast!" Said Mrs. Mitty. "What are you driving so fast for?"

"Hmm?" said Walter Mitty. He looked at his wife, in the seat beside him, with shocked astonishment. She seemed grossly unfamiliar, like a strange woman who had yelled at him in a crowd. "You were up to fifty-five," she said. "You know I don't like to go more than forty. You were up to fifty-five." Walter Mitty drove on toward Waterbury in silence, the roaring of the SN202 through the worst storm in twenty years of Navy flying fading in the remote, intimate airways of his mind.

"You're tensed up again," said Mrs. Mitty. "It's one of your days. I wish you'd let Dr. Renshaw look you over."

Walter Mitty stopped the car in front of the building where his wife went to have her hair done. "Remember to get those overshoes while I'm having my hair done," she said. "I don't need overshoes," said Mitty. She put her mirror back into her bag. "We've been all through that," she said, getting out of the car. "You're not a young man any longer." He raced the engine a little. "Why don't you wear your gloves? Have you lost your gloves?" Walter Mitty reached in a pocket and brought out the gloves. He put them on, but after she had turned and gone into the building and he had driven on to a red light, he took them off again. "Pick it up, brother!" snapped a cop as the light changed, and Mitty hastily pulled on his gloves and lurched ahead. He drove around the streets aimlessly for a time, and then he drove past the hospital on his way to the parking lot.

. . . "It's the millionaire banker, Wellington McMillan," said the pretty nurse. "Yes?" said Walter Mitty, removing his gloves slowly. "Who has the case?" "Dr. Renshaw and Dr. Benbow, but there are two specialists here, Dr. Remington from New York and Mr. Pritchard-Mitford from London. He flew over." A door opened down a long, cool corridor and Dr. Renshaw came out. He looked distraught and haggard. "Hello, Mitty," he said. "We're having the devil's own time with McMillan, the millionaire banker and close personal friend of Roosevelt. Obstreosis of the ductal tract. Tertiary. Wish you'd take a look at him." "Glad to," said Mitty.

In the operating room there were whispered introductions: "Dr. Remington, Dr. Mitty. Mr. Pritchard-Mitford, Dr. Mitty." "I've read your book on streptothricosis," said Pritchard-Mitford, shaking hands. "A brilliant performance, sir." "Thank you," said Walter Mitty. "Didn't know you were in the States, Mitty," grumbled Remington. "Coals to Newcastle, bringing Mitford and me up here for a tertiary." "You are very kind," said Mitty. A huge, complicated machine, connected to the operating table, with many tubes and wires, began at this moment to go pocketa-pocketa-pocketa. "The new anesthetizer is giving way!" shouted an interne. "There is no one in the East who knows how to fix it!" "Quiet, man!" said Mitty, in a low, cool voice. He sprang to the machine, which was now going pocketa-pocketa-queep-pocketa-queep. He began fingering delicately a row of glistening dials. "Give me a fountain pen!" he snapped. Someone handed him a fountain pen. He pulled a faulty piston out of the machine and inserted the pen in its place. "That will hold for ten minutes," he said. "Get on with the operation." A nurse hurried over and whispered to Renshaw, and Mitty saw the man turn pale. "Coreopsis has set in," said Renshaw nervously. "If you would take over, Mitty?" Mitty looked at him and at the craven figure of Benbow, who drank, and at the grave, uncertain faces of the two great specialists. "If you wish," he said. They slipped a white gown on him; he adjusted a mask and drew on thin gloves; nurses handed him shining . . .

"Back it up, Mac! Look out for that Buick!" Walter Mitty jammed on the brakes. "Wrong lane, Mac," said the parking-lot attendant, looking at Mitty closely. "Gee. Yeh," muttered Mitty. He began cautiously to back out of the lane marked "Exit Only." "Leave her sit there," said the attendant. "I'll put her away." Mitty got out of the car. "Hey, better leave the key." "Oh," said Mitty, handing the man the ignition key. The attendant vaulted into the car, backed it up with insolent skill, and put it where it belonged.

They're so damn cocky, thought Walter Mitty, walking along Main Street; they think they know everything. Once he had tried to take his chains off, outside New Milford, and he had got them wound around the axles. A man had had to come out in a wrecking car and unwind them, a young, grinning garageman. Since then Mrs. Mitty always made him drive to a garage to have the chains taken off. The next time, he thought, I'll wear my right arm in a sling; they won't grin at me then. I'll have my right arm in a sling and they'll see I couldn't possibly take the chains off myself. He kicked at the slush on the sidewalk. "Overshoes," he said to himself, and he began looking for a shoe store.

When he came out into the street again, with the overshoes in a box under his arm, Walter Mitty began to wonder what the other thing was his wife had told him to get. She had told him, twice, before they set out from their house for Waterbury. In a way he hated these weekly trips to town—he was always getting something wrong. Kleenex, he thought, Squibb's, razor blades? No. Toothpaste, toothbrush, bicarbonate, carborundum, initiative and referendum? He gave it up. But she would remember it. "Where's the what's-its-name?" she would ask. "Don't tell me you forgot the what's-its-name." A newsboy went by shouting something about the Waterbury trial.

. . . "Perhaps this will refresh your memory." The District Attorney suddenly thrust a heavy automatic at the quiet figure on the witness stand. "Have you ever seen this before?" Walter Mitty took the gun and examined it expertly. "This is my Webley-Vickers 50.80," he said calmly. An excited buzz ran around the courtroom. The Judge rapped for order. "You are a crack shot with any sort of firearms, I believe?" said the District Attorney, insinuatingly. "Objection!" shouted Mitty's attorney. "We have shown that the defendant could not have fired the shot. We have shown that he wore his right arm in a sling on the night of the fourteenth of July." Walter Mitty raised his hand briefly and the bicker-ing attorneys were stilled. "With any known make of gun," he said evenly, "I could have killed Gregory Fitzhurst at three hundred feet *with my left hand*." Pandemonium broke loose in the courtroom. A woman's scream rose above the bedlam and suddenly a lovely, dark-haired girl was in Walter Mitty's arms. The District Attorney struck at her savagely. Without rising from his chair, Mitty let the man have it on the point of the chin. "You miserable cur!" . . .

"Puppy biscuit," said Walter Mitty. He stopped walking and the buildings of Waterbury rose up out of the misty courtroom and surrounded him again. A woman who was passing laughed. "He said 'Puppy biscuit,'" she said to her companion. "That man said 'Puppy biscuit' to himself." Walter Mitty hurried on. He went into an A. & P., not the first one he came to but a smaller one farther up the street. "I want some biscuit for small, young dogs," he said to the clerk. "Any special brand, sir?" The greatest pistol shot in the world thought a moment. "It says 'Puppies Bark for It' on the box," said Walter Mitty.

His wife would be through at the hairdresser's in fifteen minutes, Mitty saw in looking at his watch, unless they had trouble drying it; sometimes they had trouble drying it. She didn't like to get to the hotel first; she would want him to be there waiting for her as usual. He found a big leather chair in the lobby, facing a window, and he put the overshoes and the puppy biscuit on the floor beside it. He picked up an old copy of *Liberty* and sank down into the chair. "Can Germany Conquer the World Through the Air?" Walter Mitty looked at the pictures of bomb-ing planes and of ruined streets.

. . . "The cannonading has got the wind up in young Raleigh, sir," said the sergeant. Captain Mitty looked up at him through touseled hair. "Get him to bed," he said wearily. "With the others. I'll fly alone." "But you can't, sir," said the sergeant anxiously. "It takes two men to handle that bomber and the Archies are pounding hell out of the air. Von Richtman's circus is between here and Saulier." "Somebody's got to get that ammunition dump," said Mitty. "I'm going over. Spot of brandy?" He poured a drink for the sergeant and one for himself. War thundered and whined around the dugout and battered at the door. There was a rending of wood and splinters flew through the room. "A bit of a near thing," said Captain Mitty carelessly. "The box barrage is closing in," said the sergeant. "We only live once, Sergeant," said Mitty, with his faint, fleeting smile. "Or do we?" He poured another brandy and tossed it off. "I never see a man could hold his brandy like you, sir," said the sergeant. "Begging your pardon, sir." Captain Mitty stood up and strapped on his huge Webley-Vickers automatic. "It's forty kilometers through hell, sir," said the sergeant. Mitty finished one last brandy. "After all," he said softly, "what isn't?" The pounding of the cannon increased; there was the rat-tat-tatting of machine guns, and from somewhere came the menacing pocketa-pocketa-pocketa of the new flame-throwers. Walter Mitty walked to the door of the dugout humming "Aupres de Ma Blonde." He turned and waved to the sergeant. "Cheerio!"

he said . . .

Something struck his shoulder. "I've been looking all over this hotel for you," said Mrs. Mitty. "Why do you have to hide in this old chair? How did you expect me to find you?" "Things close in," said Walter Mitty vaguely. "What?" Mrs. Mitty said. "Did you get the what's-its-name? The puppy biscuit? What's in that box?" "Overshoes," said Mitty. "Couldn't you have put them on in the store?" "I was thinking," said Walter Mitty. "Does it ever occur to you that I am sometimes thinking?" She looked at him. "I'm going to take your temperature when I get you home," she said.

They went out through the revolving doors that made a faintly derisive whistling sound when you pushed them. It was two blocks to the parking lot. At the drugstore on the corner she said, "Wait here for me. I forgot something. I won't be a minute." She was more than a minute. Walter Mitty lighted a cigarette. It began to rain, rain with sleet in it. He stood up against the wall of the drugstore, smoking. . . . He put his shoulders back and his heels together. "To hell with the handkerchief," said Walter Mitty scornfully. He took one last drag on his cigarette and snapped it away. Then, with that faint, fleeting smile playing about his lips, he faced the firing squad; erect and motionless, proud and disdainful, Walter Mitty the Undefeated, inscrutable to the last.

—by James Thurber

1. Mr. and Mrs. Mitty are driving to what city? _____

2. Mr. Mitty stops at several places during his trip to the city. These places are listed below in jumbled order. Number these places according to the sequence in which they are mentioned in the story.

_____ parking lot   _____ shoe store

_____ hotel lobby   _____ A & P grocery store

_____ beauty parlor

3. Walter Mitty's fantasies are influenced by his real-life experiences. The first example in the chart below illustrates the cause-and-effect relationship between an actual incident (the cause) and the daydream (the effect). Using the example as a model, identify the fantasy that stems from the real situation.

Real Incident (the cause)	Fantasy (the effect)
Speeding in his car	*Character:* Commander of a Navy plane *Situation:* Flying the plane during a dangerous storm
Driving past a hospital on his way to the parking lot.	*Character:* _____ *Situation:* _____ _____
A newspaper boy shouting about the Waterbury trial.	*Character:* _____ *Situation:* _____ _____
Reading a magazine article entitled "Can Germany Conquer the World?"	*Character:* _____ *Situation:* _____ _____

4. From Mrs. Mitty's conversations with her husband, you can infer that she is bossy and critical. Identify three lines of dialogue that support this inference.

_____
_____
_____

5. In his fantasies, Walter Mitty imagines himself as

(1) wealthy and selfish
(2) modest and shy
(3) forgetful and foolish
(4) strong and courageous
(5) tense and fearful

6. One of the major themes expressed in this passage is that

    (1) people who fantasize are emotionally disturbed
    (2) doctors know how to handle pressure
    (3) husbands resent their wives
    (4) parking lot attendants are rude
    (5) people daydream to escape the dull routine of life

7. The subject of this short story would be best suited for which of the following television shows?

    (1) a soap opera
    (2) a situation comedy
    (3) a science fiction series
    (4) a news program
    (5) a courtroom drama

FOR ANSWERS AND EXPLANATIONS, SEE PAGE 279.

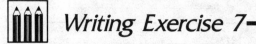

Writing Exercise 7

Like Walter Mitty, most people daydream. On a separate sheet of paper, describe a fantasy that you have had. Your description should include the answers to the following questions:

    ☐ What is the imaginary situation?

    ☐ Where and when does the fantasy occur?

    ☐ What role do you play in the fantasy?

ANSWERS WILL VARY.

★ **GED PRACTICE** ★

Exercise 13: Chapter Review

Directions: Read the following passages and answer the multiple-choice questions. Use the purpose question at the beginning of each passage to focus your reading and to help you understand the passage.

Passage 1: Popular Literature

HOW DOES A CROWD BEHAVE AT THE PREMIERE OF A HOLLYWOOD MOVIE?

Although it was still several hours before the celebrities would arrive, thousands of people had already gathered. They stood facing the theatre with their backs toward the gutter in a thick line hundreds of feet long. A big squad of policemen was trying to keep a lane open between the front rank of the
5 crowd and the facade of the theatre.

Tod entered the lane while the policeman guarding it was busy with a woman whose parcel had torn open, dropping oranges all over the place. Another policeman shouted for him to get the hell across the street, but he took a chance and kept going. They had enough to do without chasing him. He
10 noticed how worried they looked and how careful they tried to be. If they had to arrest someone, they joked good-naturedly with the culprit, making light of it until they got him around the corner, then they whaled him with their clubs. Only so long as the man was actually part of the crowd did they have to be gentle.
15 Tod had walked only a short distance along the narrow lane when he began to get frightened. People shouted, commenting on his hat, his carriage, and his clothing. There was a continuous roar of catcalls, laughter and yells, pierced occasionally by a scream. The scream was usually followed by a sudden movement in the dense mass and part of it would surge forward
20 wherever the police line was weakest. As soon as that part was rammed back, the bulge would pop out somewhere else.
The police force would have to be doubled when the stars started to arrive. At the sight of their heroes and heroines, the crowd would turn demoniac. Some little gesture, either too pleasing or too offensive, would start it moving and then
25 nothing but machine guns would stop it. Individually the purpose of its members might simply to be to get a souvenir, but collectively it would grab and rend.
A young man with a portable microphone was describing the scene. His rapid, hysterical voice was like that of a revivalist preacher whipping his
30 congregation toward the ecstasy of fits.
"What a crowd folks! What a crowd! There must be ten thousand excited, screaming fans outside Kahn's Persian tonight. The police can't hold them. Here, listen to them roar."

—Excerpted from *The Day of the Locust*
by Nathanael West

1. How did the police treat an arrested person after he was separated from the crowd?

    (1) carefully
    (2) gently
    (3) good-naturedly
    (4) jokingly
    (5) violently

2. The purpose of the second and third paragraphs is to describe

    (1) the movement of the crowd
    (2) Tod's observations of the scene
    (3) the personalities of the policemen
    (4) the effects of a woman dropping oranges
    (5) the physical appearance of individuals within the crowd

3. According to the passage, which of the following words best describes Tod's feeling toward the crowd?

    (1) excitement
    (2) surprise
    (3) resentment
    (4) fright
    (5) admiration

4. "His rapid, hysterical voice was like that of a revivalist preacher whipping his congregation toward the ecstasy of fits" (lines 28–30).
   The author uses this comparison to show that the man with the microphone

    (1) has strong religious convictions
    (2) is rehearsing the role of a preacher
    (3) enjoys listening to sermons
    (4) speaks in an agitated and manipulative tone
    (5) wants to lead a congregation

5. In this excerpt, who is telling the story?

    (1) Tod
    (2) the author acting as narrator
    (3) the man with the microphone
    (4) a policeman
    (5) a movie star

6. Which statement best expresses the theme of the passage?

    (1) When controlling a crowd, police should practice nonviolence.
    (2) When a crowd turns into a mob, people lose their individual identities.
    (3) Hollywood celebrities like their fans to show devotion.
    (4) Law and order at outdoor events should be strictly enforced.
    (5) Everyone secretly desires fame and public attention.

7. The scene described in this passage also portrays the way crowds sometimes behave at

    (1) a zoo
    (2) a rock concert
    (3) an amusement park
    (4) a basketball game
    (5) a trade show

Passage 2: Classic Literature

WHAT DOES PIP NOTICE ABOUT MISS HAVISHAM?

She was dressed in rich materials—satins, and lace, and silks—all of white. Her shoes were white. And she had a long white veil dependent from her hair, and she had bridal flowers in her hair, but her hair was white. Some bright

jewels sparkled on her neck and on her hands, and some other jewels lay
5 sparkling on the table. Dresses, less splendid than the dress she wore, and half-
packed trunks, were scattered about. She had not quite finished dressing, for
she had but one shoe on—the other was on the table near her hand—her veil
was but half arranged, her watch and chain were not put on, and some lace for
her bosom lay with those trinkets, and with her handkerchief, and gloves, and
10 some flowers, and a Prayer-book, all confusedly heaped about the looking-
glass.

It was not in the first few moments that I saw all these things, though I saw
more of them in the first moments than might be supposed. But, I saw that
everything within my view which ought to be white, had been white long ago,
15 and had lost its lustre, and was faded and yellow. I saw that the bride within the
bridal dress had withered like the dress, and like the flowers, and had no
brightness left but the brightness of her sunken eyes. I saw that the dress had
been put upon the rounded figure of a young woman, and that the figure upon
which it now hung loose, had shrunk to skin and bone. . . .

20 "Who is it?" said the lady at the table.

"Pip, ma'am."

"Pip?"

"Mr. Pumblechook's boy, ma'am. Come—to play."

"Come nearer; let me look at you. Come close."

25 It was when I stood before her, avoiding her eyes, that I took note of
surrounding objects in detail, and saw that her watch had stopped at twenty
minutes to nine, and that a clock in the room had stopped at twenty minutes to
nine.

"Look at me," said Miss Havisham. "You are not afraid of a woman who has
30 never seen the sun since you were born?"

—Excerpted from *Great Expectations* by Charles Dickens

8. The scene takes place in

   (1) a parlor
   (2) a living room
   (3) a bedroom
   (4) an attic
   (5) an enclosed porch

9. In this excerpt, the author reveals the character of Miss Havisham by

   (1) analyzing her relationship with Pip
   (2) summarizing events from her past
   (3) describing her physical appearance and surroundings
   (4) detailing the reasons for her behavior
   (5) presenting her opinion of herself

10. Based on lines 1–4, you can conclude that Miss Havisham is

   (1) wealthy
   (2) embarrassed
   (3) nervous
   (4) beautiful
   (5) greedy

11. The descriptive details in lines 14–19 suggest an atmosphere of

    (1) decay
    (2) disappointment
    (3) loneliness
    (4) frustration
    (5) desperation

12. From whose point of view is the story told?

    (1) the author's
    (2) Miss Havisham's
    (3) a bride's
    (4) Mr. Pumblechook's
    (5) Pip's

13. "... a clock in the room had stopped at twenty minutes to nine" (lines 27–28)

The author includes this observation to show that

    (1) time has stood still in this room
    (2) the watch and clock need to be repaired
    (3) Pip wants to check how long his visit is taking
    (4) Miss Havisham doesn't know how to tell time
    (5) Miss Havisham forgot to rewind her watch and clock

14. If this scene were presented in a movie, the camera would focus on

    (1) Pip
    (2) Miss Havisham
    (3) the setting
    (4) Miss Havisham's belongings
    (5) Miss Havisham's table

Passage 3: Commentary About Prose

WHAT DOES AN AUTHOR SAY ABOUT WRITING?

As I wrote, I followed, almost unconsciously, many principles of the novel which my reading of the novels of other writers had made me feel were necessary for the building of a well-constructed book. For the most part the novel is rendered in the present; I wanted the reader to feel that Bigger's story
5 was happening *now*, like a play upon the stage or a movie unfolding upon the screen. Action follows action, as in a prize fight. Wherever possible, I told of Bigger's life in close-up, slow-motion, giving the feel of the grain in the passing of time. I had long had the feeling that this was the best way to "enclose" the reader's mind in a new world, to blot out all reality except that which I was giving
10 him.

Then again, as much as I could, I restricted the novel to what Bigger saw and felt, to the limits of his feeling and thoughts, even when I was conveying *more* than that to the reader. I had the notion that such a manner of rendering

15 made for a sharper effect, a more pointed sense of the character, his peculiar type of being and consciousness. Throughout there is but one point of view: Bigger's. This, too, I felt, made for a richer illusion of reality.

I kept out of the story as much as possible, for I wanted the reader to feel that there was nothing between him and Bigger; that the story was a special *première* given in his own private theater.

20 I kept the scenes long, made as much happen within a short space of time as possible; all of which, I felt, made for greater density and richness of effect.

In a like manner I tried to keep a unified sense of background throughout the story; the background would change, of course, but I tried to keep before the eyes of the reader at all times the forces and elements against which Bigger

25 was striving.

And because I had limited myself to rendering only what Bigger saw and felt, I gave no more reality to the other characters than that which Bigger himself saw.

—Excerpted from "How 'Bigger' Was Born," the
introduction to *Native Son* by Richard Wright

15. According to the excerpt, how does the plot of Bigger's story resemble a prizefight?

(1) Action follows action in the novel.
(2) Bigger constantly faces conflicts.
(3) Bigger often resorts to physical violence.
(4) Bigger finds himself in a win-lose situation.
(5) Bigger competes with other characters.

16. The author tells the novel from whose point of view?

(1) the author's
(2) another character's
(3) Bigger's
(4) a spectator's
(5) a movie director's

17. From this excerpt, you can conclude that the author's approach to writing the novel is

(1) disorganized
(2) inflexible
(3) deliberate
(4) relaxed
(5) illogical

18. Why does the author want the reader to feel that "the story was a special première given in his own private theater" (lines 18–19)?

(1) The reader can pretend that he owns his own playhouse.
(2) The reader can feel that he personally experiences the dramatic events of Bigger's life.
(3) The reader can evaluate Bigger's story like a theater critic.
(4) The reader can imagine being a special person in show business.
(5) The reader can appreciate plays more than novels.

19. Which of the following phrases best summarizes the content of the entire passage?

    (1) similarities between plays and novels
    (2) approaches to reading a novel
    (3) techniques of novel writing
    (4) influences of movies on novel writing
    (5) methods for analyzing character

20. If Bigger were a real person rather than a fictional character, which of the following writers would be most likely to tell his life story?

    (1) a poet
    (2) a movie reviewer
    (3) a journalist
    (4) a songwriter
    (5) a playwright

FOR ANSWERS AND EXPLANATIONS, SEE PAGES 279-80.

6 POETRY

All writing communicates an observation, an opinion, or an emotion. For instance, newspaper articles convey information about daily events. You assume that newspaper articles are written accurately and summarize the most essential facts. The journalist's responsibility is to report the truth—a precise account of an incident.

On September 16, 1963, a dynamite explosion in Birmingham's Sixteenth Street Baptist Church killed four young black girls. The following excerpt from a news story highlights important details about the incident:

> The four girls killed in the blast had just heard Mrs. Ella C. Demand, their teacher, complete the Sunday School lesson for the day. The subject was "The Love That Forgives."
>
> During the period between the class and an assembly in the main auditorium, they went to the women's lounge in the basement at the northeast corner of the church.
>
> The blast occurred at about 10:25 A.M. . . .
>
> Church members said they found the girls huddled together beneath a pile of masonry debris.
>
> —Excerpted from "Four Negro Girls Killed in Birmingham Church Bombing" in *The New York Times*

Dudley Randall, a poet, retold this news story as a poem. He relates an imaginary conversation between a mother and her daughter, one of the four victims. In his interpretation, the mother mistakenly assumes that going to church is safer than marching in a civil rights demonstration. The poet, unlike the journalist, is not obliged to report the actual circumstances of an event. The poem "Ballad of Birmingham" illustrates how poets see real-life experiences in original and imaginative ways.

As you study this poem, compare and contrast its content, style, and structure with the newspaper version. The comments in the right-hand column will help to guide your reading:

The Poem	Comments on Structure and Content
Ballad of Birmingham	Title of the poem
(On the Bombing of a Church in Birmingham, Alabama, 1963)	Poet's reason for writing the poem
"Mother dear, may I go downtown Instead of out to play, And march the streets of Birmingham In a Freedom March today?"	*Stanza 1:* Daughter's spoken words Daughter asks to attend the civil rights demonstration.
5 "No, baby, no, you may not go, For the dogs are fierce and wild, And clubs and hoses, guns and jail Aren't good for a little child."	*Stanza 2:* Mother's spoken words Mother gives reasons for her refusal.
"But, mother, I won't be alone. 10 Other children will go with me, And march the streets of Birmingham To make our country free."	*Stanza 3:* Daughter's spoken words Daughter tries to change her mother's mind.
"No, baby, no, you may not go, For I fear those guns will fire. 15 But you may go to church instead And sing in the children's choir."	*Stanza 4:* Mother's spoken words Mother again denies her daughter's request.
She has combed and brushed her night-dark hair, And bathed rose petal sweet, And drawn white gloves on her small brown hands 20 And white shoes on her feet.	*Stanza 5:* Daughter's physical appearance Mother dresses her daughter.
The mother smiled to know her child Was in the sacred place, But that smile was the last smile To come upon her face.	*Stanza 6:* Mother's feelings Hints suggest that a tragic event will occur.
25 For when she heard the explosion, Her eyes grew wet and wild. She raced through the streets of Birmingham Calling for her child.	*Stanza 7:* Mother's response to the explosion Mother looks for her daughter.
She clawed through bits of glass and brick, 30 Then lifted out a shoe. "O here's the shoe my baby wore, But, baby, where are you?"	*Stanza 8:* Mother's actions and spoken words Mother discovers her daughter is dead.

—by Dudley Randall

Let's closely compare some of the characteristics of the newspaper article and the poem. The following chart analyzes the major differences.

Characteristics	Newspaper Article	"Ballad of Birmingham"
Visual Appearance and Arrangement of Words on the Page	Groups sentences into paragraphs.	Divides sentences into lines. Four lines are clustered together to form a unit called a *stanza*.
Sound of the Words	Words in the newspaper article don't rhyme.	In the second and fourth lines of each stanza, the last word rhymes. The rhyming words produce a musical effect.
Author's Purpose	To inform the reader	To affect the reader emotionally
Style of Language	Simple, direct statements **Examples:** "The blast occurred at about 10:25 A.M." "Church members said they found the girls huddled together beneath a pile of masonry debris."	Descriptive language that creates vivid images **Examples:** "Her eyes grew wet and wild." "She clawed through bits of glass and brick."

Characteristics of Poetry

Even though other poems aren't exactly like "Ballad of Birmingham," the observations in the preceding chart can help you to form generalizations about poetry. Here are some common characteristics:

1. Sentences are divided into lines. Sometimes lines are grouped in stanzas. (See example on page 182.)

2. The sounds and arrangement of words produce a musical effect.

3. Descriptive language, both literal and figurative, creates striking images that may affect the reader emotionally.

4. Like tone of voice, the tone of a poem reveals the poet's feelings and attitudes about a subject.

5. Poetry imaginatively portrays a wide range of subjects, including both serious topics and everyday experiences and observations.

In the next exercise, you will apply what you have just learned about poetry.

Exercise 1: Characteristics of Poetry

Directions: Reread Dudley Randall's poem "Ballad of Birmingham." Then complete the exercises.

1. The last words in the even-numbered lines of each stanza rhyme. In the spaces provided, write the eight pairs of rhyming words.

    Lines 2 & 4: _____ _____

    Lines 6 & 8: _____ _____

    Lines 10 & 12: _____ _____

    Lines 14 & 16: _____ _____

    Lines 18 & 20: _____ _____

    Lines 22 & 24: _____ _____

    Lines 26 & 28: _____ _____

    Lines 30 & 32: _____ _____

2. Write the specific line or lines from the poem that support(s) each of the following statements:

    (1) The streets of Birmingham, Alabama, are dangerous.

    _____

    _____

    _____

(2) The mother was crying.

_____

(3) The mother searched for her daughter at the church.

_____

(4) The mother found evidence that her daughter was dead.

_____

3. Write *true* or *false* next to each of the following statements:

(1) The poet directly states his personal reaction to the bombing.

_____

(2) The poem suggests that the girl would have lived if she had attended the "Freedom March." _____

(3) The poet reveals the mother's grief and horror. _____

(4) The words and the rhythm of the poem are similar to those of a song.

_____

FOR ANSWERS AND EXPLANATIONS, SEE PAGES 280-81.

Writing Exercise 1

Find a newspaper article that affects you emotionally. On a separate sheet of paper, write a poem about the story. Imagine the people who were involved in the incident. To make an interesting poem, add descriptive details not reported in the original article. Experiment with different ways of arranging the words on the page.

ANSWERS WILL VARY.

Suggestions for Reading Poetry

How should you read a poem? Kenneth Koch and Kate Farrell, two modern poets, offer the following advice:

The best way to begin is by reading the poem several times to get used to the style. After you get a sense of the whole poem, there are some things you can do to help yourself understand anything that's unclear—if anything still is unclear, which often it won't be. There may be a word or two you don't understand, or a reference to a person or a place that you're not familiar with. These you can look up in a dictionary or encyclopedia or ask someone about. There may be a sentence that's so long it's hard to follow, or a sentence that's left incomplete; words may be in an unusual order, or a sentence may be hard to see because it's divided into different lines. For these problems, just go through the poem slowly, seeing where the different sentences begin and end. If you understand part of a poem and not another part, try to use what you do understand to help you see what the rest means.

—Excerpted from *Sleeping on the Wing* by Kenneth Koch
and Kate Farrell

On the following lines, write four suggestions that Kenneth Koch and Kate Farrell make for reading a poem:

1. _____

2. _____

3. _____

4. _____

Did you include some of these major points?

1. Read the poem several times to get accustomed to the poet's style—the way he or she uses language.

2. Look up unfamiliar words in a dictionary or an encyclopedia.

3. Read the poem slowly. Notice where sentences begin and end. (Note: A period usually marks the end of a complete sentence. In some poems, the first word of each line is capitalized. Don't assume that the capitalization signals the beginning of a new sentence.)

4. Apply what you already understand about part of the poem to the parts that seem more difficult.

In addition to these suggestions, here are a few more guidelines: (1) Read the poem aloud. Listen to the sound and the rhythm of the words. (2) Pay attention to the title. The title may provide clues about the topic and the theme of the poem. (3) Identify the speaker of the poem. Like a narrator in a short story or a novel, the *speaker* represents a person's voice. The poet invents a voice to narrate the poem. If the poem uses the pronoun "I," don't assume that "I" refers to the poet personally. (4) Grasp the literal meaning of the poem—what the poet directly tells you. Infer the suggested meaning, if there is one.

When you interpret poetry, you practice all the reading skills presented in the first three chapters of this textbook:

☐ Understanding the literal meaning—the poem's directly stated main ideas and supporting details

☐ Making inferences based upon the literal meaning

☐ Analyzing style and structure—the way a poet uses language and arranges content

In some poems, you also will find fictional elements—for example, setting, plot, characterization, dialogue, and theme.

For practice in reading poetry, complete the next exercise.

Exercise 2: Reading a Poem

Directions: In the following poem, Janet Campbell Hale, a Native American poet, writes about a person, a place, and an event. Carefully read the poem and complete the exercise.

```
        I lay my hand
        Upon
        The coldness of the smooth
        White stone,
    5   My fingers touch the words,
        I read again:
        My father's name,
        Date of birth,
        Date of death,
   10   Veteran of
        World War I.

        "This is your
        Grandfather's grave,"
        I tell my children,
   15   Wishing I could tell them,
        That they would understand,
        That the man
        Who was my father,
        Was of that first generation,
   20   Born on old land
        Newly made reservation,
        That at twelve,
        He went to Mission School,
        To learn to wear shoes,
   25   To eat with knife and fork,
        To pray to the Catholic God,
        To painfully
        Learn English words,
        English meanings,
   30   White ways of thinking,
```

> English words,
> To speak,
> To think,
> To write,
> 35   English words,
> When we,
> My children
> And I
> Know no others.

—Excerpted from "Tribal Cemetery"
by Janet Campbell Hale

1.   The poem takes place at

    (1)   an Indian reservation
    (2)   the Mission School
    (3)   a graveyard
    (4)   a funeral parlor
    (5)   a Catholic church

2.   The speaker, the person telling the poem, is

    (1)   the father
    (2)   the father's daughter
    (3)   the grandchildren
    (4)   a priest
    (5)   a schoolteacher

3.   Why is the phrase "English words" repeated three times (Lines 28, 31, and 35)?

    (1)   to praise the superiority of the English language
    (2)   to emphasize that English was a foreign, unnatural language for the father to learn
    (3)   to show that a knowledge of English helps people to find good jobs
    (4)   to emphasize the importance of studying vocabulary, speech, and grammar
    (5)   to show that the father was a poor student

4.   How does the daughter feel about her father?

    (1)   proud
    (2)   angry
    (3)   disrespectful
    (4)   suspicious
    (5)   annoyed

5.   In the poem, you are told certain literal statements about the father who has died. These literal statements provide you with clues about the suggested meaning of the poem. The following inferences are based on the statements in the poem. If an inference *can* be based on the poem, label it *valid*. If the poem does not support a statement, label it *invalid*.

    (1)   The father was honored with medals for his bravery as a soldier.

(2) Beginning at the age of twelve, the father began to lose touch with his original heritage. _____

(3) The father practiced only his native religion all his life. _____

(4) The generations after the father are disconnected from their Native American roots. _____

(5) The purpose of the father's training at the Mission School was to make him conform to white American culture. _____

(6) Non-English-speaking immigrants arriving to the United States could probably identify with the father's difficulty in adapting to American society. _____

FOR ANSWERS AND EXPLANATIONS, SEE PAGE 281.

Understanding the Language of Poetry

One of the most striking characteristics of poetry is its attention to language. Poetic language often appeals to the senses—sights, sounds, odors, textures, and tastes.

Poets use both literal statements and figures of speech to express sensations and ideas. In this section, you will learn how poets describe their perceptions through literal and figurative language.

Literal Descriptions

Poetry uses words to literally describe the physical appearance of a person, a place, or a thing. These descriptions should help you to visualize the object of the poet's observation. The central purpose of purely descriptive poetry is to help you to "see" a detailed image.

Use your imagination to picture the man described in the following poem:

The Runner
On a flat road runs the well-train'd runner;
He is lean and sinewy, with muscular legs;
He is thinly clothed—he leans forward as he runs,
With lightly closed fists, and arms partially rais'd.

—by Walt Whitman

Can you see a clear image of the runner? Reread the poem and write the specific words or phrases that answer these questions:

1. Where is the man running? _____

2. What words describe the runner's build? _____

   _____

3. How is the runner dressed? _____

4. What pose does he strike as he runs? _____

   _____

Here are the correct responses:

1. "on a flat road"
2. "lean"; "sinewy"; "muscular legs"
3. "thinly clothed"
4. "leans forward"; "lightly closed fists"; "arms partially rais'd"

The total effect of these descriptive details creates a vivid portrait of a runner. The words produce an image as distinct as a snapshot. Compare the poem with the following photograph of Scott Tinley, winner of the 1982 and 1985 Hawaii Ironman triathlons.

Photograph by Mike Plant

Writing Exercise 2

Find a photograph of an athlete in the sports section of the newspaper. On a separate sheet of paper, write a short poem in which you re-create the image of the athlete through descriptive words and phrases. Use Walt Whitman's poem "The Runner" as a model.

ANSWERS WILL VARY.

More Practice With Descriptions

In the preceding poem, Walt Whitman directly shows you what the runner looks like. He offers no comments about the runner's personality. However, you could probably infer that the poet admires the runner's physical appearance and athletic ability.

As you already know from reading fiction, a character's physical appearance and actions often reveal his personality. In the next excerpt, a stanza from the poem "Kindergarten," the person telling the poem describes a school principal. Circle the words and phrases that create a picture in your mind.

> The principal had a long black whip
> studded through with razor blades
> and nine lashes on it.
> The principal wore a black suit
> and smoked Pall Malls
> and wrote bad notes to your father.
>
> —Excerpted from "Kindergarten" by Ronald Rogers

You can infer that the speaker of the poem fears the principal. Why? Write the descriptive details that support this inference.

_____

_____

The first three lines and the last line suggest the speaker's fearful attitude. The detailed description of the principal's "long black whip / studded through with razor blades / and nine lashes on it" presents a threatening image. The principal also "wrote bad notes to your father"—another method he apparently used to instill fear. The literal descriptions in the poem provide you with clues about the principal's character.

For further practice in understanding literal descriptions, complete the next exercise.

Exercise 3: Understanding Images

Directions: Carefully read the poem, and then answer the questions.

The Great Figure
Among the rain
and lights
I saw the figure 5
in gold
on a red
firetruck
moving
tense
unheeded
to gong clangs
siren howls
and wheels rumbling
through the dark city.

—by William Carlos Williams

1. What is the focus of the speaker's attention?

   _____

2. In what place did this observation occur? _____

3. The speaker uses the word *tense* to describe

   (1) the falling of the rain
   (2) the movement of the firetruck
   (3) the victims of the fire
   (4) the firefighters' attitude
   (5) his feelings of uneasiness

4. Write three images referring to sound.

   _____

FOR ANSWERS AND EXPLANATIONS, SEE PAGE 281.

Figurative Language*

Poets also rely on figurative language to describe observations, ideas, and feelings. However, unlike literal descriptions, figures of speech are comparisons—direct or implied—between two different things. When you read a figure of speech, visualize the two images being compared. Picturing the pair of images in your mind will help you to interpret the poet's purpose in drawing the comparison.

*For a review of figurative language, see pages 42–46, 63–65, and 136–40.

In this section, you will study three types of figurative language—**simile**, **metaphor**, and **personification**. On the GED Interpreting Literature and the Arts Test, you will be asked to interpret the meaning of figurative language. You will *not* have to identify the figures of speech according to their literary terms.

Simile and Metaphor

A direct comparison using the words *as* or *like* is called a *simile*.

direct comparison
"Oh, my love is like a red, red rose" (Robert Burns)

direct comparison
"two socks as soft as rabbits" (Pablo Neruda)

On the other hand, a *metaphor*, or implied comparison, states that something *is* something else. The words *as* and *like* are not used in a metaphor.

implied comparison
"You ain't nothin' but a hound dog" (Jerry Leiber and Mike Stoller)

If the lyrics Elvis Presley made famous had read "You act like a hound dog," he would be using a simile. In his version, this comparison is a metaphor because it is implied, not stated directly.

In the following poem, Langston Hughes uses five similes and one metaphor to explain the effects of a postponed dream. Read the poem carefully, and identify these six figures of speech.

Dream Deferred
What happens to a dream deferred?

Does it dry up
like a raisin in the sun?
Or fester like a sore—
And then run?
Does it stink like rotten meat?
Or crust and sugar over—
like a syrupy sweet?

Maybe it just sags
like a heavy load.

Or does it explode?

—by Langston Hughes

A dream deferred is like *(similes)*:

1. _____   3. _____   5. _____

2. _____   4. _____

In the last line, the speaker implies that a dream deferred is a *(metaphor)*:

6. _____

Did you state that the speaker directly compares "a dream deferred" to (1) a raisin, (2) a sore, (3) rotten meat, (4) a sweet, and (5) a heavy load? The concluding line of the poem implies a metaphor. From the word "explodes," you can assume that "a dream deferred" *is* a bomb, not like a bomb.

Did you notice that through these figures of speech, the speaker of the poem conveys his frustration over having a dream delayed? The final metaphor—an exploding bomb—illustrates a violent reaction.

Personification

A figure of speech that represents nonliving things as humans or animals is called *personification*. In the following example, the poet shows the sun speaking like a person. As you read the excerpt, look for clues that suggest whom the sun represents in the poet's imagination.

> The Sun woke me this morning loud
> and clear, saying "Hey! I've been
> trying to wake you up for fifteen
> minutes. Don't be so rude, you are
> 5   only the second poet I've ever chosen
> to speak to personally
>   so why
> aren't you more attentive? If I could
> burn you through the window I would
> 10   to wake you up. I can't hang around
> here all day."
>   "Sorry, Sun, I stayed
> up late last night talking to Hal."

—Excerpted from "A True Account of Talking to the Sun
at Fire Island" by Frank O'Hara

You probably guessed that the poet portrays the sun as another character in the poem. The sun is the person who initiates a conversation with the poet. Like a real human being, the sun reveals its personality through dialogue.

According to the sun's remarks to the poet, which word best describes the sun's behavior?

(1) apologetic
(2) polite
(3) sleepy
(4) impatient
(5) shy

You were correct if you said *impatient*. Let's examine the clues that support this inference. The sun has been trying to wake up the poet for fifteen minutes. In lines 10–11, the sun states, "I can't hang around / here all day." Therefore, you can conclude that the sun is expressing its impatience.

In the following lyrics from the song "Good Mornin', Blues," notice the personification:

> SINGER'S QUESTION: "Good mornin', blues, blues, how do you do?"
> BLUES' RESPONSE: "I'm feelin' pretty well, but pardner, how are you?"

In this example, the singer addresses the blues as though they were a real person. And like a person, the blues speak. You probably already know that the dictionary defines the blues as a feeling of depression or a style of jazz music. According to the songwriter's imagination, the blues have the power of speech.

For further practice in understanding the language of poetry—imagery and figures of speech—complete the next exercise.

Exercise 4: The Language of Poetry

Directions: In this exercise, you will read two versions of an excerpt from William Wordsworth's poem, "I Wandered Lonely as a Cloud." In Version 1, you will read the poem in its original format; in Version 2, you will read the same lines of poetry in the balloons of a comic strip. Notice how the comic strip version uses illustrations to show the poetic images and figures of speech. After you study the two versions, complete the exercise.

Version 1

I wandered lonely as a cloud
 That floats on high o'er vales and hills,
When all at once I saw a crowd,
 A host, of golden daffodils,
5 Beside the lake, beneath the trees,
Fluttering and dancing in the breeze.

Continuous as the stars that shine
 And twinkle on the milky way,
They stretched in never-ending line
10 Along the margin of a bay:
Ten thousand saw I at a glance,
Tossing their heads in sprightly dance.

The waves beside them danced; but they
 Out-did the sparkling waves in glee;

  —Excerpted from "I Wandered Lonely as a Cloud"
   by William Wordsworth

Version 2

—Excerpted from *Poetry Comics* by Dave Morice

1. The speaker of the poem observes nature from the viewpoint of

    (1) a flower
    (2) a cloud
    (3) a hill
    (4) the wind
    (5) the lake

2. In the second stanza, the speaker of the poem compares the arrangement of the daffodils with

    (1) stars in the milky way
    (2) waves in the ocean
    (3) leaves on a tree
    (4) grass on a hillside
    (5) ballerinas in a performance

3. What phrases suggest that the daffodils are people?

    _____

4. The ways that the poet uses words most closely resembles the work of

    (1) a painter
    (2) a weather forecaster
    (3) a gardener
    (4) a travel guide
    (5) a mapmaker

FOR ANSWERS AND EXPLANATIONS, SEE PAGE 281.

The Subjects of Poetry

What kinds of subjects attract poets' attention? Poets imaginatively portray a wide variety of subjects, including both serious topics and everyday experiences and observations. Below is a partial list of topics you will find in poetry:

love	work	political views
family relationships	objects	city scenes
landscapes	painful emotions	social comments
birthdays	death	memories
people	tragedies	war
philosophy	humor	paintings
music	dance	

In this section, you will study poetry about four of these subjects—family relationships, love, a person's work, and memories. The exercises for each poem will help you to develop your skills in interpreting poetry.

Exercise 5: A Poem About Family Relationships ────

Directions: Study the excerpt from Diane Wakoski's poem entitled "The Photos." Notice how the speaker in the poem portrays the members of her family. Then complete the exercise.

> My sister in her well-tailored silk blouse hands me
> the photo of my father
> in naval uniform and white hat.
> I say, "Oh, this is the one which Mama used to have on her dresser."
>
> 5 My sister controls her face and furtively looks at my mother,
> a sad rag bag of a woman, lumpy and sagging everywhere,
> like a mattress at the Salvation Army, though with no holes or tears,
> and says, "No."
>
> I look again,
> 10 and see that my father is wearing a wedding ring,
> which he never did
> when he lived with my mother. And that there is a legend on it,
> "To my dearest wife,
>   Love
> 15   Chief"
> And I realize the photo must have belonged to his second wife,
> whom he left our mother to marry.

—Excerpted from "The Photos" by Diane Wakoski

1. Identify the family members referred to in the poem. _____

_____

2. What is one of the daughters, the speaker of the poem, describing when she compares her mother to a "rag bag" (line 6) and a "mattress at the Salvation Army" (line 7)? _____

_____

3. In lines 10–15, what object does the speaker notice in her father's photograph? What does this object tell you about both his marriages? _____

_____

_____

4. In a few sentences, summarize the content of this poem in your own words.

_____

_____

_____

_____

FOR ANSWERS AND EXPLANATIONS, SEE PAGES 281-82.

Exercise 6: A Love Poem

Directions: In the following excerpt, the poet expresses his feelings about a woman. Like a love letter, the poem is addressed to a specific person. The word "you" in the poem refers, of course, to the woman the speaker loves. As you read the poem, pay close attention to the poet's awareness of the woman's physical appearance. Then complete the exercises.

> Shiny record albums scattered over
> the livingroom floor, reflecting light
> from the lamp, sharp reflections that hurt
> my eyes as I watch you, squatting among the platters,
> 5 the beer foam making mustaches on your lips.
>
> And, too,
> the shadows on your cheeks from your long lashes
> fascinate me—almost as much as the dimples:
> in your cheeks, your arms and your legs:
> 10 dimples . . . dimples . . . dimples . . .
>
> You
> hum along with Mathis—how you love Mathis!
> with his burnished hair and quicksilver voice that dances
> among the stars and whirls through canyons
> 15 like windblown snow. sometimes I think that Mathis
> could take you from me if you could be complete
> without me. I glance at my watch. it is now time.
>
> —Excerpted from "As You Leave Me"
> by Etheridge Knight

1. **(1)** Where is the woman? _____

   (2) What objects are scattered around her? _____

2. Why does the poet repeat the word *dimples* three times in line 10? _____

   _____

   _____

3. What other details does the poet notice about the woman's facial

   features? _____

   _____

4. In the third stanza, the poet imagines that he is jealous of Johnny Mathis,

   a popular singer. Why? _____

   _____

5. Why does the poet say that Mathis's voice "dances / among the stars and whirls through canyons / like windblown snow"?

    (1) to suggest that Mathis's reputation as a singer is overblown

    (2) to show that Mathis is a star performer who has reached the height of his career

    (3) to compare the power of Mathis's voice to a violent blizzard

    (4) to describe the rhythm, the softness, and the beauty of Mathis's voice

    (5) to suggest that Mathis howls and whistles when he sings

FOR ANSWERS AND EXPLANATIONS, SEE PAGE 282.

Exercise 7: A Poem About a Person's Work

Directions: "Hay for the Horses" describes a man performing his job. Just as you saw with characterization in prose fiction, this poem describes how the man's activities and language reveal details about his life and personality. As you read the poem, try to picture the man and his actions. Then complete the exercises.

Hay for the Horses

He had driven half the night
From far down San Joaquin
Through Mariposa, up the
Dangerous mountain roads,
5 And pulled in at eight a.m.
With his big truckload of hay
      behind the barn.
With winch and ropes and hooks
We stacked the bales up clean
10 To splintery redwood rafters
High in the dark, flecks of alfalfa
Whirling through shingle-cracks of light,
Itch of haydust in the
      sweaty shirt and shoes.
15 At lunchtime under Black oak
Out in the hot corral,
—The old mare nosing lunchpails,
Grasshoppers crackling in the weeds—
'I'm sixty-eight,' he said,
20 'I first bucked hay when I was seventeen.
I thought, that day I started,
I sure would hate to do this all my life.
And dammit, that's just what
I've gone and done.'

—by Gary Snyder

1. Where does the man stack hay? _____

2. According to the poem, the man began stacking hay at _____
and took a break at _____.

3. The lines "With winch and ropes and hooks / We stacked the bales up clean" describe

   (1) an emotion
   (2) a process
   (3) a person
   (4) an opinion
   (5) a character trait

4. What two images from the poem describe a texture (how something feels)?

   _____

   _____.

   What image from the poem describes a sound? _____

5. How old was the man when he first bucked hay? _____

   How old is he now? _____

6. How did the man originally feel about doing this job? _____

   _____

FOR ANSWERS AND EXPLANATIONS, SEE PAGE 282.

Writing Exercise 3

In this exercise, you will be writing a poem about memories. The following excerpt is from a book-length poem entitled *I Remember*. Joe Brainard, the poet, lists his memories. As the following example illustrates, each line of the poem begins with the words "I remember," followed by an image.

I remember that Eskimos kiss with their noses. (?)

I remember that the only friends my parents had who owned a swimming pool also owned a funeral parlor.

I remember laundromats at night all lit up with nobody in them.

I remember a very clean Catholic book-gift shop with practically nothing in it to buy.

I remember rearranging boxes of candy so it would look like not so much was missing.

I remember brown and white shoes with little decorative holes cut out of them.

I remember certain group gatherings that are hard to get up and leave from.

I remember alligators and quicksand in jungle movies. (Pretty scary)

—Excerpted from *I Remember* by Joe Brainard

Using the poem as a model, write your own poem in which you list memorable experiences and observations. Your poem may or may not rhyme. Use a separate sheet of paper for your poem. (Suggestions for remembered images: TV shows, Hollywood films, movie stars, fashion styles, relatives, friends, objects, places, vacations, etc.)

ANSWERS WILL VARY.

Writing Exercise 4

In this exercise, you will create a poem based on your social security number. Because each social security number is unique, your poem will be one of a kind.

First, read and complete the form on page 181. Make sure that you read the directions on the form before you try to complete it.

After you've completed the form, use the lines you circled on the form to fill in the following blanks and reveal your poem.

Letter	Number	Poetic Line
A	_____	_____
B	_____	_____
C	_____	_____
D	_____	_____
E	_____	_____
F	_____	_____
G	_____	_____
H	_____	_____
I	_____	_____

SOURCE: *Poetry Comics* by Dave Morice

ANSWERS WILL VARY.

SCHEDULE SE
(Form 1040)
Department of the Treasury
Internal Revenue Service

Computation of Social Security Poem ◄ ◄ ◄
▶ See Instructions for Schedule SE (Form 1040).
▶ Attach to Form 1040.

1981
23

Name of self-employed person (as shown on social security card)	Social security number of self-employed person ▶		

Your social security number determines your own unique poem hidden in a billion possible poems below. To find yours, just circle the nine digits of your social security number, one digit per column. Begin with the A-column for your first digit, and continue through I. The corresponding phrases, when read in the order of their selection, form your nine-line 1981 Social Security Poem.
Not only is it free verse, it's tax-deductible!

A
1. As the wheels
2. When other planets
3. Because her acorns
4. Since your lips
5. While those mannikins
6. If these shadows
7. After his dogs
8. Although our trucks
9. Before both dancers
0. Until their faces

B
1. were sleeping on
2. are flying around
3. don't bother
4. laughed at
5. bounced off
6. march around
7. will stumble over
8. can't taste
9. might paint
0. won't speak to

C
1. the singer's mouth,
2. his antique television,
3. her grand piano player,
4. these sad sandwiches,
5. those beautiful blue teeth,
6. that mindless table,
7. this magic Buick,
8. their golden typewriters,
9. an optical illusion,
0. a missing link,

D
1. he tried to whistle
2. she slapped him
3. he saw a ghost
4. she always grinned
5. he chuckled once
6. she wished him luck
7. he just pushed buttons
8. she read minds
9. he never sneezed
0. she almost ate dinner

E
1. down the sink.
2. against their beliefs.
3. between two mirrors.
4. at the Crystal Café.
5. like her telephone.
6. with the devil's lighter.
7. across Kansas.
8. without starlight.
9. in his dream.
0. out of sheer desire.

F
1. Her modern poetry
2. His astral projection
3. These lightning bolts
4. Their bathtub gin
5. That parking ramp
6. Random numbers
7. Your gothic romance
8. Those laser beams
9. My green thumb
0. The space shuttle

G
1. awkwardly
2. silently
3. jealously
4. haphazardly
5. neatly
6. voraciously
7. pitifully
8. gleefully
9. frankly
0. longingly

H
1. frightened the gnomes
2. pulled the plug
3. stunned the barber
4. praised the clock
5. attracted the mice
6. troubled the professor
7. boiled the shapes
8. angered the ambassador
9. caught the butterfly
0. bewildered the muse

I
1. floating in my soup.
2. upholstering his lawn.
3. naming those plants.
4. watching like an elephant.
5. looking for Fred.
6. training her cat.
7. evicting the landlord.
8. burning your toast.
9. hiding in their cellar.
0. glowing like a lamp.

Exercise 8: Chapter Review

Directions: Read the following poems and answer the multiple choice questions. Use the purpose question that precedes each poem to focus your reading.

Poem 1

WHAT KIND OF PERSON IS FLICK?

Flick stands tall among the idiot pumps—
Five on a side, the old bubble-head style,
Their rubber elbows hanging loose and low.
One's nostrils are two S's, and his eyes
5   An E and O. And one is squat, without
A head at all—more of a football type.

Once, Flick played for the high school team, the Wizards.
He was good: in fact, the best. In '46
He bucketed three hundred ninety points,
10   A county record still. The ball loved Flick.
I saw him rack up thirty-eight or forty
In one home game. His hands were like wild birds.

He never learned a trade; he just sells gas,
Checks oil, and changes flats. Once in a while,
15   As a gag, he dribbles an inner tube,
But most of us remember anyway.
His hands are fine and nervous on the lug wrench.
It makes no difference to the lug wrench, though.

Off work, he hangs around Mae's Luncheonette.
20   Grease-grey and kind of coiled, he plays pinball,
Sips lemon cokes, and smokes those thin cigars;
Flick seldom speaks to Mae, just sits and nods
Beyond her face towards the bright applauding tiers
Of Necco Wafers, Nibs, and Juju Beads.

—Excerpted from "Ex-Basketball Player" by John Updike

1. Flick currently earns his living as

   (1) a car salesman
   (2) a professional basketball player
   (3) a busboy and cook
   (4) a high school coach
   (5) a gas station attendant

2. In line 3, the phrase "rubber elbows hanging loose and low" describes

   (1) an auto mechanic's tools
   (2) the hoses on the gas pumps
   (3) the stance of a football player
   (4) Flick's long, flexible arms
   (5) Flick's injured elbows

3. What is the main idea expressed in lines 7–12?

   (1) Flick scored 390 points during the 1946 season.
   (2) Flick's high school team was named the Wizards.
   (3) Fans applauded Flick's athletic performance.
   (4) Flick was an outstanding high school basketball player.
   (5) Flick broke a county record.

4. "His hands were like wild birds" (line 12). What does this comparison show?

   (1) Flick seemed to fly on the basketball court.
   (2) Flick was an aggressive basketball player.
   (3) Flick lacked control in making jump shots.
   (4) Flick flapped and waved his hands.
   (5) Flick quickly and agilely handled the basketball.

5. You can conclude that the major point of the third stanza is that

   (1) Flick skillfully uses a lug wrench
   (2) Flick misses playing basketball
   (3) Flick pretends the inner tube is a basketball
   (4) Flick's fans remember his achievements
   (5) Flick likes to amuse himself at work

6. You can infer that "Necco Wafers, Nibs, and Juju Beads" (line 24) are the names of

   (1) ready-to-eat cereals
   (2) soft drinks
   (3) sweets
   (4) ice cream sundaes
   (5) the diner's daily specials

7. The underlying purpose of the poem is

   (1) to show that a high school athlete's fame is often short-lived
   (2) to prove that untrained people are stuck in boring jobs
   (3) to explain how high schools develop their students' talents
   (4) to show how teenagers choose their careers
   (5) to illustrate why fans admire athletes

8. Which of the following magazines would most likely publish an article about high school graduates whose situation is similar to Flick's?

   (1) *Popular Mechanics*
   (2) *Sports Illustrated*
   (3) *Car and Driver Magazine*
   (4) *Science Digest*
   (5) *Business Week*

Poem 2

WHAT DO YOU LEARN ABOUT RICHARD CORY?

Richard Cory
Whenever Richard Cory went down town,
We people on the pavement looked at him:
He was a gentleman from sole to crown,
Clean favored, and imperially slim.

5 And he was always quietly arrayed,
And he was always human when he talked;
But still he fluttered pulses when he said,
"Good-morning," and he glittered when he walked.

And he was rich—yes, richer than a king—
10 And admirably schooled in every grace:
In fine, we thought that he was everything
To make us wish that we were in his place.

So on we worked, and waited for the light,
And went without the meat, and cursed the bread;
15 And Richard Cory, one calm summer night,
Went home and put a bullet through his head.

—by Edwin Arlington Robinson

9. You can infer that "we people" (line 2), the speakers of the poem, are

   (1) wealthy and satisfied
   (2) poor and hard-working
   (3) lazy and unemployed
   (4) middle-class and successful
   (5) concerned and politically active

10. The words referring to Richard Cory—*crown, imperially,* and *king*—suggest an image of

    (1) snobbery
    (2) greed
    (3) royalty
    (4) conceit
    (5) selfishness

11. According to line 12, how do the people feel about Richard Cory's wealth?

    (1) suspicious
    (2) sad
    (3) indifferent
    (4) envious
    (5) hostile

12. What event occurs at the end of the poem?

    (1) Richard Cory is assassinated.
    (2) Richard Cory receives a death threat.
    (3) Richard Cory dies of natural causes.
    (4) Richard Cory dies in an accidental shooting.
    (5) Richard Cory commits suicide.

13. From Richard Cory's actions, you can infer that he

    (1) resents the townspeople
    (2) knows he is going bankrupt
    (3) conceals serious personal problems
    (4) behaves like a coward
    (5) wishes he had closer friends

14. The phrase "waited for the light" (line 13) means

    (1) hoped for better times
    (2) wanted new lamps
    (3) looked forward to the sunrise
    (4) expected an inheritance
    (5) prayed for sparkling jewels

15. If the major theme were stated as the title of a magazine article, what would the title be?

    (1) "People Learn to Cope with Poverty"
    (2) "Society Frowns upon Suicide"
    (3) "Wealth Impresses People"
    (4) "Money Doesn't Ensure Happiness"
    (5) "People Reveal Their True Feelings"

Poem 3

WHAT IS IT LIKE TO HOE AN ONION FIELD?

Daybreak
In this moment when the light starts up
In the east and rubs
The horizon until it catches fire,

We enter the fields to hoe,
5 Row after row, among the small flags of onion,
Waving off the dragonflies
That ladder the air.

And tears the onions raise
Do not begin in your eyes but in ours,
10 In the salt blown
From one blister into another;

They begin in knowing
You will never waken to bear
The hour timed to a heart beat,
15 The wind pressing us closer to the ground.

When the season ends,
And the onions are unplugged from their sleep,
We won't forget what you failed to see,
And nothing will heal
20 Under the rain's broken fingers.

—by Gary Soto

16. What occurrence is described in the first stanza?

    (1) a campfire
    (2) an early sunrise
    (3) a blazing field
    (4) a person striking a match
    (5) a forest fire

17. The person addressed in the poem as *you* is

    (1) the reader
    (2) another farmer
    (3) the rain
    (4) a grocery store owner
    (5) the sky

18. Lines 10–11 suggest an image of

    (1) the heat forming blisters on the soil
    (2) insects creating blisters on the onion's surface
    (3) the intensity of the hot sun
    (4) the onion pickers' emotional wounds
    (5) the painful, blistered hands of the onion pickers

19. "And the onions are unplugged from their sleep" (line 17)
What is the meaning of this figure of speech?

    (1) The onions look like electrical sockets.
    (2) The farm workers are drowsy.
    (3) The onions are uprooted from the ground.
    (4) The onions are dead.
    (5) Electrical machines pick the onions.

20. The personification in line 20—"the rain's broken fingers"—describes the way raindrops

    (1) brutally strike the ground
    (2) form huge puddles
    (3) damage the onion crop
    (4) beat on the farm workers' heads
    (5) soak into the soft earth

21. The purpose of the poem is to reveal

    (1) the conflicts between farm workers
    (2) the beauty and splendor of nature
    (3) the process of picking onions
    (4) the oppressive conditions and hardships of the field workers
    (5) the characteristics of an onion field

22. Which of the following groups would be most likely to identify with the farm workers' experience?

    (1) secretaries
    (2) factory workers
    (3) lawyers
    (4) nurses
    (5) photographers

FOR ANSWERS AND EXPLANATIONS, SEE PAGES 282-83.

☐ 7 DRAMA

Drama is a type of literature, as well as a form of entertainment. Plays are intended for a live performance in a theater. Members of the audience immediately respond to the characters, represented by actors who recite lines of dialogue and perform their roles in the play's events. When you watch a theatrical performance onstage, you see the story unfold before your eyes. This experience is similar to viewing a television show or a movie. You directly witness the characters and their actions.

On the GED Interpreting Literature and the Arts Test, you will be asked multiple-choice questions about passages from drama. This chapter will prepare you to answer those questions correctly. You will acquire the reading skills necessary for interpreting the content of drama and analyzing its elements.

Comparing Drama and Prose

Studying drama as a work of literature is similar to reading a short story or a novel. Playwrights and fiction writers both tell a story. They create imaginary settings in which characters act out the events of the plot. However, their methods of presentation differ.

The following passages illustrate some of the similarities and differences between drama and fictional prose. The first excerpt is from John Steinbeck's novel *Of Mice and Men*. In the second excerpt, Steinbeck rewrote the scene from the novel in play form. Study the novel version and the play version carefully. Look for the similarities and differences by answering these two questions: (1) What methods of storytelling are used? and (2) How do the visual appearance and arrangement of the words on the printed page differ?

Novel Version

Lennie got up on his knees and looked down at George. "Ain't we gonna have no supper?"

"Sure we are, if you gather up some dead willow sticks. I got three cans of beans in my bindle. You get a fire ready. I'll give you a match when you get the sticks together. Then we'll heat the beans and have supper."

Lennie said, "I like beans with ketchup."

"Well, we ain't got no ketchup. You go get wood. An' don't you fool around. It'll be dark before long."

Lennie lumbered to his feet and disappeared in the brush. George lay where he was and whistled softly to himself. There were sounds of splashings down the river in the direction Lennie had taken. George stopped whistling and listened. "Poor bastard," he said softly, and then went on whistling again.

In a moment Lennie came crashing back through the brush. He carried one small willow stick in his hand. George sat up. "Awright," he said brusquely, "Gi'me that mouse!"

But Lennie made an elaborate pantomime of innocence. "What mouse, George? I ain't got no mouse."

George held out his hand. "Come on. Give it to me. You ain't puttin' nothing over."

Lennie hesitated, backed away, looked wildly at the brush line as though he contemplated running for his freedom. George said coldly, "You gonna give me that mouse or do I have to sock you?"

"Give you what, George?"

"You know God damn well what. I want that mouse."

Lennie reluctantly reached into his pocket. His voice broke a little. "I don't know why I can't keep it. It ain't nobody's mouse. I didn't steal it. I found it lyin' right beside the road."

George's hand remained outstretched imperiously. Slowly, like a terrier who doesn't want to bring a ball to its master, Lennie approached, drew back, approached again. George snapped his fingers sharply, and at the sound Lennie laid the mouse in his hand.

"I wasn't doin' nothing bad with it, George. Jus' strokin' it."

George stood up and threw the mouse as far as he could into the darkening brush, and then he stepped to the pool and washed his hands. "You crazy fool. Don't you think I could see your feet was wet where you went acrost the river to get it?" He heard Lennie's whimpering cry and wheeled about. "Blubberin' like a baby! Jesus Christ! A big guy like you." Lennie's lip quivered and tears started in his eyes. "Aw, Lennie!" George put his hand on Lennie's shoulder. "I ain't takin' it away jus' for meanness. That mouse ain't fresh, Lennie; and besides, you've broke it pettin' it. You get another mouse that's fresh and I'll let you keep it a little while."

—Excerpted from the novel *Of Mice and Men*
by John Steinbeck

Play Version

LENNIE: [*Gets up on his knees and looks down at GEORGE, plaintively.*] Ain't we gonna have no supper?

GEORGE: Sure we are. You gather up some dead willow sticks. I got three cans of beans in my bindle. I'll open 'em up while you get a fire
5 ready. We'll eat 'em cold.

LENNIE: [*Companionably.*] I like beans with ketchup.

GEORGE: Well, we ain't got no ketchup. You go get the wood, and don't you fool around none. Be dark before long. [*LENNIE lumbers to his feet and disappears into the brush. GEORGE gets out the*
10 *bean cans, opens two of them, suddenly turns his head and listens. A little sound of splashing comes from the direction that LENNIE has taken. GEORGE looks after him; shakes his head. LENNIE comes back carrying a few small willow sticks in his hand.*] All right, give me that mouse.

15 LENNIE: [*With elaborate pantomime of innocence.*] What, George? I ain't got no mouse.

GEORGE: [*Holding out his hand.*] Come on! Give it to me! You ain't puttin' nothing over. [*LENNIE hesitates, backs away, turns and looks as if he were going to run. Coldly.*] You gonna give me that mouse
20 or do I have to take a sock at you?

LENNIE: Give you what, George?

GEORGE: You know goddamn well, what! I want that mouse!

LENNIE: [*Almost in tears.*] I don't know why I can't keep it. It ain't nobody's mouse. I didn't steal it! I found it layin' right beside the
25 road. [*GEORGE snaps his fingers sharply, and LENNIE lays the mouse in his hand.*] I wasn't doin' nothing bad with it. Just stroking it. That ain't bad.

GEORGE: [*Stands up and throws the mouse as far as he can into the brush, then he steps to the pool, and washes his hands.*] You crazy fool!
30 Thought you could get away with it, didn't you? Don't you think I could see your feet was wet where you went in the water to get it? [*LENNIE whimpers like a puppy.*] Blubbering like a baby. Jesus Christ, a big guy like you! [*LENNIE tries to control himself, but his lips quiver and his face works with effort. GEORGE puts*
35 *his hand on LENNIE'S shoulder for a moment.*] Aw, Lennie, I ain't takin' it away just for meanness. That mouse ain't fresh. Besides, you broke it pettin' it. You get a mouse that's fresh and I'll let you keep it a little while.

—Excerpted from the play *Of Mice and Men*
by John Steinbeck

As you probably noticed, both the novel and the play depict the same episode. Which of the following statements best summarizes the central action of these passages?

(1)   George and Lennie cook beans for dinner.
(2)   George gets angry with Lennie for petting a mouse to death.
(3)   Lennie acts like a crybaby.
(4)   Lennie gathers willow sticks for the campfire.
(5)   George threatens to punch Lennie.

Answer (2) is the correct response. When George says that Lennie "broke" the mouse, George means that Lennie killed the mouse by petting it. The dialogue in both excerpts focuses on this incident.

Now let's examine how the novel and the play present this moment from the plot. The following chart compares and contrasts two characteristics mentioned earlier—storytelling methods and format:

How the Story *Of Mice and Men* Is Told

Characteristics	Novel Version	Play Version
Storytelling method	An outside narrator who doesn't participate in the action tells the story. He comments on the characters and describes plot details. He uses past-tense verbs to show that the action has already occurred. **Example of Narrator's Comment:** Lennie got up on his knees and looked down at George.	No narrator is present. Instead, **_stage directions_**—words, phrases, and sentences in *italicized print* and enclosed in brackets— explain to the actors what their tone of voice, facial expressions, and gestures should be. The stage directions use present-tense verbs to show that the action is happening now. **Example of Stage Directions:** LENNIE: [*Gets up on his knees and looks down at GEORGE plaintively.*]

Characteristics	Novel Version	Play Version
Format (Visual appearance and arrangement of the words on the page)	Sentences are grouped into paragraphs. The characters' dialogue is enclosed in quotation marks. When the conversation switches to another speaker, a new paragraph begins. Words not enclosed in quotation marks identify the speaker, comment on the characters, or describe actions. **Example:** But Lennie made an elaborate pantomime of innocence. "What mouse, George? I ain't got no mouse."	The play is written in script form consisting of **dialogue** and stage directions. The character's dialogue appears next to his name. The stage directions correlate the character's speech with his emotions and physical movements. Stage directions also guide the actor who portrays the character on stage. **Example:** LENNIE: [*With elaborate pantomime of innocence.*] What, George? I ain't got no mouse.

In the next exercise, you will apply what you have just learned about drama.

Exercise 1: Characteristics of Drama

Directions: Look over the play version of *Of Mice and Men* on page 190, and answer the questions below.

1. Write the stage direction that describes each of the following actions. Remember, the stage directions are the italicized words enclosed in brackets.

    (1) Lennie looks as though he is about to cry.

    _____

    (2) George gets rid of the mouse.

    _____

    (3) George tries to comfort Lennie.

    _____

2. Write the dialogue that supports each of the following statements:

    (1) George says that Lennie is acting childish.

    _____

    (2) Lennie lies to George.

    _____

(3) George knows where Lennie went to get the mouse.

_____

3. Decide whether the following inferences about the play are *valid* or *invalid*. When you say an inference is valid, you mean it is reasonable based on the passage. If you say that it is invalid, you mean it is contradicted by the passage.

(1) George is totally insensitive to Lennie's feelings. _____

(2) Lennie and George use formal language in their speech.

_____

(3) George dominates Lennie. _____

(4) Lennie is simple-minded. _____

FOR ANSWERS AND EXPLANATIONS, SEE PAGE 283.

Format of Scripts

The excerpt from the play *Of Mice and Men* illustrates how drama tells a story in script form. This section will discuss the format of a script in more detail. Your ability to read and interpret a play will improve once you recognize the distinctive features of a script.

Acts and Scenes: Structuring the Plot

Long plays are organized into major sections called ***acts***. Sometimes acts are divided into ***scenes***—specific episodes from the story set in one place and occurring during a fixed time period. For example, here is the organization of Lorraine Hansberry's play *A Raisin in the Sun*.

The action of the play is set on Chicago's South Side,
sometime between World War II and the present.

Act One
SCENE 1. Friday morning.
SCENE 2. The following morning.

Act Two
SCENE 1. Later, the same day.
SCENE 2. Friday night, a few weeks later.
SCENE 3. Moving day, one week later.

Act Three
An hour later.

—Excerpted from *A Raisin in the Sun*
by Lorraine Hansberry

When you pay attention to the shifts in acts and scenes, you get clues about how the plot of the play is structured. Furthermore, you also gain an overview of the time span in which the events unfold. For example, you can infer that *A Raisin in the Sun* presents action occurring over a month's time.

A Cast List: Introducing the Characters

The first page of most scripts lists the characters who perform in the play. As you will notice in the example that follows, the cast list includes the following information about the main characters:

1. Name

2. Age

3. Occupation

4. Physical description or personality traits

Cast

NOLA BARNES is thirty. She is a single mother who divides her time between her son and her career as a social worker. Proud and determined, she commands respect from those around her.

SAM MILLER, thirty-four, is Nola's ex-husband. A star athlete in high school, Sam relies too much on his physical strength and appearance to impress people. He is a steelworker who would like to spend more time with Nola and David.

DAVID, Nola's eleven-year-old son, is thinner and smaller than his classmates. He is working to overcome a learning disability that has slowed his progress in school. He is a loner who shares his feelings more with his tutor at school than with his father.

DWIGHT PARKS, David's tutor, is twenty-eight. He laughs easily, is a good listener, and cares more about his students than he admits. He has never met Nola, but when she comes to pick up David, Dwight watches for her by the window.

JUAN MORALES lives in Nola's building. He is seventeen and has been arrested several times for petty theft and trespassing. He has a deep scar on his chin and looks out at the world through black, expressionless eyes.

BEATRICE LUIS, Juan's grandmother, has taken care of Juan since he was a child. Now in declining health, she worries about her grandson and would like to ask Nola for help.

LUCITA
ESMERALDA
LU-KEE   } Nola and David's neighbors
JOE
EXTRAS

Writing Exercise 1

Using the cast list you just read, write your own cast list on a separate sheet of paper. Choose five people—friends or relatives—and introduce them as play characters.

Include the following information: (1) name, (2) age, (3) occupation, and (4) physical appearance or personality traits.

ANSWERS WILL VARY.

Stage Directions: Establishing the Setting

As you have already learned, playwrights use stage directions to indicate a character's tone of voice, feelings, facial expressions, gestures, and actions. Stage directions also explain the setting—where and when the action takes place.

Terms such as *stage right, stage left,* and *down right* inform the actors of where events should take place onstage. The *wing* refers to the area on either side of the stage that is not visible to the audience.

Stage directions are given for the benefit of the actors, who face the audience from the stage. Therefore, action which occurs *stage right*—to the actors' right as they face the audience—takes place on the audience's left.

The following excerpt shows how the setting should appear on the stage. As you read these stage directions, try to picture in your mind what this room looks like. Notice the colors as well as the condition and the arrangement of the furniture. Remember that the actors will perform their roles in this imaginary place.

Scene: *Stark, low-rent motel room on the edge of the Mojave Desert. Faded green plaster walls. Dark brown linoleum floor. No rugs. Cast iron four-poster single bed, slightly off center, favoring stage right, set horizontally to audience. Bed covered with faded blue chenille bedspread. Metal table with well-worn yellow Formica top. Two matching metal chairs in the fifties "S" shape design with yellow plastic seats and backs, also well-worn.*

—Excerpted from *Fool for Love* by Sam Shepard

Writing Exercise 2

Imagine a room in your house or apartment as the setting for a play. Using the preceding example as a model, write a paragraph or two of stage directions explaining the physical appearance of the room. Describe the furniture and how it is arranged. Also include noticeable features about the room—the size, the condition, the color of the walls and floor, etc. Use a separate sheet of paper for this description.

ANSWERS WILL VARY.

Dialogue: Revealing Character and Advancing the Plot

A script mainly consists of dialogue—conversations among the characters. Dramatic dialogue, however, differs from everyday conversations with people. The playwright carefully chooses dialogue that reveals character and advances the plot. The action progresses as the characters recite their lines and participate in the events of the story. Therefore, when you read a play, your attention is focused on interpreting the characters' spoken words in the context of a dramatic situation.

Here are some suggestions for reading the dialogue in a script:

1. Notice the punctuation. Playwrights sometimes use a dash (—) or an ellipsis (. . .) to indicate pauses or interruptions in the characters' speech.

2. Study the stage directions printed before and after the characters' dialogue. Look for clues that explain how the characters deliver their lines. Descriptions of voice, attitude, or actions heighten the meaning of the spoken words.

Apply these suggestions as you read the dialogue between two World War I veterans—Harold and Kenner:

HAROLD: I want to *remember*—the good things.

KENNER: Like being over there. Scared to death. Watching guys screamin' and bleeding to death.

HAROLD: I wasn't scared . . . not like you tell it.

KENNER: Damn . . . everybody was. Didn't you ever wake up in sweats and shivers? I used to put my blanket in my mouth and . . .

HAROLD: [*shakes his head, no.*]

KENNER: Well . . . I was scared. Everybody was.

HAROLD: [*softly*] That's a lie.

—Excerpted from the televison adaptation of
"Soldier's Home" by Ernest Hemingway
(screenplay by Robert Geller)

The dash (—) and the ellipsis (. . .) show pauses or interruptions in speech. How does Harold speak when he says, "That's a lie"? If you said "softly," you correctly recognized how the stage directions corresponded to Harold's statement.

The plot of "Soldier's Home" recounts how Harold Krebs, the main character, adjusts to civilian life following his combat experience overseas. The preceding dialogue contributes to the story's development. Harold's conversation reveals his feelings about fighting in the war. You can infer that he is still affected by his wartime memories.

Writing Exercise 3

Choose two characters from your cast list (from Writing Exercise 1). On a separate sheet of paper, write a brief dialogue in script form between these two people. Include stage directions describing how they deliver their lines. Remember that the dialogue should imitate the speech of each character.

ANSWERS WILL VARY.

Exercise 2: Reading a Script

Directions: In this exercise, you will apply your skills in reading a script. The following excerpt is from the play *The Odd Couple,* a comedy about two divorced men who are roommates. Study the script carefully, and then complete the exercises.

FELIX: What's wrong? [*Crosses back to tray, puts down glasses, etc.*]

OSCAR: There's something wrong with this system, that's what's wrong. I don't think that two single men living alone in a big eight-room apartment should have a cleaner house than my mother.

5 FELIX: [*Gets rest of dishes, glasses and coasters from table.*] What are you talking about? I'm just going to put the dishes in the sink. You want me to leave them here all night?

OSCAR: [*Takes his glass which FELIX has put on tray and crosses to bar for refill.*] I don't care if you take them to bed with you. You can
10 play Mr. Clean all you want. But don't make *me* feel guilty.

FELIX: [*Takes tray into kitchen, leaving swinging door open.*] I'm not asking you to do it, Oscar. You don't have to clean up.

OSCAR: [*Moves up to door.*] *That's* why you make me feel guilty. You're always in my bathroom hanging up my towels. . . . Whenever I
15 smoke you follow me around with an ashtray. . . . Last night I found you washing the kitchen floor shaking your head and moaning, "Footprints, footprints"! [*Paces Right.*]

FELIX: [*Comes back to the table with silent butler into which he dumps the ashtrays; then wipes them carefully.*] I didn't say they were
20 yours.

OSCAR: [*Angrily; sits Down Right in wing chair.*] Well, they *were* mine, damn it. I have feet and they make prints. What do you want me to do, climb across the cabinets?

FELIX: No! I want you to walk on the floor.

25 OSCAR: I appreciate that! I really do.

FELIX: [*Crosses to telephone table and cleans ashtray there.*] I'm just trying to keep the place livable. I didn't realize I irritated you that much.

OSCAR: I just feel *I* should have the right to decide when my bathtub
30 needs a going over with Dutch Cleanser. . . . It's the democratic way!

—Excerpted from *The Odd Couple* by Neil Simon

1. Where does the scene take place?

   (1) a house
   (2) a hotel
   (3) a dormitory
   (4) an apartment
   (5) a bar

2. The stage directions referring to Felix show his

   (1) tone of voice
   (2) facial expressions
   (3) actions
   (4) emotions
   (5) clothing

3. What is Oscar's tone of voice when he says, "Well, they *were* mine, damn it" (lines 21–22)?

   (1) guilty
   (2) angry
   (3) comic
   (4) insincere
   (5) selfish

4. Write two household chores that Felix does while he talks to Oscar.

   (1)_____

   (2)_____

5. According to this scene, what causes the tension between Felix and Oscar?

   (1) They are both unmarried.
   (2) They have different housekeeping habits.
   (3) Oscar is a smoker and Felix is a nonsmoker.
   (4) Oscar is overly attached to his mother.
   (5) Felix wants to earn his living as a professional butler.

FOR ANSWERS AND EXPLANATIONS, SEE PAGE 283.

Story Elements of Drama

In plays, you will find many of the story elements that were discussed in the chapter on fictional prose. Let's review the definitions of these elements as they apply to drama.

Setting: The place, the time, and the atmosphere in which dramatic situations occur. Setting in plays is conveyed by the stage directions and the characters' comments about the physical surroundings.

Plot: The series of events tracing the action of a story. The plot of a play relies almost entirely on the characters' performance—the way they immediately respond to ongoing situations. Therefore, the plot stems from the characters, whose purpose is to act out events.

Characters involved in conflicts create moments of tension in the plot. Plays usually contain scenes showing conflicts among the characters. For example, the conflict in the scene from *Of Mice and Men* (page 190) results when George discovers that Lennie has snatched a mouse and unintentionally killed it. George's initial reaction is anger; George scolds Lennie. George resolves the conflict by telling Lennie to "get a mouse that's fresh."

Characterization: The methods of revealing character—appearance, personality, and behavior. Because plays are written in script form, you learn about the characters from reading the dialogue and the stage directions. Therefore, look for clues in the dialogue and stage directions that suggest character traits. Your understanding of characterization is largely based on the inferences you make.

Theme: A general statement that explains the underlying meaning of a story. As a rule, you would have to read the entire play, rather than an excerpt, to determine the significance of the dramatic action. However, the dialogue in some scenes expresses beliefs or opinions about life and human behavior. The topic of conversation and the characters' statements about that topic may reveal the major or minor theme of the play.

In the next exercise, you will apply your understanding of fictional elements to drama.

Exercise 3: The Story Elements of a Script ——————

Directions: The following excerpt is from a TV script for "Hill Street Blues," a popular police series. In this scene, police officers J. D. LaRue and Neal Washington are investigating the shooting of another police officer. Study the passage carefully. Try to imagine the actors reciting their lines. Then answer the questions that follow.

[*Interior front desk area—with a discouraged LARUE and WASHINGTON*]

LARUE: [*under his breath*] Coming up empty.

WASHINGTON: Detective work, babe. Every twenty haystacks there's
5   bound to be a needle.

[*Under which, they're approaching one of the last of their interviewees—are intercepted by SID—*]

SID: Hey, J.D, Neal.

LARUE: Sid.

10 WASHINGTON: How you doin', Sidney? Make your parole?

SID: Made my parole, I'm having a little bad luck since I'm out.

WASHINGTON: Takes time readjusting Sid.

[*LARUE and WASHINGTON are glad to see him, both are ready to move on—*]

15 SID: Heard you guys are questioning bookies 'bout a cop that
           got hit.

[*Which gets their attention—*]

WASHINGTON: Harry Garibaldi.

SID: Black-hair, pretty good looking, maybe thirty-two?

20 LARUE: [*nods*] What've you got?

SID: I'm gonna be absolutely straight with you fellas. I had some
           paper confiscated in a numbers pop this morning—any
           conceivable way you could get that back for me?

WASHINGTON: You just admitted to frequenting a gambling establishment
25   Sid—that's a parole violation—

SID: Fellas it was a thirty-six hundred dollar score—

[*LARUE puts SID against the wall—*]

LARUE: Garibaldi.

SID: Horse-room on Jefferson and Utica. Guy I'm talking about
30   used to go in there, he had a line of credit—I heard a
           couple people say he was a cop—[*resignedly readjusting
           his ambitions*] So would it at least be worth half a c?

WASHINGTON: Which corner of Jefferson and Utica?

35

SID: South . . . [*turns, points like a weather-vane*] I get all confused. Southwest side.

[*WASHINGTON moves to tell the other detectives. LARUE goes to his pockets—*]

LARUE: If there's anything in it you get another fifty.

40

[*LARUE hurries off to join the other cops—SID figures he's fifty ahead of where he was—*]

—Excerpted from "Seoul on Ice"
by Jeffrey Lewis and David Milch

1. Where does the scene occur?

    _____

2. How do LaRue and Washington initially feel about seeing Sid?

    (1) hostile
    (2) suspicious
    (3) annoyed
    (4) glad
    (5) frightened

3. Write the line of Sid's dialogue that captures LaRue's and Washington's

    attention. _____

    _____

4. **(1)** What is the name of the police officer who was shot?

    _____

    (2) Briefly summarize Sid's description of the police officer's appearance.

    _____

5. Why does LaRue put Sid against the wall?

    (1) to punish Sid for violating parole by frequenting gambling establishments
    (2) to demand the names of illegal gambling establishments
    (3) to pressure Sid into revealing information about the shooting
    (4) to force Sid into confessing that he committed the crime
    (5) to frisk Sid for illegal weapons and forged documents

6. Which of the following character traits does LaRue reveal in this scene?

    (1) honesty
    (2) aggression
    (3) greediness
    (4) stupidity
    (5) selfishness

7. Which of the following character traits does Washington reveal in this scene?

    (1) understanding
    (2) cruelty
    (3) boredom
    (4) weakness
    (5) cautiousness

8. Which word best describes the dialogue in this scene?

    (1) sarcastic
    (2) realistic
    (3) formal
    (4) phony
    (5) unemotional

FOR ANSWERS AND EXPLANATIONS, SEE PAGES 283-84.

Characters: Performers of Drama

In drama, the characters participate in the ongoing events of the story. Their performance is the central focus of your attention. Why? Because scripts consist almost entirely of characters' dialogue and actions. The roles the characters play develop these elements of drama—plot, characterization, and theme.

Unlike prose fiction, plays usually do not have a narrator who comments on the characters and summarizes events. Instead, you directly observe the characters performing the action. You see how they respond to past or present situations. You also imaginatively "hear" their remarks about themselves or other characters.

Based on your observations, you make inferences about the characters' dramatic role in a play. Do they cause conflicts? Do they influence events? Do they make decisions that affect the outcome of the play?

You also form opinions about the characters' personalities and relationships with other people. Do they communicate honestly, or do their words disguise their true feelings? Does their dialogue show an understanding of another character's viewpoint?

In the next exercise, you will closely examine these aspects of the characters' performance:

☐ comments about themselves

☐ comments about other people

☐ responses to each other's comments

☐ reactions to events

Exercise 4: Two Characters' Performances

Directions: In the following passage, Nora confronts her husband, Torvald Helmer. Study the dialogue and the stage directions carefully. Then complete the exercise.

NORA: Sit down. This'll take some time. I have a lot to say.

HELMER: [*sitting at the table directly opposite her*] You worry me, Nora. And I don't understand you.

NORA: No, that's exactly it. You don't understand me. And I've never understood you either—until tonight. No, don't interrupt. You can just listen to what I say. We're closing out accounts, Torvald.

HELMER: How do you mean that?

NORA: [*after a short pause*] Doesn't anything strike you about our sitting here like this?

10 HELMER: What's that?

NORA: We've been married now eight years. Doesn't it occur to you that this is the first time we two, you and I, man and wife, have ever talked seriously together?

HELMER: What do you mean—seriously?

15 NORA: In eight whole years—longer even—right from our first acquaintance, we've never exchanged a serious word on any serious thing.

HELMER: You mean I should constantly go and involve you in problems you couldn't possibly help me with?

20 NORA: I'm not talking of problems. I'm saying that we've never sat down seriously together and tried to get to the bottom of anything.

HELMER: But dearest, what good would that ever do you?

NORA: That's the point right there: you've never understood me. I've been wronged greatly, Torvald—first by Papa, and then by you.

25 HELMER: What! By us—the two people who've loved you more than anyone else?

NORA: [*shaking her head*] You never loved me. You've thought it fun to be in love with me, that's all.

HELMER: Nora, what a thing to say!

30 NORA: Yes, it's true now, Torvald. When I lived at home with Papa, he told me all his opinions, so I had the same ones too; or if they were different I hid them, since he wouldn't have cared for that. He used to call me his doll-child, and he played with me the way I played with my dolls. Then I came into your house—

35   HELMER: How can you speak of our marriage like that?

NORA: [*unperturbed*] I mean, then I went from Papa's hands into yours. You arranged everything to your own taste, and so I got the same taste as you—or I pretended to; I can't remember. I guess a little of both, first one, then the other. Now when I look back, it seems as if I'd lived here like a beggar—just from hand to mouth. I've lived by doing tricks for you, Torvald. But that's the way you wanted it. It's a great sin what you and Papa did to me. You're to blame that nothing's become of me.

HELMER: Nora, how unfair and ungrateful you are! Haven't you been happy here?

NORA: No, never. I thought so—but I never have.

HELMER: Not—not happy!

NORA: No, only lighthearted. And you've always been so kind to me. But our home's been nothing but a playpen. I've been your doll-wife here, just as at home I was Papa's doll-child. And in turn the children have been my dolls. I thought it was fun when you played with me, just as they thought it fun when I played with them. That's been our marriage, Torvald.

HELMER: There's some truth in what you're saying—under all the raving exaggeration. But it'll all be different after this. Playtime's over; now for the schooling.

NORA: Whose schooling—mine or the children's?

HELMER: Both yours and the children's, dearest.

NORA: Oh, Torvald, you're not the man to teach me to be a good wife to you.

HELMER: And you can say that?

NORA: And I—how am I equipped to bring up children?

HELMER: Nora!

NORA: Didn't you say a moment ago that that was no job to trust me with?

HELMER: In a flare of temper! Why fasten on that?

NORA: Yes, but you were so very right. I'm not up to the job. There's another job I have to do first. I have to try to educate myself. You can't help me with that. I've go to do it alone. And that's why I'm leaving you now.

—Excerpted from *The Doll House* by Henrik Ibsen.

1. Where are Nora and Helmer seated during their conversation?

   _____

2. What does Nora mean by the phrase "closing out accounts" (line 6)?

   (1) paying the household bills
   (2) transferring the savings account to another bank
   (3) filing for bankruptcy
   (4) discussing financial investments
   (5) ending the marriage

3. What does Nora mean when she says, "I've been your doll-wife here, just as at home I was Papa's doll-child" (lines 49–50)?

   (1) She has always been pretty as a doll.
   (2) She has a cute and playful personality.
   (3) Neither her husband nor her father has treated her like a human being.
   (4) Her husband and father collect lifelike dolls.
   (5) Nora toys with her father's and Helmer's affection.

4. According to this passage, what is the significance of the play's title, *The Doll House?* _____

   _____

   _____

5. Label each of the following statements as *true* or *false*.

   (1) Helmer discusses serious issues with Nora. _____

   (2) Helmer is satisfied with the marriage. _____

   (3) Nora and Helmer disagree about the definition of love. _____

   (4) Helmer considers Nora his equal. _____

   (5) Helmer understands his wife's point of view. _____

   (6) Helmer has not physically abused Nora. _____

6. In a short paragraph, write your opinion of either Nora or Helmer. Explain your feelings about the character's behavior and role as either a wife or a husband.

   _____

   _____

   _____

   _____

   _____

   _____

   _____

FOR ANSWERS AND EXPLANATIONS, SEE PAGE 284.

Reading a Complete Scene from a Play

In this section, you will read an entire scene from a play. Unlike a shorter passage, a complete scene presents a more detailed development of character and plot.

Use the following questions as study aids for understanding the literal meanings, the suggested meanings, and the structural elements of drama:

1. Where and when does the scene occur?

2. What is the topic of conversation?

3. What is the literal meaning of the speaker's statements?

4. What is the relationship between the stage directions and the dialogue? Do the speaker's tone of voice and actions emphasize or change the literal meaning of the spoken words?

5. What do other characters say in response to the first speaker? Based on these responses, can you make inferences about the relationships of the characters involved in the conversation?

6. Does the dialogue show a conflict between the characters? Is the conflict resolved?

7. Do the characters in the scene discuss other people? What do the characters' comments reveal about those people?

8. Does the dialogue reveal the speaker's personality, behavior, or background?

9. What specific incidents of plot are depicted in the scene?

10. Do characters express their beliefs or opinions about life or human behavior? If so, do their comments suggest a theme—a general statement explaining the significance of the dramatic action?

Exercise 5: A Complete Scene from a Play

This excerpt is longer than those you'll see on the GED Interpreting Literature and the Arts Test. However, when you read the entire scene, you will see how all of the elements of drama work together.

Directions: Arthur Miller's play *Death of a Salesman* tells the story of Willy Loman, a sixty-year-old sales representative who is approaching the end of his career. In the following scene from Act II, Willy meets with his boss, Howard. Willy proposes a change in his position with the firm. Read the script carefully. Then complete the exercise.

[*HOWARD WAGNER, thirty-six, wheels in a small typewriter table on which is a wire-recording machine and proceeds to plug it in. This is on the left forestage . . . HOWARD is intent on threading the machine and only glances over his shoulder as WILLY appears.*]

WILLY: Pst! Pst!

HOWARD: Hello, Willy, come in.

WILLY: Like to have a little talk with you, Howard.

HOWARD: Sorry to keep you waiting. I'll be with you in a minute.

WILLY: What's that, Howard?

HOWARD: Didn't you ever see one of these? Wire recorder.

WILLY: Oh. Can we talk a minute?

HOWARD: Records things. Just got a delivery yesterday. Been driving me crazy, the most terrific machine I ever saw in my life. I was up all night with it.

WILLY: What do you do with it?

HOWARD: I bought it for dictation, but you can do anything with it. Listen to this. I had it home last night. Listen to what I picked up. The first one is my daughter. Get this. [*He flicks the switch and "Roll out the Barrel" is heard being whistled.*] Listen to that kid whistle.

WILLY: That is lifelike, isn't it?

HOWARD: Seven years old. Get that tone.

WILLY: Ts, ts. Like to ask a little favor if you. . .

[*The whistling breaks off, and the voice of HOWARD'S DAUGHTER is heard.*]

HIS DAUGHTER: "Now you, Daddy."

HOWARD: She's crazy for me! [*Again the same song is whistled.*] That's me! Ha! [*He winks.*]

WILLY: You're very good!

[*The whistling breaks off again. The machine runs silent for a moment.*]

HOWARD: Sh! Get this now, this is my son.

HIS SON: "The capital of Alabama is Montgomery; the capital of Arizona is Phoenix; the capital of Arkansas is Little Rock; the capital of California is Sacramento . . ." [*And on, and on.*]

HOWARD: [*holding up five fingers*] Five years old, Willy!

WILLY: He'll make an announcer some day!

40 HIS SON: [*continuing*] "The capital . . ."

HOWARD: Get that—alphabetical order! [*The machine breaks off suddenly.*] Wait a minute. The maid kicked the plug out.

WILLY: It certainly is a—

45 HOWARD: Sh, for God's sake!

HIS SON: "It's nine o'clock, Bulova watch time. So I have to go to sleep."

WILLY: That really is—

HOWARD: Wait a minute. The next is my wife.

50 [*They wait.*]

HOWARD'S VOICE: "Go on, say something." [*Pause.*] "Well, you gonna talk?"

HIS WIFE: "I can't think of anything."

HOWARD'S VOICE: "Well, talk—it's turning."

55 HIS WIFE: [*shyly, beaten*] "Hello." [*Silence.*] "Oh, Howard, I can't talk into this . . ."

HOWARD: [*snapping the machine off*] That was my wife.

WILLY: That is a wonderful machine. Can we—

HOWARD: I tell you, Willy, I'm gonna take my camera, and my
60 bandsaw, and all my hobbies, and out they go. This is the most fascinating relaxation I ever found.

WILLY: I think I'll get one myself.

HOWARD: Sure, they're only a hundred and a half. You can't do without it. Supposing you wanna hear Jack Benny,
65 see? But you can't be at home at that hour. So you tell the maid to turn the radio on when Jack Benny comes on, and this automatically goes on with the radio . . .

WILLY: And when you come home you . . .

HOWARD: You can come home twelve o'clock, one o'clock, any
70 time you like, and you get yourself a Coke and sit yourself down, throw the switch, and there's Jack Benny's program in the middle of the night!

WILLY: I'm definitely going to get one. Because lots of time I'm on the road, and I think to myself, what I must be
75 missing on the radio!

HOWARD: Don't you have a radio in the car?

WILLY: Well, yeah, but who ever thinks of turning it on?

HOWARD: Say, aren't you supposed to be in Boston?

WILLY: That's what I want to talk to you about, Howard. You
80   got a minute?

          [*He draws a chair in from the wing.*]

HOWARD: What happened? What're you doing here?

WILLY: Well . . .

HOWARD: You didn't crack up again, did you?

85 WILLY: Oh, no. No . . .

HOWARD: Geez, you had me worried there for a minute. What's
          the trouble?

WILLY: Well, to tell you the truth, Howard, I've come to the
          decision that I'd rather not travel any more.

90 HOWARD: Not travel! Well, what'll you do?

WILLY: Remember, Christmas time, when you had the party
          here? You said you'd try to think of some spot for me
          here in town.

HOWARD: With us?

95 WILLY: Well, sure.

HOWARD: Oh, yeah, yeah. I remember. Well, I couldn't think of
          anything for you, Willy.

WILLY: I tell ya, Howard. The kids are all grown up, y'know. I
          don't need much any more. If I could take home—well,
100   sixty-five dollars a week, I could swing it.

HOWARD: Yeah, but Willy, see I —

WILLY: I tell ya why, Howard. Speaking frankly and between
          the two of us, y'know—I'm just a little tired.

HOWARD: Oh, I could understand that, Willy. But you're a road
105   man, Willy, and we do a road business. We've only got
          a half-dozen salesmen on the floor here.

WILLY: God knows, Howard, I never asked a favor of any man.
          But I was with the firm when your father used to carry
          you in here in his arms.

110 HOWARD: I know that, Willy, but—

WILLY: Your father came to me the day you were born and
          asked me what I thought of the name of Howard, may
          he rest in peace.

HOWARD: I appreciate that, Willy, but there just is no spot here

115   for you. If I had a spot I'd slam you right in, but I just don't have a single, solitary spot.

                [*He looks for his lighter. WILLY has picked it up and gives it to him. Pause.*]

WILLY: [*with increasing anger*] Howard, all I need to set my
120   table is fifty dollars a week.

HOWARD: But where am I going to put you, kid?

WILLY: Look, it isn't a question of whether I can sell merchandise, is it?

HOWARD: No, but it's a business, kid, and everybody's gotta pull
125   his own weight.

WILLY: [*desperately*] Just let me tell you a story, Howard—

HOWARD: 'Cause you gotta admit, business is business.

WILLY: [*angrily*] Business is definitely business, but just listen for a minute. You don't understand this. When I was a
130   boy—eighteen, nineteen—I was already on the road. And there was a question in my mind as to whether selling had a future for me. Because in those days I had a yearning to go to Alaska. See, there were three gold strikes in one month in Alaska, and I felt like
135   going out. Just for the ride, you might say.

HOWARD: [*barely interested*] Don't say.

WILLY: Oh, yeah, my father lived many years in Alaska. He was an adventurous man. We've got quite a little streak of self-reliance in our family. I thought I'd go out with
140   my older brother and try to locate him, and maybe settle in the North with the old man. And I was almost decided to go, when I met a salesman in the Parker House. His name was Dave Singleman. And he was eighty-four years old, and he'd drummed merchandise
145   in thirty-one states. And old Dave, he'd go up to his room, y'understand, put on his green velvet slippers— I'll never forget—and pick up his phone and call the buyers, and without ever leaving his room, at the age of eighty-four, he made his living. And when I saw that,
150   I realized that selling was the greatest career a man could want. 'Cause what could be more satisfying than to be able to go, at the age of eighty-four, into twenty or thirty different cities, and pick up a phone, and be remembered and loved and helped by so many
155   different people? Do you know? when he died—and by the way he died the death of a salesman, in his green velvet slippers in the smoker of the New York, New Haven, and Hartford, going into Boston—when he

160 died, hundreds of salesmen and buyers were at his funeral. Things were sad on a lotta trains for months after that. [*He stands up. HOWARD has not looked at him.*] In those days there was personality in it, Howard.

165 There was respect, and comradeship, and gratitude in it. Today, it's all cut and dried, and there's no chance for bringing friendship to bear—or personality. You see what I mean? They don't know me any more.

HOWARD: [*moving away, to the right*] That's just the thing, Willy.

WILLY: If I had forty dollars a week—that's all I'd need. Forty dollars, Howard.

170 HOWARD: Kid, I can't take blood from a stone, I—

WILLY: [*desperation is on him now*] Howard, the year Al Smith was nominated, your father came to me and—

HOWARD: [*starting to go off*] I've got to see some people, kid.

WILLY: [*stopping him*] I'm talking about your father! There
175 were promises made across this desk! You mustn't tell me you've got people to see—I put thirty-four years into this firm, Howard, and now I can't pay my insurance! You can't eat the orange and throw the peel away—a man is not a piece of fruit! [*After a pause.*]
180 Now pay attention. Your father—in 1928 I had a big year. I averaged a hundred and seventy dollars a week in commissions.

HOWARD: [*impatiently*] Now, Willy, you never averaged—

WILLY: [*banging his hand on the desk*] I averaged a hundred
185 and seventy dollars a week in the year of 1928! And your father came to me—or rather, I was in the office here—it was right over this desk—and he put his hand on my shoulder—

HOWARD: [*getting up*] You'll have to excuse me, Willy, I gotta see
190 some people. Pull yourself together. [*Going out*] I'll be back in a little while.

[*On HOWARD'S exit, the light on his chair grows very bright and strange.*]

WILLY: Pull myself together! What the hell did I say to him?
195 My God, I was yelling at him! How could I! [*WILLY breaks off, staring at the light, which occupies the chair, animating it. He approaches this chair, standing across the desk from it.*] Frank, Frank, don't you remember what you told me that time? How you put your hand
200 on my shoulder, and Frank . . . [*He leans on the desk and as he speaks the dead man's name he accidentally switches on the recorder, and instantly—*]

HOWARD'S SON: "... of New York is Albany. The capital of Ohio is Cincinnati, the capital of Rhode Island is ..." [*The recitation continues.*]

205

WILLY: [*leaping away with fright, shouting*] Ha! Howard! Howard! Howard!

HOWARD: [*rushing in*] What happened?

WILLY: [*pointing at the machine, which continues nasally, childishly, with the capital cities*] Shut it off! Shut it off!

210

HOWARD: [*pulling the plug out*] Look, Willy ...

WILLY: [*pressing his hands to his eyes*] I gotta get myself some coffee. I'll get some coffee ...

[*WILLY starts to walk out. HOWARD stops him.*]

HOWARD: [*rolling up the cord*] Willy, look ...

215

WILLY: I'll go to Boston.

HOWARD: Willy, you can't go to Boston for us.

WILLY: Why can't I go?

HOWARD: I don't want you to represent us. I've been meaning to tell you for a long time now.

220

WILLY: Howard, are you firing me?

HOWARD: I think you need a good long rest, Willy.

WILLY: Howard—

HOWARD: And when you feel better, come back, and we'll see if we can work something out.

225

WILLY: But I gotta earn money, Howard. I'm in no position—

HOWARD: Where are your sons? Why don't your sons give you a hand?

WILLY: They're working on a very big deal.

HOWARD: This is no time for false pride, Willy. You go to your sons and tell them that you're tired. You've got two great boys, haven't you?

230

WILLY: Oh, no question, no question, but in the meantime ...

HOWARD: Then that's that, heh?

WILLY: All right. I'll go to Boston tomorrow.

235

HOWARD: No, no.

WILLY: I can't throw myself on my sons. I'm not a cripple!

HOWARD: Look, kid, I'm busy this morning.

WILLY: [*grasping HOWARD'S arm*] Howard, you've got to let
240   me go to Boston!

HOWARD: [*hard, keeping himself under control*] I've got a line of
people to see this morning. Sit down, take five
minutes, and pull yourself together, and then go home,
will ya? I need the office, Willy. [*He starts to go, turns,*
245   *remembering the recorder, starts to push off the table*
holding the recorder.] Oh, yeah. Whenever you can this
week, stop by and drop off the samples. You'll feel
better, Willy, and then come back and we'll talk. Pull
yourself together, kid, there's people outside.

250   [*HOWARD exits, pushing the table off left. WILLY stares*
into space, exhausted.]

—Excerpted from *Death of a Salesman* by Arthur Miller

1. As the scene opens, why does Howard insistently play with the wire recorder?

    (1) to show his enthusiasm for new machines
    (2) to avoid talking to Willy
    (3) to explain how a wire recorder operates
    (4) to introduce his family to Willy
    (5) to persuade Willy to buy a wire recorder

2. "I've come to the decision that I'd rather not travel any more" (lines 88–89). What action occurs as a result of this statement?

    (1) a friendly conversation
    (2) a job interview
    (3) a heated argument
    (4) a fair debate
    (5) a fistfight

3. Willy tries to negotiate his weekly pay with Howard. List the three salaries that Willy requests:

    _____   _____   _____

4. What is the major point of Willy's long speech (lines 137–66)?

    (1) Hundreds of salesmen and buyers attended David Singleman's funeral.
    (2) Willy's father was an adventurous man who lived in Alaska.
    (3) The advantages of a sales career outweigh the disadvantages.
    (4) Salesmen used to value respect and personal relationships as well as commissions.
    (5) Willy decided not to settle in the North.

5. How long has Willy worked for the firm? _____

6. Write two statements from Howard's dialogue that indirectly say to Willy, "You are fired." _____

_____

7. From Willy's and Howard's actions, you can make judgments about their personality and behavior.

    (1) Circle three of the following character traits that Willy reveals in this scene:

        proud   greedy
        composed   frustrated
        desperate   ambitious
        grateful

    (2) Circle three of the following character traits that Howard reveals in this scene:

        appreciative   concerned
        insensitive   bored
        impatient   respectful
        generous

FOR ANSWERS AND EXPLANATIONS, SEE PAGE 284.

 Writing Exercise 4━━━━━━━━━━━━━━━━

On a separate sheet of paper, write a short scene in script form portraying a conflict between a boss and an employee. Write down the following information before you begin writing the dialogue:

    ☐ time   ☐ characters

    ☐ place   ☐ conflict

ANSWERS WILL VARY.

★ **GED PRACTICE** ★

Exercise 6: Chapter Review━━━━━━━━━━━━━━

Directions: Read the following passages and answer the multiple-choice questions. Use the purpose question to focus your reading.

Passage 1

WHAT DO YOU NOTICE ABOUT MAY AND EDDIE'S RELATIONSHIP?

EDDIE: I'm not leavin'. I don't care what you think anymore. I don't care what you feel. None a' that matters. I'm not leavin'. I'm stayin' right

here. I don't care if a hundred "dates" walk through that door—I'll take every one of 'em on. I don't care if you hate my guts. I don't
5   care if you can't stand the sight of me or the sound of me or the smell of me. I'm never leavin'. You'll never get rid of me. You'll never escape me either. I'll track you down no matter where you go. I know exactly how your mind works. I've been right every time. Every single time.

10 MAY: You've gotta' give this up, Eddie.

EDDIE: I'm not giving it up!

[*Pause.*]

MAY: [*calm*] Okay. Look. I don't understand what you've got in your head anymore. I really don't. I don't get it. *Now* you desperately need
15   me. *Now* you can't live without me. *NOW* you'll do anything for me. Why should I believe it this time?

EDDIE: Because it's true.

MAY: It was supposed to have been true every time before. Every other time. Now it's true again. . . . Fifteen years I've been a yo-yo for
20   you. I've never been split. I've never been two ways about you. I've either loved you or not loved you. And now I just plain don't love you. Understand? Do you understand that? I don't love you. I don't need you. I don't want you. Do you get that? Now if you can still stay, then you're either crazy or pathetic.

25   [*She crosses down left to table, sits in upstage chair facing audience, takes slug of tequila from bottle, slams it down on table.*]

—Excerpted from *Fool for Love* by Sam Shepard

1. According to lines 3–7, what is the emotional basis for Eddie's attachment to May?

   (1) loneliness and depression
   (2) pity and guilt
   (3) obligation and commitment
   (4) love and respect
   (5) jealousy and possessiveness

2. From this excerpt, you can infer that May and Eddie's relationship is

   (1) unhealthy
   (2) caring
   (3) compassionate
   (4) unemotional
   (5) casual

3. Which of the following words best describes May's impression of Eddie's behavior?

   (1) stable
   (2) unpredictable
   (3) calm
   (4) mature
   (5) sympathetic

4. May "takes slug of tequila from bottle, slams it down on table" (line 26). The playwright includes this stage direction to show May's

   (1) alcoholism
   (2) clumsiness
   (3) thirst
   (4) anger
   (5) strength

5. If May wrote a letter to Ann Landers or another advice columnist, which of the following questions would she most likely ask?

   (1) Am I too young to get married?
   (2) Will Eddie make a good husband?
   (3) Where can I find a shelter for battered women?
   (4) How can I resolve my situation with Eddie?
   (5) How long should a couple be engaged?

Passage 2

WHY IS MARGARET ANGRY?

[*At the rise of the curtain someone is taking a shower in the bathroom, the door of which is half open. A pretty young woman, with anxious lines in her face, enters the bedroom and crosses to the bathroom door.*]

5 MARGARET: [*shouting above the roar of water*] One of those no-neck monsters hit me with a hot buttered biscuit so I have t'change!

[*MARGARET'S voice is both rapid and drawling. In her long speeches she has the vocal tricks of a priest delivering a liturgical chant, the lines are almost sung, always continuing a little beyond her breath so she has to gasp for another. Sometimes she intersperses the lines with a little wordless singing, such as "Da-da-daaaa!"*]

[*Water turns off and BRICK calls out to her, but is still unseen. A tone of politely feigned interest, masking indifference, or worse, is characteristic of his speech with MARGARET.*]

BRICK: Wha'd you say, Maggie? Water was on s' loud I couldn't hear ya . .

MARGARET: Well, I!—just remarked that!—one of th' no-neck monsters
20   messed up m' lovely lace dress so I got t'—cha-a-ange. . . .

           [*She opens and kicks shut drawers of the dresser.*]

BRICK: Why d'ya call Gooper's kiddies no-neck monsters?

MARGARET: Because they've got no necks! Isn't that a good enough
           reason?

25 BRICK: Don't they have necks?

MARGARET: None visible. Their fat little heads are set on their fat little
           bodies without a bit of connection.

BRICK: That's too bad.

MARGARET: Yes, it's too bad because you can't wring their necks if they've
30   got no necks to wring! Isn't that right, honey?

           [*She steps out of her dress, stands in a slip of ivory satin and
           lace.*]

           Yep, they're no-neck monsters, all no-neck people are
           monsters . . .

35   [*children shriek downstairs.*]

           Hear them? Hear them screaming? I don't know where their
           voice-boxes are located since they don't have necks. I tell you
           I got so nervous at that table tonight I thought I would throw
           back my head and utter a scream you could hear across the
40   Arkansas border an' parts of Louisiana an' Tennessee. I said
           to your charming sister-in-law, Mae, honey, couldn't you feed
           those precious little things at a separate table with an oilcloth
           cover? They make such a mess an' the lace cloth looks *so*
           pretty! She made enormous eyes at me and said, "Ohhh,
45   noooooo! On Big Daddy's birthday? Why, he would never
           forgive me!" Well, I want you to know, Big Daddy hadn't been
           at the table two minutes with those five no-neck monsters
           slobbering and drooling over their food before he threw down
           his fork and shouted, "Fo' God's sake, Gooper, why don't you
50   put them pigs at a trough in th' kitchen?"—Well, I swear, I
           simply could have di-ieed!

—Excerpted from *Cat on a Hot Tin Roof*
by Tennessee Williams

6. Which of the following words best describes Brick's attitude toward
   Margaret's remarks?

   (1) interested
   (2) indifferent
   (3) critical
   (4) excited
   (5) impolite

7. You can infer that this scene takes place

    (1) in the South
    (2) in the Midwest
    (3) on the West Coast
    (4) in New England
    (5) in the Southwest

8. Gooper is Brick's

    (1) father
    (2) nephew
    (3) uncle
    (4) brother-in-law
    (5) brother

9. Why does Big Daddy refer to the children as "pigs at a trough" (line 50)?

    (1) They make snorting noises.
    (2) They look like hogs.
    (3) They have mud on their faces.
    (4) They eat like slobs.
    (5) They play with other barnyard animals.

10. What is the main topic of Margaret's conversation?

    (1) the children's appearance and behavior
    (2) her fondness for Big Daddy
    (3) the birthday celebration
    (4) her low opinion of her sister-in-law
    (5) the description of her dress

11. If this scene were adapted to a movie, the camera would focus on

    (1) Brick
    (2) the children
    (3) Big Daddy
    (4) Margaret
    (5) Mae

Passage 3

WHAT DO YOU LEARN ABOUT BIG WALTER?

RUTH: [*Studying her mother-in-law furtively and concentrating on her ironing, anxious to encourage without seeming to*] Well, Lord knows, we've put enough rent into this here rat trap to pay for four houses by now . . .

5   MAMA: [*Looking up at the words "rat trap" and then looking around and leaning back and sighing—in a suddenly reflective mood—*] "Rat trap"—yes, that's all it is. [*Smiling*] I remember just as well the day me and Big Walter moved in here. Hadn't been married but two weeks and wasn't planning on living here no more than a

10   year. [*She shakes her head at the dissolved dream*] We was going to set away, little by little, don't you know, and buy a little place out in Morgan Park. We even picked out the house. [*Chuckling a little*] Looks right dumpy today. But Lord, child, you should know all the dreams I had 'bout buying that house and fixing it up and

15   making me a little garden in the back— [*She waits and stops smiling*] And didn't none of it happen.

[*Dropping her hands in a futile gesture*]

RUTH: [*Dropping her head down, ironing*] Yes, life can be a barrel of disappointments, sometimes.

20 MAMA: Honey, Big Walter would come in here some nights back then and slump down on that couch there and just look at the rug, and look at me and look at the rug and then back at me—and I'd know he was down then . . . really down. [*After a second very long and thoughtful pause; she is seeing back to times that only

25   she can see*] And then, Lord, when I lost that baby—little Claude—I almost thought I was going to lose Big Walter too. Oh, that man grieved hisself! He was one man to love his children.

RUTH: Ain't nothin' can tear at you like losin' your baby.

MAMA: I guess that's how come that man finally worked hisself to death

30   like he done. Like he was fighting his own war with this here world that took his baby from him.

RUTH: He sure was a fine man, all right. I always liked Mr. Younger.

MAMA: Crazy 'bout his children! God knows there was plenty wrong with Walter Younger—hard-headed, mean, kind of wild with women—

35   plenty wrong with him. But he sure loved his children. Always wanted them to have something—be something. That's where Brother gets all these notions, I reckon. Big Walter used to say, he'd get right wet in the eyes sometimes, lean his head back with the water standing in his eyes and say, "Seem like God didn't see

40   fit to give the black man nothing but dreams—but He did give us children to make them dreams seem worthwhile." [*She smiles*] He could talk like that, don't you know.

RUTH: Yes, he sure could. He was a good man, Mr. Younger.

MAMA: Yes, a fine man—just couldn't never catch up with his dreams,

45   that's all.

—Excerpted from *A Raisin in the Sun*
by Lorraine Hansberry

12. Which of the following words best describes Mama and Ruth's attitude toward Big Walter?

(1) frustration
(2) respect
(3) disappointment
(4) resentment
(5) guilt

13. What was the major cause of Big Walter's grief?

    (1) his baby's death
    (2) his financial troubles
    (3) his shabby surroundings
    (4) his war experiences
    (5) his demanding job

14. From Mama's comments about her husband, Big Walter, you can infer that she was

    (1) a hot-tempered wife
    (2) a pampered wife
    (3) a selfish wife
    (4) an insensitive wife
    (5) an understanding wife

15. According to Mama, what overall goal was Big Walter unable to accomplish?

    (1) growing a garden
    (2) buying a house
    (3) fulfilling his dreams
    (4) financing his children's education
    (5) earning a high salary

16. Why does the playwright include the gesture *Dropping her head down, ironing* (line 18) before Ruth's line of dialogue?

    (1) to show that Ruth is only concerned about her housework
    (2) to emphasize that Ruth, too, understands life's disappointments
    (3) to show that Ruth is afraid to look directly at Mama
    (4) to reveal Ruth's hardworking personality
    (5) to show that Ruth is bored with the conversation

17. If Big Walter were still alive, which of the following statements would he most likely support?

    (1) Children are a burden to their parents.
    (2) Children should behave as maturely as adults.
    (3) Parents should ignore their children.
    (4) Children represent the hopes for the future.
    (5) Parents should spoil their children.

FOR ANSWERS AND EXPLANATIONS, SEE PAGES 284-85.

8
COMMENTARIES ON THE ARTS

Nearly 25 percent of the GED Interpreting Literature and the Arts Test consists of questions about commentaries on the arts. Commentaries on the arts—a type of nonfiction prose—include reviews, critical essays, and informative essays about these topics:

Television and Film	Performing Arts	Visual Arts	Literature
TV shows	music	painting	nonfiction
movies	dance	architecture	fiction
	theatrical	sculpture	poetry
	performances	photography	drama

The author's approach to writing about these artistic works depends on his purpose and the response he expects from his readers. Let's examine the purpose of three kinds of commentaries: (1) reviews, (2) critical essays, and (3) informative essays.

Reviews

Reviews of movies, plays, books, and other art forms appear in newspapers and magazines. Intended for the general reading public, reviews briefly describe the content of a piece and evaluate its strengths and weaknesses. The reviewer assumes that most readers are unfamiliar with his subject. His purpose is to sway the readers' opinion. For instance, after reading a movie review, you should ask yourself this question: "According to the reviewer's recommendations, should I see the movie?" Your decision may be influenced by the reviewer's overall comments and a rating, such as "I give this movie three stars."

Critical Essays

Critical essays present a more in-depth analysis of the arts than reviews do. Critical essays are usually directed to readers who already have a solid base of knowledge about the particular art form. The author of critical essays often interprets artistic techniques, such as style and structure. She may also explain the meaning of a work of art and judge its merits. For example, a critical essay about the jazz singer Billie Holiday might analyze how her voice incorporated the technical and emotional qualities of Louis Armstrong's trumpet playing. (Note: The commentary selections on the GED Literature Test do *not* require you to know anything in advance about the art forms they cover.)

Informative Essays

In informative essays, the author's intention is to educate the readers about art and artists. He may provide historical background, descriptive summaries, or biographical sketches. In purely informative essays, the author withholds personal judgments. His purpose is to instruct readers rather than to persuade them to agree with his opinions. For example, an informative essay about art appreciation might tell readers how to look at a painting.

To prepare you for the GED Interpreting Literature and the Arts Test, this chapter will present a wide range of commentaries on the arts. You will apply the reading skills discussed throughout this book. In addition, you will focus on some of the elements that reviewers, critics, and authors use in developing their topics:

☐ Facts and opinions

☐ Descriptive language

Recognizing these elements will help you to determine the author's viewpoint as well as the style and the structure of commentaries on the arts.

Facts and Opinions

In Chapter 1 of this book (Exercise 4), you learned that the fiction writer Ralph Ellison attended Tuskegee Institute in Alabama, where he studied music and composing. Through research you could prove that this statement is true. A true statement can be proven as a **fact**.

Suppose a literary critic commented, "Ralph Ellison's musical training strongly influenced his prose style. His rhythmical sentences, his attention to the sound of words, the balanced structure of his stories—all reveal how his craft as a musician was transferred to his writing." The critic's statement is an **opinion**— a judgment about Ralph Ellison's prose style. Although the critic supports her opinion with examples, it is still an opinion, a reflection of her own interpretation.

You can verify the truth of factual information. In contrast, a critic's interpretation may or may not be accurate. When you read commentaries on the arts, you need to distinguish between facts and opinions. You cannot dispute the accuracy of proven facts. However, you have the option to agree or disagree with an author's opinion. Recognizing the difference between facts and opinions will enhance your understanding of commentaries in the following ways:

1. Your literal understanding of the passage will improve if you grasp the factual information.

2. You will be able to pinpoint sentences in the passage that express the author's beliefs.

3. You will be able to identify facts that are used to support the critic's opinions or main idea.

Practice your skills in distinguishing facts from opinions. The following are statements about the original television series, "The Twilight Zone." Label each statement *fact* or *opinion*.

1. Rod Serling was the series' host and narrator. _____

2. In 1960 and 1961, Rod Serling won an Emmy Award for "Outstanding Writing Achievements in Drama." _____

3. During the 1960s, Rod Serling was the most talented and imaginative scriptwriter in Hollywood. _____

4. Art Carney starred in an episode entitled "The Night of the Meek." He played a department store Santa Claus who was fired for drinking. Later in the episode, he discovered that he actually *was* Santa Claus. _____

5. Art Carney's role as a drunken department store Santa Claus projects a disturbing image to young viewers. _____

6. "The Night of the Meek" is a moving, sensitive story about a man's generosity and Christmas miracles. _____

7. The series was telecast on CBS from 1959 to 1965. _____

8. The music introducing each episode was spooky. _____

Did you label statements 1, 2, 4, and 7 as facts? Did you label statements 3, 5, 6, and 8 as opinions? If so, you correctly distinguished facts from opinions.

Let's examine these responses more closely. The accuracy of the factual statements 1, 2, 4, and 7 can be verified by research.

As you probably noticed, the descriptive words in statements 3, 5, 6, and 8 reflect the author's opinion. Statement 3 praises Rod Serling's writing as "talented" and "imaginative." Statement 5 criticizes Art Carney's portrayal of Santa Claus as "disturbing" to young viewers. In statement 6, the words "moving" and "sensitive" describe possible emotional reactions to an episode of "The Twilight Zone." In statement 8, "spooky" describes the feeling that the music might suggest to some listeners.

For further practice in distinguishing facts from opinions, complete the next exercise.

Exercise 1: Facts and Opinions

Part I

Directions: Carefully read the four short commentaries about Ntozake Shange's play *For Colored Girls Who Have Considered Suicide/When the Rainbow Is Enuf.* After each commentary, label each statement *fact* or *opinion.*

1. *For Colored Girls Who Have Considered Suicide/When the Rainbow Is Enuf* is a "choreopoem"—a theatrical production combining music, dance, and poetry. Seven black women, each wearing a dress in one of the rainbow colors, relate their personal experiences onstage. Written by Ntozake Shange, the show was first produced in November 1975. Soon after, the show was staged on Broadway for two years. The show's continued popularity reflects Shange's insightful portrayal of black women.

   (1) A "choreopoem" combines music, dance, and poetry. _____

   (2) The show was staged on Broadway for two years. _____

   (3) Shange insightfully portrays the experiences of black women. _____

2. "[This play is a] stirringly acted, intimate production of Ntozake Shange's Tony Award-winning drama that explores the lives of seven black women, presented by Pegasus Players."
   —Excerpted from a drama review in the *Chicago Tribune,*
   July 25, 1986

   (1) The show was a Tony Award-winning drama. _____

   (2) The show explores the lives of seven black women. _____

   (3) The production is stirringly acted and intimate. _____

3. "When Ntozake Shange wrote this 'choreopoem' ten years ago, it seemed like an outspoken affirmation of black women. Today, it sounds like the seven black women in this plotless play think only about black men. The adolescent poetry is flaccid and self-indulgent, and the production, despite some high-energy performances, can't pump much strength into it."
   —Excerpted from a drama review in *Chicago* magazine,
   August 1986

   (1) Despite some good performances, the play is dated. _____

(2) Shange's poetry is adolescent. _____

(3) The production of the play is weak. _____

4. *"Colored Girls*, as directed by Sydney Daniels, suffers from a slow start, but as Ntozake Shange's lovely poetry gets rolling, the pace picks up. And it isn't long before the Pegasus Players cast begins to make a strong connection. The tale-telling session becomes comfortable and irresistible in this cleanly delivered and forcefully presented production."

—Excerpted from a drama review in the *Chicago Sun-Times*, July 27, 1986

(1) Sydney Daniels is the director. _____

(2) The acting is performed by the Pegasus Players cast. _____

(3) Shange's poetry is lovely. _____

(4) The production is cleanly delivered and forcefully presented.

_____

Part II
Directions: Reread the preceding commentaries. Then write the number of the commentary that correctly answers each of the following questions.

_____ **1.** Which commentary expresses the most negative opinion of the production?

_____ **2.** Which commentary praises Shange's poetry?

_____ **3.** Which commentary does not judge a specific production of the show?

_____ **4.** Which commentary implies that the show is dated?

FOR ANSWERS AND EXPLANATIONS, SEE PAGE 285.

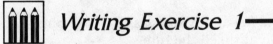 *Writing Exercise 1*

Watch your favorite television show, and write a short commentary in which you include both factual information and your opinion. In the first paragraph, record facts about the show. (Suggestions: Include the title of the show, the names of the leading actors and the characters they portray, a brief summary of the plot, etc.)

In the second paragraph, state your opinion of the show. Address the following questions: Why is the show your favorite? How would you rate the actors' performances? Would you recommend the show to a friend? Use a separate sheet of paper for your commentary.

ANSWERS WILL VARY.

Descriptive Language

Descriptive language often characterizes the writing style of commentaries on the arts. As you have already observed, reviewers rely on colorful adjectives in phrasing their opinions. An adjective is a part of speech that describes a person, a place, a thing, or an idea. The following are examples of adjectives used in movie and play reviews:

- hilarious

- wild, witty, and wonderful

- sensational, clever, and warm-hearted

- delightful, funny, and sophisticated

You probably noticed that all of these adjectives are flattering. The reviewers have chosen words praising the movie or play described.

On the other hand, you can also infer a reviewer's disapproval of a play or a movie from the descriptive language. The following adjectives from play and movie reviews are uncomplimentary:

- unimaginative and predictable

- strained and clumsy

- trivial and simple-minded

- offensive

Recognizing descriptive language enables you to determine the reviewer's opinion—positive or negative—about an artistic work. The following statement is excerpted from Sid Smith's review of *The Toxic Avenger*, a horror film. Circle the descriptive words that reveal the reviewer's impression of the movie.

"The Toxic Avenger" is a monstrously crude, blatantly tasteless film reminiscent of the now by-gone drive-in movies.

Did you circle "monstrously crude" and "blatantly tasteless"? These phrases express Sid Smith's viewpoint. He obviously disliked the film.

In the next exercise, you will study several examples showing how reviewers convey their opinions through descriptive language.

Exercise 2: Identifying Descriptive Language in Reviews

Directions: The following are reviewers' statements about a theater company, a singer, a novel, and a movie. Carefully read these statements and complete the exercises.

Part I: Comments about Steppenwolf Theatre Company

"Nervy, electric, physically charged style"

—Michael Billington, *The Guardian*

"Steppenwolf Theatre Company is not merely good. It's simply great!"

—Glenna Syse, *Sun-Times*

"Steppenwolf, as always, is spectacular. . . ."

—Linda Winer, *USA Today*

"The strongest, most energetic theatre company in America today"

—*Vogue* magazine

From the preceding statements, write four adjectives that praise the Steppenwolf Theatre Company.

_____   _____

_____   _____

Part II: Comments about singer Pia Zadora

"A big, brash, pop singing voice . . ."

—*The New York Times*

"Her voice is . . . strong, mature, and it envelops the lyrics with a caress."

—*Variety*

"She has a tremendous voice . . . big, clear and good . . . the audience went crazy."

—*Detroit Free Press*

Write four adjectives from the preceding comments that describe Pia Zadora's singing voice.

_____   _____

_____   _____

Part III: Comments about Ernest Hemingway's novel *The Garden of Eden*

"A highly readable story"

—E. L. Doctorow, *The New York Times Book Review*

"Wonderful writing . . . Hemingway at the top of his form"

—Charles P. Corn, *San Francisco Chronicle*

"Hemingway dialogue at its best . . . a novel worth having"
—Peter S. Prescott, *Newsweek*

Write two adjectives from the preceding comments that describe the quality of Hemingway's writing.

_____   _____

Part IV: Comments about the movie, *The Children*

"A nuclear power plant releases a radioactive mist that turns some school-children into monsters. The nasty tykes commit such despicable acts as killing their parents with deadly hugs. It's a cheaply made, lackluster horror film with a predictable script, dreadful acting, and the usual amount of gore."

—Excerpted from a review of *The Children*
in *Rating the Movies* by Jay Brown
and the editors of *Consumer Guide*

1. Write the adjective describing the script. _____

2. Write the adjective describing the acting. _____

FOR ANSWERS AND EXPLANATIONS, SEE PAGE 285.

 Writing Exercise 2 —————————————

On the following lines, write three adjectives describing each of the following topics:

1. The voice of your favorite singer

    Singer's name: _____

    Adjectives: _____ _____ _____

2. A movie that you disliked

    Movie title: _____

    Adjectives: _____ _____ _____

3. A TV series that you would recommend to a friend

    Series title: _____

    Adjectives: _____ _____ _____

ANSWERS WILL VARY.

Additional Suggestions for Reading Commentaries on the Arts

Use the following list of suggestions to develop your skills in reading commentaries:

1. Find the main idea to focus your reading.

2. If the author expresses an opinion, look for facts, examples, or other evidence that he uses to support his impressions.

3. To understand the context of an author's comments, pay close attention to brief summaries or descriptions about the artistic work.

4. Notice characteristics of style and structure—the author's choice of language and arrangement of information. Evaluate the overall effects of these techniques.

5. Draw your own conclusions based on the ideas and supporting details presented in the commentary.

Apply these suggestions in the next exercise.

Exercise 3: Interpreting a Commentary

Directions: Carefully study the following passage and complete the exercises about the Harlem Unit's black production of Shakespeare's *Macbeth*. (The Harlem Unit was part of the Federal Theatre Project, a theatrical program organized in 1935.)

When Rose McClendon died in 1936 at the age of fifty-one, John Houseman carried on the directorial duties of the Harlem unit alone. One of its first major productions was a black version of *Macbeth*. The black actors and actresses of the Harlem unit wanted to prove that they could perform the
5   classics as well as portray servants, but this would be no ordinary version of Shakespeare's play.

Macbeth is about a power-mad Scottish nobleman who murders the king of Scotland with the help of his wife. He is urged to commit the crime by a group of witches who prepare mysterious potions and chant, "Double, double, toil and
10   trouble, fire burn and cauldron bubble!" Because Houseman wanted an experienced director with a flair for the dramatic to stage this exciting play, he hired a young white man named Orson Welles, who had just wound up a tour of Shakespeare's *Romeo and Juliet*.

It was unanimously decided to change the locale of the play from Scotland
15   to Haiti. Haiti, famous for its "voodoo" and witchcraft, made a much more exciting setting than Scotland and allowed the black-magic theme of the drama to be played to the hilt.

When Welles discovered a touring African dance group stranded in New York for lack of return passage, he immediately signed them up. He also hired
20 a practicing African witch doctor whom he had somehow found in New York. The musical score for the show was full of voodoo drums and witches' cries, and the jungle sets were exotic and eerie. All the roles were played by blacks: Jack Carter and Edna Thomas were Lord and Lady Macbeth, Canada Lee played Banquo, and Eric Burroughs played the evil Hecate.
25 The show was a tremendous success. Drama critic Brooks Atkinson praised the Haitian setting as follows in his review of the production: "The witches have always worried the life out of the polite tragic stage. . . . But ship the witches down to the rank and fever-stricken jungle of Haiti, dress them in fantastic costumes, crowd the stage with mad and gabbing throngs of evil
30 worshippers, beat the jungle drums, raise the voices until the jungle echoes, stuff a gleaming, naked witch doctor into the cauldron, hold up Negro masks in baleful light—and there you have a witches' scene that is logical and stunning and a triumph of theatre art."

—Excerpted from "The Harlem Unit"
by James Haskins

1. What is the main idea of the passage?

  (1) Classic dramas continue to attract large audiences.
  (2) The cast of *Macbeth* consisted of black actors and actresses.
  (3) Shakespeare was fascinated by witches and the supernatural.
  (4) The Harlem Unit staged an unusual production of *Macbeth*.
  (5) Macbeth, the main character, was a cold-blooded murderer.

2. In your own words, briefly summarize the plot of Shakespeare's play

  Macbeth. _____

  _____

  _____

3. What is the setting for Shakespeare's version of *Macbeth*? _____

4. Where does the play take place in the Harlem Unit's production? _____

5. How does the author describe the musical score for the show?

  _____

6. Label each of the following statements *fact* or *opinion*.

  (1) Shakespeare wrote *Macbeth* and *Romeo and Juliet*.

  _____

  (2) Orson Welles directed the Harlem Unit's production of *Macbeth*.

  _____

(3) Orson Welles was a remarkably gifted and creative individual.

_____

(4) Haiti is a more exciting country than Scotland. _____

(5) An African dance group and a practicing African witch doctor were cast for the show. _____

(6) Edna Thomas played the role of Lady Macbeth. _____

7. Which of the following statements expresses drama critic Brooks Atkinson's impression of the show?

(1) The show was a popular success.
(2) The jungle sets were exotic and eerie.
(3) The witches' scene was a theatrical masterpiece.
(4) The hiring of a practicing African witch doctor made the show authentic.
(5) Shakespeare's _Macbeth_ is an exciting play.

8. Which of the following words best describes the tone of Brooks Atkinson's review?

(1) enthusiastic
(2) unemotional
(3) technical
(4) disapproving
(5) indifferent

FOR ANSWERS AND EXPLANATIONS, SEE PAGES 285-86.

Commentaries on the Arts: Reading Selections

The remainder of this chapter will provide you with extensive practice in interpreting commentaries on the arts. You will read passages and complete exercises on the following subjects:

• Television and film

• Performing arts

• Visual arts

• Literature

The purpose question for each passage will help to focus your reading. As you study the commentaries, be sure to apply the reading skills presented in this book.

Television and Film

Television and film are popular forms of entertainment. You probably have experience talking about TV shows and movies with your friends. The next two commentaries illustrate how professional writers discuss these topics.

Exercise 4: Commentary on a TV Show

Directions: Carefully read the passage and answer the questions.

WHAT ARE THE HIGHLIGHTS OF THE TV SHOW "THE HONEYMOONERS"?

It is doubtful whether Ralph and Alice Kramden ever actually went on a honeymoon. Their home was on Chauncy Street in Brooklyn, a cheap apartment that reminded one of a flophouse with only one bed. A telephone, at least to penny-pinching Ralph, was an outrageous luxury, far beyond the
5   means of a man earning barely $60 a week. The apartment was stripped to the barest minimum in furnishings—a table, chairs, bureau, and an incredibly ancient stove, kitchen sink and icebox. (The iceman kept complaining about traveling across town in the hot summer to deliver one melting block of ice.)

Certainly *The Honeymooners* was Gleason's most realistic creation. Almost
10   everyone knew someone who constantly roared off such colorful phrases as "Oh, you're a regular riot, Alice! Har-de-HAR-de-har-har!" or "You're askin' for a knuckle sandwich, Alice!" or the classic "One of these days, Alice . . . *one of these days* . . . POW! Right in the kisser!"

But Alice put up with Ralph, whose scatterbrained schemes to get rich
15   always resulted in tragedy. She loved Ralph but could raise her own voice enough to put him in his place and leave him speechless. In the end Ralph always realized his blunder, admitting, "You know why I did that, Alice? 'Cause I'm a BLABBERMOUTH!" Then, before the final fade-out, he'd give his wife a big hug and kiss, saying, "Baby, you're the greatest!"

20   Much of the humor of *The Honeymooners* resulted from Ralph's weight problem. Apparently Ralph was only concerned with his weight when someone made a remark about it. Otherwise he and Norton were never reluctant to go to the local pizza parlor or Chinese restaurant. The Ralph Kramden "fat" jokes became as familiar as the "cheap" jokes made about Jack Benny.

25   RALPH: Alice, your mother is not stepping foot in this house!

     ALICE: Why not?

     RALPH: Before you know it, she'll be starting in with the cracks. Remember what she went around telling everyone at our wedding? "I'm not losing a daughter, I'm gaining a ton."

—Excerpted from *The Great Television Heroes*
by Donald F. Glut and Jim Harmon

1. The passage focuses on the show's

    (1) popularity
    (2) humor
    (3) production crew
    (4) flaws
    (5) scriptwriters

2. The main purpose of the first paragraph is

    (1) to reveal Alice's personality
    (2) to summarize the plot
    (3) to describe the setting
    (4) to judge acting performances
    (5) to analyze household appliances

3. What main technique do the authors use to familiarize the readers with the TV show?

    (1) interviews with the starring characters
    (2) examples of dialogue from the script
    (3) responses of TV viewers
    (4) examples of Jackie Gleason's creative suggestions
    (5) comparisons with the Jack Benny Show

4. The authors quote a joke about Ralph's

    (1) mother-in-law
    (2) cheapness
    (3) get-rich-quick schemes
    (4) jealousy
    (5) weight problem

5. The authors of the passage want the readers to conclude that "The Honeymooners"

    (1) is a cruel TV series
    (2) appeals only to working-class audiences
    (3) portrays unbelievable characters
    (4) is an entertaining situation comedy
    (5) is a sensitive urban drama

FOR ANSWERS AND EXPLANATIONS, SEE PAGE 286.

Exercise 5: Commentary on a Film

Directions: Carefully read the passage and answer the questions.

WHAT EVENTS OCCUR IN *THE 39 STEPS*?

One of the all-time classics, this thrilling espionage adventure was the first film to establish Hitchcock as the Master of Suspense. What are the "39 Steps," and where do they lead? Which vital secrets are in the mind of a performer named Mr. Memory? Can the British Empire be saved from imminent destruc-

5   tion? These are only some of the baffling questions faced by Richard Hannay, a happy-go-lucky Canadian tourist who innocently visits a London music hall and ends up in a terrifying chase across the country. After the music hall show is abruptly interrupted by a gunshot, a strange woman asks Hannay for his protection from deadly secret agents. Later, she appears in his room—with a

10   knife in her back! Pursued by the police for the murder, Hannay sets out to find the spy organization's sinister leader, who can be identified only by the fact that part of his finger is missing. Like many later Hitchcock heroes, Hannay is an ordinary man suddenly caught up in a chaotic world where nothing is certain and all appearances are deceptive.

—Excerpted from a description of *The 39 Steps*
in *Video Yesteryear*

1. In lines 2–5, why does the author pose questions?

    (1) to test the reader's knowledge
    (2) to arouse the reader's curiosity
    (3) to plant misleading clues in the reader's mind
    (4) to imitate a lawyer's speaking style
    (5) to baffle the main character

2. According to the excerpt, many heroes in Hitchcock films are

    (1) notorious murderers
    (2) happy-go-lucky tourists
    (3) sinister spies
    (4) tough police officers
    (5) ordinary men

3. Moments from the movie's plot are listed here in jumbled order. Rearrange the plot details according to the sequence described in the passage. Number the statements 1 through 6 to show the correct order.

    _____ Suspected of murder, Richard Hannay is pursued by the police.

    _____ A strange woman asks Richard Hannay to protect her from deadly secret agents.

    _____ Richard Hannay tries to track down the spy organization's sinister leader.

_____ Richard Hannay visits a London music hall.

_____ The strange woman appears in Richard Hannay's room with a knife in her back.

_____ A gunshot interrupts the music show.

4. Which of the following newspaper headlines would most likely intrigue Alfred Hitchcock?

(1) FBI Agents Screened for Drug Use
(2) Detectives Undergo Rigorous Training
(3) Police Officers Demand Higher Wages
(4) Suburban Man Finds Dead Body in Car Trunk
(5) Local Politician Ticketed for Speeding

5. Which of the following statements best summarizes the author's opinion of _The 39 Steps?_

(1) The film represents Hitchcock's best work.
(2) The stereotyped characters are unbelievable.
(3) The thrilling spy adventure is masterfully directed.
(4) The plot is overly complicated.
(5) The film is excessively violent.

FOR ANSWERS AND EXPLANATIONS, SEE PAGE 286.

 Writing Exercise 3

In a paragraph, summarize the highlights from a movie that impressed you. Write your summary on a separate sheet of paper.

ANSWERS WILL VARY.

Performing Arts

Performing arts are presented live before an audience. In this section, you will read commentaries about music, dance, and theater. Part of the effectiveness of these reviews is in helping you, the reader, to "see" and "hear" the performances.

Exercise 6: Commentary on Music

Directions: Carefully read the passage and answer the questions.

WHAT DOES LORETTA LYNN COMMUNICATE IN HER MUSIC?

Kitty Wells paved the way for woman-to-woman "message music" when she sang "It Wasn't God Who Made Honky Tonk Angels" in 1952, but it wasn't until a decade later that the fans found their real Pied Piper. Loretta Lynn was her name, and she sang to and about the frustrations of millions of blue-collar

5   housewives, women who didn't want independence from a man so much as a man they could depend on. Loretta's pure, strong, soulful voice hit them from their radios, and Loretta was here to stay.

      "Don't come home a-drinkin' with lovin' on your mind," was one of Loretta's messages, and as Minnie Pearl notes, "Loretta sang what these women were

10   thinking." Loretta sang about men who fooled around, having a good time for themselves while their wives stayed at home changing diapers, wiping noses, and scrimping enough to make it out of the grocery store every week. Within a remarkably short time, she had become the spokeswoman for every woman who had gotten married too early, gotten pregnant too often, and felt trapped

15   by the tedium and drudgery of her life. Betty Freidan and Gloria Steinem couldn't reach these women; Loretta, who expressed her disinterest in "the movement" by falling asleep in Betty Freidan's presence on *The David Frost Show*, could. Her message was straightforward and practical: "We know we can't leave the farms, can't abandon our children, can't all have careers, can't

20   even get out of the kitchen—but we *can* show our men that what's fair for the goose is fair for the gander, and we have just as much right to get some fun out of life as they do." While Tammy Wynette, ever the romanticist, was singing, "Stand By Your Man," Loretta was saying "stand up to your man."

      The fans knew that Loretta was singing from personal experience. They

25   knew songs like "Don't Come Home A-Drinkin'" and "You Ain't Woman Enough To Take My Man" were aimed directly at her husband, Mooney ("Doo") Lynn. She had lived it, too. She was one of them, and that gave her the right to speak for all of them.

              —Excerpted from *Singers & Sweethearts: The Women of Country Music*
                                  by Joan Drew

1.   Who is Loretta Lynn's primary audience? _____

2.   According to the excerpt, which of the following phrases best describes Loretta Lynn's singing voice?

    (1) powerful and moving
    (2) angry and frustrated
    (3) romantic and sentimental
    (4) exciting and fun-loving
    (5) straightforward and honest

3.   What is the major difference between Tammy Wynette and Loretta Lynn?

    (1) their voices
    (2) their popularity
    (3) their success
    (4) their talent
    (5) their message

4.   Why does the author list two examples of Loretta Lynn's song titles (lines 25–26)?

    (1) to show how Tammy Wynette influenced Loretta Lynn's style
    (2) to oppose Betty Freidan's and Gloria Steinem's ideas
    (3) to represent the attitudes of all women
    (4) to show that Loretta Lynn writes songs about her personal relationships
    (5) to illustrate Loretta Lynn's creativity in composing song lyrics

5. Which of the following statements best summarizes Loretta Lynn's opinion?

(1) Young mothers feel trapped by their responsibilities.
(2) Women have the right to enjoy life as much as men.
(3) The women's movement ignores the problems of housewives.
(4) Women should seek total independence from men.
(5) Women identify with a singer whose music reveals personal experience.

FOR ANSWERS AND EXPLANATIONS, SEE PAGE 286.

 Writing Exercise 4

On a separate sheet of paper, write a letter to your favorite performing artist, such as a singer, a comedian, a musician, or an actor. Tell the person why you admire him or her. Use specific details to support your opinion.

ANSWERS WILL VARY.

Exercise 7: Commentary on Dance

Directions: The following passage is about the Nicholas Brothers, a famous tap-dancing team. Carefully read the passage and answer the questions.

HOW DID THE NICHOLAS BROTHERS SUCCEED IN SHOW BUSINESS?

"We never had teachers," Nicholas says. "Fayard could watch and pick up things. . . . He was a natural."

After mastering the basics, the brothers began choreographing their own routines.

5 "When they found out that we had something going," Nicholas says, "our folks stopped doing their jobs to take care of us. They decided to manage us."

By the late-'30s, the Nicholas family moved back to New York and the brothers entered the world of vaudeville at Harlem's famed Cotton Club.

"That was the main job we had when we were kids," Nicholas says.

10 At the Cotton Club they performed on the same bill with some of the most acclaimed black performers of the era including Cab Calloway and Duke Ellington. Unlike most of the black stars, the young Nicholas Brothers were allowed to mingle with the all-white audience. But Nicholas says that their privileges didn't hold much significance for him at the time.

15 "It didn't matter to me. We were so young," he says. "Nothing mattered. I just enjoyed the work."

The enthusiastic response the Nicholas Brothers received at the Cotton Club led one of its managers to take charge of the budding tap dancing act. In 1940, the brothers, then 10 and 16 respectively, were contracted to Hollywood's

20 20th Century-Fox studio for their dance routines. They debuted in "Down Argentine Way."

Choreographer Nick Castle designed many of the Nicholas Brothers' routines, including their famed Staircase Dance in "Stormy Weather" in which the hoofers leapt over each other's backs all the way down a giant staircase,

25 landing in full splits. Castle worked with the duo throughout their movie career

and also helped Harold develop some of his signature stunts such as backflipping into a split, and sliding through a tunnel of open legs.

30   "He thought of all the crazy, impossible things for us to do," Nicholas says. "My brother and I started something different in tap dancing when we did the movies. People always asked us if we studied ballet because we used our hands so much."

—Excerpted from "Star of 'Tap Dance Kid' Started Living
Title Role More Than Half a Century Ago"
by Robert Blau

1. How did the Nicholas Brothers learn to dance?

   _____

2. Where was the Cotton Club located?

   _____

3. You can infer that a choreographer is a person who

   (1) manages entertainers
   (2) recruits new talent
   (3) reviews dance performances
   (4) designs dances
   (5) supervises a nightclub

4. Whose point of view does the author rely on to trace the Nicholas Brothers' career?

   (1) Cab Calloway's
   (2) one of the Nicholas brother's
   (3) Nick Castle's
   (4) Duke Ellington's
   (5) one of the dancing team's fan's

5. Which of the following words best describes the Nicholas Brothers' dance routine in the film *Stormy Weather*?

   (1) acrobatic
   (2) dainty
   (3) clumsy
   (4) slow-paced
   (5) childish

FOR ANSWERS AND EXPLANATIONS, SEE PAGE 286.

Exercise 8: Commentary on Theater

Directions: Carefully read the passage and answer the questions.

WHAT KINDS OF SHOWS DOES THE ZAPATO PUPPET THEATER PERFORM?

The Zapato Puppet Theater, a two-person company run by Michael and Laura Montenegro, utilizes several types of puppets as well as 2-foot masks. Much of its current production "The Rickety Wheel Makes the Most Noise," is comic, yet in its dreamlike and serious approach appeals to both adults and
5 children. On Saturday, this Evanston-based theater company performs an hour of vignettes at the Chicago Public Library Cultural Center, 78 E. Washington St.

Among its pieces, the show includes Chilean folktales told by Saldania, a cantankerous old man; a dance performed by La Ilorona, a tragic character from New Mexican folklore; and a mask scene between a man and woman. For
10 this the Montenegros have created 2-foot masks that entirely cover their heads.

As Laura Montenegro explains, "The reason the puppets really appeal to us is they sort of live in the world between the conscious and the unconscious. When you go into a museum you see little characters—wooden figures, masks and puppets—and they have a certain life.

15 "But when they're used and they're moved and they come alive, they reveal something mythic about our humanness. It's kind of an ancient thing. It's almost ritualistic, something that people don't have a chance to experience very much anymore. What we'd like to accomplish is to make people get a little more insight into our humanness."

20 To get that insight, the Montenegros dip frequently into folktales for the source of their vignettes and treat them in a dreamlike manner.

Chilean folktales in particular have been a source of material for the Montenegros, reflecting Michael Montenegro's roots. "My father was born in Chile," he says, "and his father was a writer, a foreign correspondent for the
25 New York Times, and among other writing endeavors he put together two volumes of Chilean folktales. And this tradition of storytelling and folklore, especially Hispanic folklore, was a very strong influence on myself and my brothers."

—Excerpted from "Puppet Theater Can Make All Our
Dreams Come True" by Robert Wolf

1. What is the title of the Zapato Puppet Theater's current production?

_____

2. Write three adjectives that the author uses to describe this production.

_____   _____   _____

3. Where was Michael Montenegro's father born? _____

4. According to Laura Montenegro, the major goal of the Zapato Puppet Theater is to

   (1) represent an ancient form of entertainment
   (2) depict ridiculous characters
   (3) imitate art exhibits at museums
   (4) display lifelike wooden masks
   (5) provide insights into human nature

5. What is the author's attitude toward the Montenegros?

   (1) cynical
   (2) joking
   (3) boastful
   (4) respectful
   (5) ridiculing

6. The following sentences draw conclusions based on the passage. Label each conclusion *valid* or *invalid*. If the passage supports the conclusion, write *valid*. If the passage does not support the conclusion, write *invalid*.

   (1) Puppet shows appeal only to children. _____

   (2) Hispanic folklore influences the subjects of Michael Montenegro's art.

   _____

   (3) Folktales and myths express stories about a particular culture.

   _____

   (4) Puppet shows are more creative than plays performed by human actors.

   _____

   (5) All artists intentionally portray their cultural heritage in their art.

   _____

FOR ANSWERS AND EXPLANATIONS, SEE PAGES 286-87.

Visual Arts

   Sculpture, painting, and photography are all examples of the visual arts. In commentaries about the visual arts, the authors often recreate the physical appearance of the art in words. Therefore, when you read descriptions, try to imagine how the work of art looks. Authors may also interpret the emotions or the message that the art seems to convey.

Exercise 9: Commentary on Sculpture

Directions: The picture below is described in the passage that follows. Carefully read the passage and answer the questions.

Old Arrow Maker, 1872, by Edmonia Lewis
National Museum of American Art, Smithsonian Institution, Gift of Joseph Sinclair

WHAT DOES EDMONIA LEWIS PORTRAY IN HER SCULPTURE?

Edmonia Lewis, the daughter of a black father and a Chippewa mother, was drawn to subjects from both her racial backgrounds. In this sculpture, she examines her Indian heritage by showing a moment of quiet reflection being enjoyed by father and daughter—a universal theme that transcends ethnic
5   boundaries. The work is small, so that the viewer feels the intimacy of the moment as well as the gentleness of a race often characterized elsewhere as brutal and savage. The arrowmaker wears an animal-skin loincloth, moccasins, and a bear-tooth necklace; his daughter is clothed in a fur bodice, long skirt,

moccasins, and a necklace of stones. An arrow, perhaps just freshly made, rests
10 near the father's left foot, and a dead deer lies at his feet, a symbol of the
traditional hunt. The marble shows an impressive variety of textures that display
Lewis's skill gained in her studies in Rome, where she spent most of her career.

One of several women sculptors working in Rome, Lewis settled there in
1865 to learn marble-carving techniques (although late in her career she, like
15 other sculptors, directed assistants in the actual carving), to pursue her career
with greater artistic freedom, and to avoid much of the racial discrimination that
she had faced in America. She was successful on every count.

—Reprinted with the permission of the National Museum
of American Art, Smithsonian Institution

1. Which part of Lewis's racial background is reflected in the sculpture, "Old
Arrow Maker"? _____

2. List three reasons why Edmonia Lewis decided to live in Rome.

(1) _____

(2) _____

(3) _____

3. According to the critic, American Indians are often characterized as

(1) gentle
(2) savage
(3) intimate
(4) quiet
(5) impressive

4. The critic thinks that the small size of the statue is effective because it

(1) was easier for the sculptor to work on
(2) is easier to reproduce than a large work
(3) captures the intimacy of the father-daughter relationship
(4) shows texture better than a larger statue would
(5) made it easier to transport it from Rome to the Smithsonian

FOR ANSWERS AND EXPLANATIONS, SEE PAGE 287.

Exercise 10: Commentary on a Folk Art

Directions: Carefully read the passage and answer the questions.

IS TATTOOING AN ART?

Tattoo artists have always felt that their work deserved more acceptance as an art and that it was discredited because of the nature of the medium. But if the medium is put aside, it is easy to see the craft, the fancy, the individuality, and the art of the practitioner. Whatever one may think of tattooing itself, one
5   must acknowledge that it is a true folk art.

Tattooing as the art of marking the human skin is quite ancient. One of the earliest known examples was discovered recently on the body of a Scythian chieftain found, frozen and perfectly preserved, in a tomb in Russia dating back to 2500 B.C. The earliest records of the use of the tattoo are Egyptian ones
10   dating to 2000 B.C., and tattoo markings have been revealed on mummies. Libyan figures from the tomb of Set I, built in 1330 B.C., are tattooed symbols of the Egyptian goddess Neith which, in a simplified form, are still employed as tattoo designs in North Africa today. Tattooing existed in southwest China in 1100 B.C. In Japan it thrived in the middle of the first century A.D., but has also
15   been traced to its origin in the sixth century B.C. It is now thought that from Japan it was taken to the South Sea Islands, where today one still sees the most intricate and delicate patterns in the raised skin of the natives.

—Excerpted from *America's Forgotten Folk Arts*
by Frederick and Mary Fried

1. According to the passage, tattoo artists would probably believe that

   (1) more tattoo parlors should open in the suburbs
   (2) all women should wear tattoos to express their individuality
   (3) replicas of their work should be exhibited in art museums
   (4) marking human skin is an uncivilized practice
   (5) the designs of Chinese tattoos are outdated

2. How have the authors supported their view that tattooing is an ancient art?

   (1) They conducted research in African and Asian museums.
   (2) They traveled around the world looking for evidence.
   (3) They specified dates and countries where tattooing was practiced.
   (4) They interviewed South Seas natives whose ancestors wore tattoos.
   (5) They described historical photographs belonging to tattoo artists.

3. You can conclude that the authors

   (1) dislike highly decorated tattoo designs
   (2) practice tattooing as a hobby
   (3) prefer African tattoos to Russian tattoos
   (4) discredit the craftsmanship of modern tattoo artists
   (5) appreciate the artistic qualities of tattooing

FOR ANSWERS AND EXPLANATIONS, SEE PAGE 287.

Literature

In earlier chapters you practiced reading fiction and nonfiction. The next three exercises will allow you to practice reading commentaries about different types of literature.

Exercise 11: Commentary on Fiction

Directions: Carefully read the passage and answer the questions.

WHAT DO YOU LEARN ABOUT DETECTIVE FICTION?

The novel rode out of Spain on the horse and donkey of Don Quixote and Sancho Panza, and the modern short story had its early masters in Russia, France and England. But the hard-boiled detective was born in America. His popularity has remained in force for half a century. He can be seen on
5 countless shelves of paperbacks and hardcovers, and he has appeared on prime time since the first vacuum tube was plugged in. The TV series *Spenser: For Hire* and *Mike Hammer* are two of his latest hangouts. As he was in the films of the '40s, so he is today, in Raymond Chandler's memorable phrase, a man "who is neither tarnished nor afraid" as he walks down America's mean streets.

10 Good cases have been made for locating his origins in the boot steps of the lonesome pioneer. Robert B. Parker, creator of Spenser, a private investigator so sure of himself that he needs only one name, even wrote a Ph.D. thesis on the subject. According to the traditional ideal, to survive with dignity on the American frontier required a touch of ruthlessness and a personal code of
15 honor. "When the wilderness disappeared at the end of the 19th century," says Parker, the hero "became a man, alone, facing an urban wilderness." A more precise definition of the breed came naturally enough from Chandler, the American-born, British-educated creator of Philip Marlowe, the detective who got more similes to the mile than anybody before or since ("as inconspicuous
20 as a tarantula on a slice of angel food"). Laid down in his essay *The Simple Art of Murder*, Chandler's description of the fictional American detective has the power of an ecclesiastical oath: "He is a relatively poor man, or he would not be a detective at all. He is a common man or he could not go among common people. He has a sense of character, or he would not know his job. He will take
25 no man's money dishonestly and no man's insolence without a due and dispassionate revenge. He is a lonely man and his pride is that you will treat him as a proud man or be very sorry you ever saw him. He talks as the man of his age talks—that is, with rude wit, a lively sense of the grotesque, a disgust for sham, and a contempt for pettiness."

—Excerpted from "Neither Tarnished nor Afraid"
by R. Z. Sheppard

1. The passage focuses on which of the following fictional elements?

   (1) plot
   (2) setting
   (3) point of view
   (4) theme
   (5) characterization

2. The hard-boiled detective originated in

   (1) Spain
   (2) America
   (3) Russia
   (4) France
   (5) England

3. According to Robert B. Parker, the portrayal of fictional detectives was influenced by

   (1) detectives in TV series
   (2) pioneers in the 19th century
   (3) heroes of modern short stories
   (4) characters in Spanish novels
   (5) private investigators in movies

4. According to Raymond Chandler, a fictional American detective is *not*

   (1) lonely
   (2) proud
   (3) wealthy
   (4) witty
   (5) honest

5. What kind of language does Philip Marlowe often use in his speech (line 19)?

   (1) literal language
   (2) formal language
   (3) ungrammatical language
   (4) figurative language
   (5) technical language

FOR ANSWERS AND EXPLANATIONS, SEE PAGE 287.

Exercise 12: Commentary on Nonfiction

Directions: Carefully read the passage and answer the questions.

HOW SHOULD NEWS REPORTERS WRITE STORIES?

Unlike the novelist and the poet, the journalist cannot spend hours searching for the truth, much less the right word. No other writer is asked to commit words to paper with such speed, under such pressure. All the more reason, then, for the journalist to borrow from those whose struggles have
5   cleared paths toward good writing. There are writing rules that apply to a three-paragraph item about a service station holdup and to a detailed investigative story on the state's deposits in non-interest-bearing bank accounts.

We might start with Tolstoy who, in describing the strength of his masterwork *War and Peace*, said, "I don't tell; I don't explain. I show; I let my
10   characters talk for me."

In short, one of the reporter's first writing rules might be: Show, don't tell. Telling makes the reader or listener passive. Showing engages him. Good

writers let the words and actions of the participants do the work. John Ciardi elaborates on Tolstoy's advice: "One of the skills of the good poet is to enact his
15   experiences rather than to talk about having had them. 'Show it, don't tell it,' he says. 'Make it happen, don't talk about its happening.' "

When the reporter makes it happen, the reader moves into the story. The reporter disappears as middleman between the event and the reader.

Covering the funeral of a child killed by a sniper, a reporter wrote, "The
20   grief-stricken parents wept during the service." Another reporter wrote, "The parents wept quietly. Mrs. Franklin leaned against her husband for support." The first reporter tells us the parents are "grief-stricken." The other reporter shows us with the picture of the mother leaning against her husband.

—Excerpted from *News Reporting and Writing*
by Melvin Mencher

1. How does a journalist's writing process differ from a novelist's or a poet's?

    (1) A journalist spends more time researching stories
    (2) A journalist is pressured to meet strict deadlines.
    (3) A journalist pays more attention to elements of style.
    (4) A journalist is unconcerned with his choice of words.
    (5) A journalist borrows techniques from other creative writers.

2. Why does the author quote the novelist Leo Tolstoy and the poet John Ciardi?

    (1) to impress the reader with his literary background
    (2) to show that fiction and poetry are more interesting than news stories
    (3) to support the validity of the writing rule, "Show, don't tell"
    (4) to explain why novelists and poets admire news reporters
    (5) to suggest that novelists and poets teach journalism classes

3. Check the sentence in each pair that creates the more specific picture of the action described:

    (1) _____ **(a)** The baseball coach was angry about the umpire's decision.
          _____ **(b)** After the "strike three" call, the baseball coach rushed from the dugout and shook his fist in the umpire's face.

    (2) _____ **(a)** Two police officers at City Hall arrested the mayor for possessing an unregistered handgun.
          _____ **(b)** The police officers took the man into custody because he had an illegal weapon.

    (3) _____ **(a)** Because she took the initiative to develop her skills, the office worker was moved into a position with more responsibilities.
          _____ **(b)** After completing evening management courses at XYZ Community College, the secretary was promoted to office supervisor.

FOR ANSWERS AND EXPLANATIONS, SEE PAGE 287.

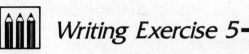 *Writing Exercise 5*

On a separate sheet of paper, write a paragraph in which you report an event. It could be an event that you witnessed in person or something that you saw on TV or in a movie. Use words and details that create a vivid picture of the action in the reader's mind.

ANSWERS WILL VARY.

Exercise 13: Commentary—A Book Review

The following excerpt from a book review is longer than the reading selections on the GED Interpreting Literature and the Arts Test. However, by reading a longer excerpt, you will acquire a better understanding of this type of commentary.

Directions: Carefully read the passage and answer the questions.

WHAT IS A BOOK REVIEWER'S OPINION OF *THE WONDERFUL WIZARD OF OZ*?

Once upon a time, 86 years ago in the city of Chicago, a man named Lyman Frank Baum sat down at the insistence of his mother-in-law to write out a bedtime story that he liked to tell to his children. The yarn was about a little girl named Dorothy, her feisty dog Toto, cyclones, Kansas and an enchanted

5   kingdom of silver slippers, flying monkeys, fighting trees, and good and bad witches. Baum and his illustrator, W. W. Denslow, had to agree to share the publishing costs, but when "The Wonderful Wizard of Oz" appeared, it quickly became the best selling children's book of 1900, and Dorothy was established as America's most famous and endearing astral explorer.

10   By the time Baum died in Hollywood in 1919, he had written 14 Oz books, each of which had its magical and enduring moments. But "The Wonderful Wizard" has remained his most famous. The gray of Kansas—the word is used 10 times in five paragraphs—gives way to the colorful rainbow of potential available in Oz, and we enter a compensatory, utopian landscape in which the

15   power of Good is greater than the power of Evil, and where the pastoral, wilderness, and technological aspects of our culture exist in beneficent harmony. Cast ashore in this forbidding territory with one fresh dress, some worn-out shoes and a picnic basket, the bedraggled Dorothy becomes a Miss Liberty, liberating the Munchkins and Winkies from the oppressive rule of the

20   Wicked Witches and leading the Scarecrow, Tin Woodman, and Cowardly Lion to kingship, glory and self-confidence. Her struggles to get back home mirror her life and flights of fancy as a prairie child, from the bran and pins of the Scarecrow's brain to the way the Wicked Witch imprisons her with housework, and she revenges herself by "liquidating" the villainess with a bucket of cleaning

25   water.

Although a continuing favorite with children, Oz has never received the admiration, or critical attention, of Lewis Carroll's famous Alice adventures. It is a less astonishing book—more traditional in concept, more commonplace in detail, less playfully daring, and more truly devoted to seeing the world with a

30   child's eye. And, as befits the pleasant adventure, W. W. Denslow's original illustrations are charming and silly rather than striking in their own right. [Dover

offers a fine paperback reprint of the original edition.] But whether you
remember "Oz" through Denslow's amusing, squat little figures or as immortal-
ized in the radiant technicolor of the 1939 film, color has always been an
35 essential part of the story's spell: a way to distinguish character and demonstrate how reality changes depending on the distorting lenses you're looking
through.

　All this has changed. Barry Moser and his Pennyroyal Press have been
coming up with startling new visions of old classics for some time, many of
40 which have been reissued in trade editions by the University of California—
"Alice's Adventures in Wonderland" and "Through the Looking-Glass," "Fran-
kenstein," "Adventures of Huckleberry Finn." Now Moser has turned his eye
and mind to "Oz." The result is a visually stunning, if suspiciously adult, reading
of Baum's homely tale.

—Excerpted from "New Illustrations Make 'Oz' a Sadder,
More Adult World" by Paul Skenazy

1. Label each of the following statements as *fact* or *opinion*.

　(1) *The Wonderful Wizard of Oz* became a best-selling children's book in 1900. _____

　(2) W. W. Denslow was the first artist to illustrate *The Wonderful Wizard of Oz.* _____

　(3) Denslow's illustrations are silly and charming. _____

　(4) *Alice's Adventures in Wonderland* is a better written and more imagina-tive book than *The Wonderful Wizard of Oz.* _____

　(5) Dorothy is America's most famous explorer of new worlds.

　　_____

　(6) *The Wonderful Wizard of Oz* is told from a child's point of view.

　　_____

　(7) The film *The Wizard of Oz* was released in 1939. _____

　(8) Barry Moser's illustrations reveal an adult interpretation of the book.

　　_____

2. How does Dorothy kill the Wicked Witch of the West?

_____

3. Why does the author begin the book review with the phrase "Once upon a time"?

　(1) He is telling a bedtime story.
　(2) His description of L. Frank Baum is imaginary.
　(3) He is writing the review for children.
　(4) He is poking fun at children's literature.
　(5) His topic is a children's fairy tale.

4. What is the major theme of *The Wonderful Wizard of Oz*?

  (1) Cyclones endanger people's lives.
  (2) Animals behave like humans.
  (3) Goodness overpowers evil.
  (4) Adults deceive children.
  (5) Life is a dream.

FOR ANSWERS AND EXPLANATIONS, SEE PAGE 287.

For additional examples of commentaries on the arts, see the following passages that you read in earlier chapters:

Television:
"Unreality of TV," Chapter 3, pages 76–77
"Soap Operas: A Healthy Habit, After All?," Chapter 4, pages 95–96

Performing Arts:
Balanchine's Complete Stories of the Great Ballets, Chapter 1, page 13

Visual Arts:
"Portraits of a Cop," Chapter 4, pages 104–105

Literature:
Modern Black Stories, Chapter 1, pages 20–21
"On Form, Not Plot, in the Short Story," Chapter 2, page 53
"How 'Bigger' Was Born," Chapter 5, pages 154–55
Sleeping on the Wing, Chapter 6, pages 161–62

★ **GED PRACTICE** ★

Exercise 14: Chapter Review

Directions: Read the following passages and answer the multiple-choice questions. Use the purpose question to focus your reading.

Passage 1

WHAT IS THE ARCHITECTURE OF THE NATIVE AMERICAN INDIAN CENTER?

The building that houses the Native American Indian Center in Niagara Falls is, by any standards, an unconventional one. Built for noncommercial purposes—to house an Indian Cultural Center and to serve as a symbol of the Iroquois nation—the structure was designed in the shape of a turtle. There were
5　several motives for choosing the design. Graphically, it was a strong image and would surely make a vivid impression on the observer. In addition, the turtle was a universal symbol of good luck, long life, and toughness. The turtle had a special meaning to the Iroquois, who call North America "the great turtle island" and whose myths hold that the earth was created on the back of a turtle. The
10　building was designed by Dennis Sun Rhodes, an Arapaho architect, who believed that it was important that modern architecture be adapted to traditional Indian values.

15

20

25

The turtle is 63,000 square feet and three stories high. Inside its multipurpose body is a 250-seat amphitheatre and exhibit hall; the surrounding concrete walls support a geodesic dome, 160 feet in diameter. The hall is illuminated by a huge skylight in the shape of a thunderbird. All the turtle's appendages are functional spaces: the four legs contain a Contemporary Crafts Hall, a National Indian Art Gallery, a museum workshop, and the building's mechanical systems. The head and neck area contain a restaurant and a dining galley (in the turtle's mouth), administration offices, and, at the top of the head, an apartment for the center's artist in residence. The forehead holds an observation deck, from which the visitor can view "the smoking waters"—Niagara Falls. Throughout the building are traditional Indian symbols, including a large circle, set into the central wooden floor, representing the continuity of life, and a compass design representing the four winds.

—Excerpted from *The Well-Built Elephant*
by J. C. C. Andrews

1. What is unique about the Native American Indian Center?

   (1) It is located in Niagara Falls.
   (2) It is three stories high.
   (3) It is designed in the shape of a turtle.
   (4) It is used for cultural purposes.
   (5) It is an example of modern architecture.

2. Which of the following statements best represents Dennis Sun Rhodes's opinion about architecture?

   (1) Buildings should make a vivid impression on the observer.
   (2) Modern architecture should be adapted to traditional values.
   (3) Architectural design should imitate forms found in nature.
   (4) Buildings should be used for noncommercial purposes.
   (5) Modern architecture should reflect contemporary American culture.

3. The main purpose of the second paragraph is to

   (1) discuss the architect's creativity
   (2) describe the anatomy of a turtle
   (3) interpret the symbols of Native American culture
   (4) describe the building's physical structure
   (5) convince readers to visit the Indian center

4. Which of the following words best describes the tone of the passage?

   (1) informative
   (2) persuasive
   (3) critical
   (4) entertaining
   (5) personal

5. Which of the following buildings also strongly shows how meaningful cultural symbols influence architectural design?

    (1) churches
    (2) skyscrapers
    (3) apartment complexes
    (4) factories
    (5) department stores

Passage 2

DOES THE TV SERIES "L.A. LAW" RESEMBLE "HILL STREET BLUES?"

Welcome to *L.A. Law*—and to the fictional corporate law firm of McKenzie, Brackman, Chaney and Kuzak.

[Steven] Bochco and [Terry Louise] Fisher created *L.A. Law*, wrote the pilot script and are now supervising a series that NBC expects to be the hottest
5   show of the fall season.

Given Bochco's role in the new show, comparisons between *L.A. Law* and *Hill Street Blues* are inevitable: both are one-hour dramas laced with humor, and both have ensemble casts, multiple storylines and are semi-serial in format—i.e., some story strands begin in one episode and continue into one or more
10 future episodes.

But the differences between *Hill Street* and *L.A. Law* are, Bochco insists, "profound." *Hill Street*, he says, was "dark," both in actual lighting and in content. "It was a show quite literally about life and death, about a beleaguered group of men and women laboring to keep despair at arm's length . . . about
15 people with much responsibility and no real authority. *L.A. Law* is brighter, more colorful, about well-educated overachievers who do win, who do have impact."

Hill Street was generally a very well written show, but Bochco and others involved with *L.A. Law* say this show must be better written.
20 "This show is talking heads," Fisher says. "The talk better be good. We can't cut to a car chase on this show. We've learned already [in the first few scripts] that when the words aren't good, the show is awful, the scenes endlessly boring."

—Excerpted from "The Partner Lay There Dead . . .
Face Down in a Dish of Beans" by David Shaw

6. Which of the following people is *not* a fictional attorney on "L.A. Law?"

    (1) McKenzie
    (2) Brackman
    (3) Chaney
    (4) Kuzak
    (5) Bochco

7. The author's purpose in the third and fourth paragraphs is to

    (1) analyze the characteristics of one-hour TV dramas
    (2) prove that "L.A. Law" is a better show than "Hill Street Blues"
    (3) describe the bleak atmosphere of "Hill Street Blues"
    (4) compare and contrast "L.A. Law" with "Hill Street Blues"
    (5) explain the continued popularity of "Hill Street Blues"

8. According to the passage, you can assume that the attorneys on "L.A. Law" are portrayed as

    (1) relaxed and compassionate
    (2) pushy and talkative
    (3) successful and influential
    (4) powerless and boring
    (5) frustrated and depressed

9. Which word best describes the author's evaluation of "Hill Street Blues?"

    (1) well-written
    (2) colorful
    (3) awful
    (4) hot
    (5) despairing

10. What is the implication of Fisher's statement, "This show is talking heads" (line 20)?

    (1) The camera focuses on the actors' heads.
    (2) The show's success depends on the quality of the dialogue.
    (3) The actors practice good speech habits.
    (4) Lawyers must know how to communicate with clients.
    (5) Characters' spoken words reveal their personalities.

11. A real attorney watching "L.A. Law" would probably be most concerned with how the show

    (1) entertains a general audience
    (2) creates a dramatic impact
    (3) depicts the legal profession
    (4) develops the plot
    (5) uses action scenes

Passage 3

WHAT DO YOU LEARN ABOUT EMILY DICKINSON'S POETRY?

Emily Dickinson, born in 1830 in Amherst, Massachusetts, lived a very secluded life. She was alone most of the time; she didn't know other writers. Almost no one knew she wrote poetry. She wrote her poems in the midst of doing other things. She wrote them on the backs of envelopes and on other
5   scraps of paper. These poems were discovered, and published, only after her death. These circumstances probably have something to do with the peculiar way her poetry is written, the way it's unlike anyone else's—with its odd use of capitals, dashes, and strange rhymes—and with its peculiar point of view. She seems to have been, more than other poets, writing just for herself.
10   Her way of looking at things seems, at first, innocent, like the innocence of children. But Emily Dickinson knows and feels things that children don't. Her

view is not so much innocent, really, as it is gentle and resigned to the way things are. It's as if she felt that simply watching were the only thing left to do. She watches nature—trees, brooks, bees, flies, flowers, snakes, wind. She
15 watches people. She seems even to watch herself in the same way she watches everything else—with impartial curiosity and from a distance.

In Emily Dickinson's poetry, the whole universe becomes very private and domestic. It is as if all of nature, all its gentle and violent forces, were noticed and wondered about with the kind of simple familiarity with which you might
20 wonder about your neighbors. And everything that happens seems almost equally important. The arrival of winter, a storm, or the coming of death gets no more space than a bird's song or a fly's buzz. This makes her poems about death seem particularly strange and chilling.

—Excerpted from *Sleeping on the Wing*
by Kenneth Koch and Kate Farrell

12. Which of the following statements expresses an opinion about Emily Dickinson?

   (1) She was born in 1830 in Amherst, Massachusetts.
   (2) She wrote some poems about death.
   (3) Her poems were published after she died.
   (4) She punctuates her poetry with dashes.
   (5) Her poems show her gentle, resigned view of the world.

13. According to the excerpt, who was probably Emily Dickinson's intended audience for her poems?

   (1) other poets
   (2) herself
   (3) children
   (4) neighbors
   (5) women

14. The main purpose of the second paragraph is to discuss Emily Dickinson's

   (1) childlike innocence
   (2) style of observation
   (3) interest in people
   (4) subjects of poetry
   (5) curiosity about herself

15. Which of the following is *not* reflected in Emily Dickinson's poetry?

   (1) a private view of the universe
   (2) a unique way of writing
   (3) an impression of everyday events
   (4) a morbid fear of death
   (5) a familiarity with nature

16. You can infer from the passage that Emily Dickinson was

    (1) sociable
    (2) ambitious
    (3) solitary
    (4) immature
    (5) awesome

17. You can conclude from the passage that Emily Dickinson did *not* write a poem entitled

    (1) "Bee! I'm Expecting You!"
    (2) "Because I Could Not Stop for Death"
    (3) "I Heard a Fly Buzz"
    (4) "A Bird Came Down the Walk"
    (5) "Juke Box Love Song"

FOR ANSWERS AND EXPLANATIONS, SEE PAGES 287-88.

INTERPRETING LITERATURE AND THE ARTS POSTTEST

Directions: This Interpreting Literature and the Arts Posttest will give you the opportunity to evaluate your readiness for the actual GED Interpreting Literature and the Arts Test.

This posttest contains forty-five questions. These questions are based on passages of fiction and nonfiction prose, poetry, drama, and commentaries on literature and the arts.

You should take approximately sixty-five minutes to complete this test. At the end of sixty-five minutes, stop and mark your place. Then finish the test. This will give you an idea of whether or not you can finish the real GED Test in the time allotted. Try to answer as many questions as you can. A blank will count as a wrong answer, so make a reasonable guess for questions you are not sure of.

When you are finished with the test, turn to the evaluation charts on page 271. Use the charts to evaluate whether or not you are ready to take the actual GED Test, and if not, what areas need more work.

Posttest Answer Grid

1 ① ② ③ ④ ⑤	16 ① ② ③ ④ ⑤	31 ① ② ③ ④ ⑤
2 ① ② ③ ④ ⑤	17 ① ② ③ ④ ⑤	32 ① ② ③ ④ ⑤
3 ① ② ③ ④ ⑤	18 ① ② ③ ④ ⑤	33 ① ② ③ ④ ⑤
4 ① ② ③ ④ ⑤	19 ① ② ③ ④ ⑤	34 ① ② ③ ④ ⑤
5 ① ② ③ ④ ⑤	20 ① ② ③ ④ ⑤	35 ① ② ③ ④ ⑤
6 ① ② ③ ④ ⑤	21 ① ② ③ ④ ⑤	36 ① ② ③ ④ ⑤
7 ① ② ③ ④ ⑤	22 ① ② ③ ④ ⑤	37 ① ② ③ ④ ⑤
8 ① ② ③ ④ ⑤	23 ① ② ③ ④ ⑤	38 ① ② ③ ④ ⑤
9 ① ② ③ ④ ⑤	24 ① ② ③ ④ ⑤	39 ① ② ③ ④ ⑤
10 ① ② ③ ④ ⑤	25 ① ② ③ ④ ⑤	40 ① ② ③ ④ ⑤
11 ① ② ③ ④ ⑤	26 ① ② ③ ④ ⑤	41 ① ② ③ ④ ⑤
12 ① ② ③ ④ ⑤	27 ① ② ③ ④ ⑤	42 ① ② ③ ④ ⑤
13 ① ② ③ ④ ⑤	28 ① ② ③ ④ ⑤	43 ① ② ③ ④ ⑤
14 ① ② ③ ④ ⑤	29 ① ② ③ ④ ⑤	44 ① ② ③ ④ ⑤
15 ① ② ③ ④ ⑤	30 ① ② ③ ④ ⑤	45 ① ② ③ ④ ⑤

Passage 1

WHAT DO YOU NOTICE ABOUT COMMUNITIES CALLED BARRIOS?

The train, its metal wheels squealing as they spin along the silvery tracks, rolls slower now. Through the gaps between the cars blinks a streetlamp, and this
5 pulsing light on a barrio streetcorner beats slower, like a weary heartbeat, until the train shudders to a halt, the light goes out, and the barrio is deep asleep.

Throughout Aztlán (the Nahuatl term
10 meaning "land to the north"), trains grumble along the edges of a sleeping people. From Lower California, through the blistering Southwest, down the Rio Grande to the muddy Gulf, the darkness
15 and mystery of dreams engulf communities fenced off by railroads, canals, and expressways. Paradoxical communities, isolated from the rest of the town by concrete columned monuments of progress,
20 and yet stranded in the past. They are surrounded by change. It eludes their reach, in their own backyards, and the people, unable and unwilling to see the future, or even touch the present, perpet-
25 uate the past.

Leaning from the expressway or jolting across the tracks, one enters a different physical world permeated by a different attitude. The physical dimensions are
30 impressive. It is a large section of town which extends for fifteen blocks north and south along the tracks, and then advances eastward, thinning into nothingness beyond the city limits. Within the
35 invisible (yet sensible) walls of the barrio, are many, many people living in too few houses. The homes, however, are much more numerous than on the outside.

Members of the barrio describe the
40 entire area as their home.

—Excerpted from "The Barrio"
by Robert Ramirez

1. Which word best describes the barrio?

    (1) isolated
    (2) sleepy
    (3) invisible
    (4) silvery
    (5) impressive

2. The purpose of the third paragraph is to

    (1) describe the homes found in the barrio
    (2) analyze why barrios are located near cities
    (3) detail the barrio's physical appearance
    (4) compare barrios with other city neighborhoods
    (5) describe the residents living in the barrios

3. Housing conditions in the barrios are

    (1) comfortable
    (2) overcrowded
    (3) modern
    (4) unusual
    (5) inhuman

4. The characteristics of the barrio most closely resemble those of

    (1) a wealthy city neighborhood
    (2) a farming community
    (3) a prison camp
    (4) a suburban community
    (5) an American Indian reservation

Passage 2

WHAT BUSINESS VIRTUE DO AMERICANS FIND MOST DAZZLING?

They bear little resemblance to Mercury, the Roman god with the winged sandals, but they move with heroic speed. Clad in their red, white and blue
5   polyester uniforms, the drivers for Domino's Pizza spring from their vehicles with cardboard cartons and sprint up the sidewalks of millions of U.S. homes. Customers often clock them to the second, since
10   the 2,000-shop chain promises a discount if the pie takes longer than 30 minutes to arrive. To help drive home the point, Domino's sponsored a race car that finished fifth in the Indianapolis 500, with Al
15   Unser Jr. behind the wheel.

Americans may value such business virtues as courtesy, reliability, economy and all that, but in the end, what really dazzles them is speed. How else to ex-
20   plain such an affinity for one-hour photo developing, instant replay, touch-tone phones and suntanning parlors? America's entrepreneurs have responded to that imperative with some of the world's
25   fastest products and services, ranging from frozen food to instant bank loans. Like Domino's Pizza, many U.S. corporate empires were built for people in a hurry: McDonald's, Federal Express, Polaroid
30   and Southland Corp., the operator of 7-Eleven stores. "America values speed," observes Felipe Castro, assistant professor of psychology at the University of California, Los Angeles. "The more you hus-
35   tle, the more money you can make."

The culture of quickness has inspired smaller operators to accelerate their pace as well. In Los Angeles, for example, time-conscious consumers can flip
40   through the telephone book to find Speedy Attorney Service, Fast Glass & Screens, Rapid Brake Service, Instant Wedding Chapel and Swift Secretarial Service. The dry-cleaning listings of any
45   phone directory look like a thesaurus entry for the word fast, including the omnipresent 1-Hour Martinizing shops and archrivals with such names as Prompt Cleaners, Presto Cleaners and One-Hour
50   Lusterizing.

—Excerpted from "Life in the Express Lane"
by Stephen Koepp

5. How are the drivers for Domino's Pizza like Mercury, the Roman god?

    (1) They wear winged sandals.
    (2) They move with heroic speed.
    (3) They compete in car races.
    (4) They wear patriotic uniforms.
    (5) They're America's fastest sprinters.

6. You can conclude that a thesaurus (line 45) is most similar to a

    (1) phone book
    (2) dictionary
    (3) consumer handbook
    (4) spelling book
    (5) store directory

7. What is the main idea of the passage?

    (1) Dry-cleaning stores advertise prompt service.
    (2) McDonald's is the most famous fast-food restaurant.
    (3) Americans are time-conscious consumers.
    (4) The goal of American business is customer satisfaction.
    (5) Consumers clock Domino's Pizza delivery trucks.

8. The quotation from Felipe Castro (lines 31–35) is effective because it

    (1) interprets why Americans value speed
    (2) analyzes why professors are interested in making money
    (3) defines the phrase "culture of quickness"
    (4) suggests that universities support major corporations
    (5) proves that Americans are greedy and impatient

9. Which of the following examples would the author *not* use to support his viewpoint?

    (1) microwave ovens
    (2) automatic bank-teller machines
    (3) overnight mail service
    (4) hand-operated meat grinders
    (5) instant cake mixes

Passage 3

WHAT DO YOU LEARN ABOUT THESE WOMEN DETECTIVES?

WASHINGTON—Sam Spade and Philip Marlowe wouldn't know what to make of it—private eyes who are dames.

That's right. Bonnie Goldstein and
5   Sally Denton are in the same line of work as Spade and Marlowe and all the other tough-talking, hard-drinking private detectives from the Hall of American Archetypal Heroes, Male Division.

10   The fact that the business has gone coed might bother the guys for a while, but it's something they'd probably get over soon enough. After all, they'd say, it finally comes down to whether you can
15   do the job, not whether you wear mascara and skirts.

It's the other thing that would be harder to figure, which is the kind of practice they have.

20   These two females are members of a new breed of private investigator. They don't go in for any of the rough, old-fashioned, down-and-dirty stuff. They don't do undercover work; they don't tail
25   anyone; they don't take anything messy like divorces or spouses who have flown the coop; they don't pack heat—no delicate little derringer in a handbag—and they've never had a case where anyone
30   turned up dead.

Their card reads Goldstein & Denton, Washington, D.C., and if you hear one of them saying something as corny as, "It's a jungle out there," it's because she's
35   standing at a window in their offices at 3000 Connecticut Ave., NW, pointing toward the entrance to the National Zoo, which is directly across the street.

In other words, they have little in
40   common with the savvy shamuses from the detective novels of the past, and nothing at all with the TV fantasy world of Sabrina Duncan, Jill Munroe and Kelly Garrett, those spunky airheads we gazed
45   at briefly a few years ago on "Charlie's Angels."

—Excerpted from "Women in a Business Bogie Wouldn't Recognize" by Paul Galloway

10. As used in the passage, what does the word *heat* mean (line 27)?

   (1) warmth
   (2) gun
   (3) excitement
   (4) stress
   (5) police

11. The detectives' office is located in

   (1) Washington, D.C.
   (2) Connecticut
   (3) the Northwest
   (4) the National Zoo
   (5) the Hall of American Heroes

12. What technique does the author use to explain Goldstein and Denton's work?

   (1) He interviews the private investigators in their office.
   (2) He analyzes their reasons for choosing their profession.
   (3) He criticizes them for entering a male-dominated profession.
   (4) He compares and contrasts them with fictional detectives in novels and TV.
   (5) He lists their challenging cases and famous clients.

13. Goldstein and Denton's choice of career is similar to that of women who work as

   (1) nurses
   (2) teachers
   (3) engineers
   (4) waitresses
   (5) secretaries

Passage 4

WHAT ACTION OCCURS AT THIS DINER?

George looked up at the clock.

"If anybody comes in you tell them the cook is off, and if they keep after it, you tell them you'll go back and cook
5 yourself. Do you get that, bright boy?"

"All right," George said. "What you going to do with us afterward?"

"That'll depend," Max said. "That's one of those things you never know at
10 the time."

George looked up at the clock. It was a quarter past six. The door from the street opened. A streetcar motorman came in.
15 "Hello, George," he said. "Can I get supper?"

"Sam's gone out," George said. "He'll be back in about half an hour."

"I'd better go up the street," the mo-
20 torman said. George looked at the clock. It was twenty minutes past six.

"That was nice, bright boy," Max said. "You're a regular little gentleman."

"He knew I'd blow his head off," Al
25 said from the kitchen.

"No," said Max. "It ain't that. Bright boy is nice. He's a nice boy. I like him."

At six fifty-five George said: "He's not coming."
30 Two other people had been in the lunchroom. Once George had gone out to the kitchen and made a ham-and-egg sandwich "to go" that a man wanted to take with him. Inside the kitchen he saw
35 Al, his derby hat tipped back, sitting on a stool beside the wicket with the muzzle of a sawed-off shotgun resting on the ledge. Nick and the cook were back to back in the corner, a towel tied in each
40 of their mouths. George had cooked the sandwich, wrapped it up in oiled paper, put it in a bag, brought it in, and the man had paid for it and gone out.

"Bright boy can do everything," Max
45 said. "He can cook and everything. You'd make some girl a nice wife, bright boy."

"Yes?" George said. "Your friend, Ole Andreson, isn't going to come."

"We'll give him ten minutes," Max
50 said.

Max watched the mirror and the clock. The hands of the clock marked seven o'clock, and then five minutes past seven.
55 "Come on, Al," said Max. "We better go. He's not coming."

"Better give him five minutes," Al said from the kitchen.

—Excerpted from "The Killers" by Ernest Hemingway

14. Which word best describes the atmosphere of the diner in this scene?

  (1) formal
  (2) tense
  (3) casual
  (4) dull
  (5) friendly

15. What tone of voice does Max use when he speaks to George?

  (1) sarcastic
  (2) polite
  (3) calm
  (4) agitated
  (5) sincere

16. You can conclude that Max and Al's intended victim is

  (1) Nick
  (2) Sam
  (3) the motorman
  (4) George
  (5) Ole Andreson

17. The conversation in the passage would also be effective in a script for a

  (1) situation comedy
  (2) gangster movie
  (3) soap opera
  (4) science fiction movie
  (5) horror movie

Passage 5

WHAT ARE THE CHARACTERS' IMPRESSIONS OF A JOCKEY NAMED BITSY BARLOW?

The three men at the corner table were a trainer, a bookie, and a rich man. The trainer was Sylvester—a large, loosely built fellow with a flushed nose
5 and slow blue eyes. The bookie was Simmons. The rich man was the owner of a horse named Seltzer, which the jockey had ridden that afternoon. The three of them drank whiskey with soda, and a
10 white-coated waiter had just brought on the main course of the dinner.

It was Sylvester who first saw the jockey. He looked away quickly, put down his whiskey glass, and nervously mashed
15 the tip of his red nose with his thumb. 'It's Bitsy Barlow,' he said. 'Standing over there across the room. Just watching us.'

'Oh, the jockey,' said the rich man. He was facing the wall and he half
20 turned his head to look behind him. 'Ask him over.'

'God no,' Sylvester said.

'He's crazy,' Simmons said. The bookie's voice was flat and without in-
25 flection. He had the face of a born gambler, carefully adjusted, the expression a permanent deadlock between fear and greed.

'Well, I wouldn't call him that ex-
30 actly,' said Sylvester. 'I've known him a long time. He was O.K. until about six months ago. But if he goes on like this, I can't see him lasting another year. I just can't.'

35 'It was what happened in Miami,' said Simmons.

'What?' asked the rich man.

Sylvester glanced across the room at the jockey and wet the corner of his
40 mouth with his red, fleshy tongue. 'A accident. A kid got hurt on the track. Broke a leg and a hip. He was a particular pal of Bitsy's. A Irish kid. Not a bad rider, either.'

45 'That's a pity,' said the rich man.

—Excerpted from "The Jockey"
by Carson McCullers

18. Where does the scene occur?

    (1) a local tavern
    (2) a racetrack
    (3) a locker room
    (4) Miami Beach
    (5) a dining room

19. The details in the first paragraph are arranged to

    (1) reveal the jockey's behavior
    (2) establish a conflict in the plot
    (3) introduce three different characters
    (4) create an atmosphere of suspense
    (5) show the drinking habits of alcoholics

20. How did Sylvester react when he first noticed the jockey?

    (1) He invited the jockey to the table.
    (2) He looked away quickly.
    (3) He glanced across the room.
    (4) He ordered another round of drinks.
    (5) He criticized the jockey's career.

21. What had caused a change in Bitsy Barlow's character?

    (1) He drank too much whiskey and soda.
    (2) He broke his leg and hip.
    (3) He lost a race and went crazy.
    (4) His close friend was injured on the track.
    (5) He lost his money in a gambling bet.

Passage 6

WHAT RESTRICTIONS DOES A MOTHER PLACE ON HER CHILD?

A Song in the Front Yard
I've stayed in the front yard all my life.
I want a peek at the back
Where it's rough and untended and
    hungry weed grows.
5 A girl gets sick of a rose.

I want to go in the back yard now
And maybe down the alley,
To where the charity children play.
I want a good time today.

10 They do some wonderful things.
They have some wonderful fun.
My mother sneers, but I say it's fine
How they don't have to go in at a quarter
    to nine.

15 My mother she tells me that Johnnie Mae
Will grow up to be a bad woman.
That George'll be taken to jail soon or
    late.
(On account of last winter he sold our
20   back gate.)

But I say it's fine. Honest I do.
And I'd like to be a bad woman too,
And wear the brave stockings of night-
    black lace.
25 And strut down the street with paint on
    my face.

        —by Gwendolyn Brooks

22. The poem is told from whose point of view?

    (1) George's
    (2) Johnnie Mae's
    (3) a young girl's
    (4) a mother's
    (5) a neighbor's

23. Where does the girl play?

    (1) in the back yard
    (2) in the alley
    (3) in the street
    (4) in an empty lot
    (5) in the front yard

24. The details in the poem are arranged to

    (1) classify types of city neighborhoods
    (2) contrast two types of upbringings
    (3) trace the stages of criminal behavior
    (4) explain the process of child development
    (5) analyze the social causes of juvenile delinquency

25. The girl's mother would most likely agree that

    (1) parents stifle their children's imagination
    (2) children should ignore their parents' rules
    (3) children should choose their own friends
    (4) children require close supervision
    (5) children should imitate other people's behavior

Passage 7

WHAT IS THIS DAUGHTER FEELING AND DESCRIBING?

I'm Just a Stranger Here,
Heaven Is My Home
The first sign was your hair,
unstraightened, shortened from worry,
and it had only been a year since the
    wedding,
5   but you had grown older, Mama.
I felt your usual care
in the mustard greens, sweet potatoes
    and chicken,
yet you smelled of whiskey and prayer.
10   I showed you the pictures,
asked which ones you'd like remade
and watched you fidget, unable to see
    them.
Raising your arm, you spoke of your
15   rheumatism,
it seems like life left your arm first,
like crumbs given to front yard robins.
Age and need, those simple weeds,
were gathering around and taking you
20   away.

              —by Carole Clemmons

26. What best expresses the main idea of this poem?

   (1) When you become an alcoholic, you neglect yourself.
   (2) You should visit your parents more often so that you can take care of their needs.
   (3) Even when they're old, mothers care for their children.
   (4) Age and need have brought about noticeable changes in Mama.
   (5) All mothers suffer from illness, old age, and depression.

27. The tone of this poem is

   (1) ironic
   (2) pleasant
   (3) sorrowful
   (4) humorous
   (5) angry

28. What is the poet describing with the phrase "those simple weeds" (line 18)?

   (1) a garden
   (2) whiskey and prayer
   (3) mama's life
   (4) age and need
   (5) rheumatism

Passage 8

WHAT IS THE CONFLICT BETWEEN TOM AND HIS MOTHER?

AMANDA: You're going to listen, and no more insolence from you! I'm at the end of my patience! [*He comes back toward her.*]

5 TOM: What do you think I'm at? Aren't I supposed to have any patience to reach the end of, Mother? I know, I know. It seems unimportant to you, what I'm *doing*—what I *want* to do—having a little *difference* between them! You don't think that—

AMANDA: I think you've been doing things that you're ashamed of. That's why you act like this. I don't believe that you go every night to the movies. Nobody goes to the movies night after night. Nobody in their right minds goes to the movies as often as you pretend to. People don't go to the movies at nearly midnight, and movies don't let out at two A.M. Come in stumbling. Muttering to yourself like a maniac! You get three hours' sleep and then go to work. Oh, I can picture the way you're doing down there. Moping, doping, because you're in no condition.

35 TOM: [*wildly*] No, I'm in no condition!

AMANDA: What right have you got to jeopardize your job? Jeopardize the security of us all? How do you think we'd manage if you were—

TOM: Listen! You think I'm crazy *about the warehouse*? [*He bends fiercely toward her slight figure.*] You think I'm in love with the Continental Shoemakers? You think I want to spend fifty-five *years* down there in that—*celotex interior*! with—*fluorescent— tubes*! Look! I'd rather somebody picked up a crowbar and battered out my brains—than go back

55 mornings! I *go*! Every time you come in yelling that God damn *"Rise and Shine!" "Rise and Shine!"* I say to myself "How *lucky dead people are*!" But I get up. I

60 *go*! For sixty-five dollars a month I give up all that I dream of doing and being *ever*! And you say self—*self's*

65 all I ever think of. Why, listen, if self is what I thought of, Mother, I'd be where he is—GONE! [*Pointing to father's picture.*] As far as the

70 system of transportation reaches! [*He starts past her. She grabs his arm.*] Don't grab at me, Mother!

AMANDA: Where are you going?

75 TOM: I'm going to the *movies*!

AMANDA: I don't believe that lie!

—Excerpted from *The Glass Menagerie* by Tennessee Williams

29. Which statement best summarizes the main idea of lines 14–34?

(1) Tom mutters to himself like a maniac.
(2) Tom gets three hours of sleep every night.
(3) Tom mopes because he is overtired.
(4) Amanda doesn't believe that Tom goes to the movies every night
(5) Normal people don't routinely attend midnight movies.

30. Which word best describes the emotions conveyed through Tom's language?

(1) patience
(2) anger
(3) respect
(4) humor
(5) indifference

31. You can conclude that Tom's father was

(1) suicidal
(2) lucky
(3) irresponsible
(4) idealistic
(5) hard-working

32. Who would be best suited to analyze the conflict in this passage?

(1) a shoemaker
(2) a factory owner
(3) a filmmaker
(4) a child psychologist
(5) a family counselor

Passage 9

WHY IS CHELSEA COMPLAINING TO HER MOTHER?

ETHEL: Can't you be home for five minutes without getting started on the past?

5 CHELSEA: This house seems to set me off.

ETHEL: Well, it shouldn't. It's a nice house.

CHELSEA: I act like a big person everywhere else. I do. I'm in
10 charge in Los Angeles. I guess I've never grown up on Golden Pond. Do you understand?

ETHEL: I don't think so.

CHELSEA: It doesn't matter. There's just
15 something about coming back here that makes me feel like a little fat girl.

ETHEL: Sit down and tell me about your trip.

20 CHELSEA: [*An outburst*] I don't want to sit down. Where were you all that time? You never bailed me out.

ETHEL: I didn't know you needed
25 bailing out.

CHELSEA: Well, I did.

ETHEL: Here we go again. You had a miserable childhood. Your father was overbearing, your
30 mother ignored you. What else is new? Don't you think everyone looks back on their childhood with some bitterness or regret about
35 something? You are a big girl now, aren't you tired of it all? You have this unpleasant chip on your shoulder which is very unattractive. You only come
40 home when I beg you to, and when you get here all you can do is be disagreeable about the past. Life marches by, Chelsea, I suggest you get on
45 with it.

[*ETHEL stands and glares at CHELSEA*]

—Excerpted from *On Golden Pond* by Ernest Thompson

33. When Chelsea visits Golden Pond, she feels like

   (1) a grown-up
   (2) a little fat girl
   (3) a house guest
   (4) a released prisoner
   (5) an unwelcome stranger

34. The tone of Chelsea's dialogue is

   (1) calm
   (2) insensitive
   (3) horrifying
   (4) mature
   (5) emotional

35. What is the main point of Ethel's dialogue in lines 27–45?

   (1) Chelsea has an overbearing father and a neglectful mother.
   (2) Chelsea avoids visiting her parents at Golden Pond.
   (3) Everyone looks back at his or her childhood with some bitterness or regret.
   (4) Chelsea should pay more attention to events in her past.
   (5) Chelsea's unhappiness as an adult stems from her miserable childhood.

36. Ethel would probably agree that

   (1) parents ruin their children's lives
   (2) people shouldn't bear grudges
   (3) mothers don't confront the past
   (4) children are forced to grow up too quickly
   (5) relationships with parents improve over time

Passage 10

HOW DID THE MOVIE *M**A*S*H CHANGE THE REVIEWER'S THINKING ABOUT WAR?

Nurses flirt outrageously over the operating table and use clamps to scratch their noses before applying them to erupting blood vessels. "I can't really
5 see—it's like the Mississippi River in there," says a surgeon, peering into an open chest wound. When the electricity goes off in the surgical ward, all the personnel instinctively forget their dying pa-
10 tients and hum a snappy chorus of "When the Lights Go Out All Over the World." The blood bank is full of cold beer. The helicopter landing strip for emergency wounded is used as a golf
15 course. Blood donations are taken from unsuspecting commanding officers in their sleep. Elliott Gould and Donald Sutherland are two hot-shot surgeons who, at one point, operate in golf shoes and
20 Japanese kimonos.

It is all totally offensive, of course, but after a while it all makes a very heavy point about American humor and where it is right now. I found myself
25 angry at first for having such a good time watching such irreverence. Then I got with it and I *knew*. War *is* obscene. War *is* offensive. War *is* a charade of vulgarity, an endless variety act of uncom-
30 promising stupidity. In short, war is a joke, and unless we can laugh at it, the joke's on us. The routines in *M**A*S*H are outrageous; only the corpses keep changing.
35 I've never held to the theory that the theater of war could also conceivably be a theater of comedy. I took it all very seriously, because I grew up with bitter doses of the kind of patriotic slush peo-
40 ple like General Patton had dished out. *M**A*S*H is the kind of film that will hopefully change that kind of thinking for today's youth.

—Excerpted from *Big Screen, Little Screen*
by Rex Reed

37. According to the passage, the *M**A*S*H surgeons get blood donations from

(1) dying patients
(2) civilian volunteers
(3) wounded soldiers
(4) unsuspecting nurses
(5) sleeping commanding officers

38. The author's purpose in the first paragraph is to

(1) introduce the actors cast in leading roles
(2) list examples of comic situations in *M**A*S*H
(3) explain why all audiences will enjoy the movie
(4) criticize the nurses' and the surgeons' conduct
(5) outline the plot of the movie

39. The reviewer states that the routines in *M**A*S*H are

(1) outrageous
(2) stupid
(3) obscene
(4) vulgar
(5) bitter

40. What conclusion does the reviewer reach about the significance of *M**A*S*H?

(1) The movie will instill patriotic feelings about the military.
(2) Theaters will stop portraying wars as serious dramas.
(3) The movie will cause war veterans to laugh at themselves.
(4) The movie will change traditional views about the meaning of war.
(5) The movie shows a distorted picture of wartime experience.

41. Which of the following films most closely resembles *M**A*S*H in its subject of humor?

(1) *The Odd Couple*, a comedy about two divorced roommates
(2) *Dr. Strangelove*, a comedy about nuclear destruction
(3) *Blazing Saddles*, a comic takeoff on popular Westerns
(4) *Back to School*, a comedy about a middle-aged college student
(5) *Some Like It Hot*, a comedy about two musicians fleeing from mobsters

Passage 11

WHAT SORT OF STORIES DOES STEPHEN KING WRITE?

Stephen King, an industry and virtually a brand name, writes about childhood terrors, about the inner lives of small people.

5 We all remember being small and most of us at times re-live awful fears based, almost invariably, on being powerless in nightmare-like moments.

To small children, every object can
10 seem to hold danger in dim light or at lonely times. To King's children, whether they are near-infants, adolescents, or grown-ups, there can be menace in cars and drains, streets and skylines, the
15 space beneath the bed—sometimes all of them at once.

King goes a step beyond such potential menace and asks: What if the fears of childhood were actual? What if cars
20 and forests and inner beings turned on us, as we so often feared they might?

Dickens and Kafka, among others, asked those same questions. In answering them, they examined values—how we
25 saw experience, and what, in fact, we saw. King works by accepting conventional values and then exaggerating them. He has not shown himself to be a great artist but he has been a powerful
30 entertainer and his readers are legion and loyal.

—Excerpted from "Horror's King Stephen Strikes Again" by Frederick Busch

42. According to the reviewer, what overall question does Stephen King ask?

    (1) Why do streets and skylines seem menacing?
    (2) What creature hides underneath the bed?
    (3) Why do objects appear dangerous in dimly lighted rooms?
    (4) What terrifies small children and teenagers?
    (5) What if the fears of childhood were actual?

43. The reviewer concludes that Stephen King is

    (1) a great artist
    (2) a gifted novelist
    (3) a powerful entertainer
    (4) a loyal reader
    (5) a childish author

44. You can predict that the atmosphere of Stephen King's stories would be

    (1) depressing
    (2) realistic
    (3) conventional
    (4) horrifying
    (5) unexciting

45. Stephen King would be *least* likely to write a story about

    (1) a teenager whose supernatural powers are destructive
    (2) a typical day in a suburban high school
    (3) children who belong to an evil cult
    (4) a creature who lives in the sewer
    (5) machines that take control over people

POSTTEST ANSWERS AND EXPLANATIONS

1. **(1)** Line 18 directly states that these communities are "isolated from the rest of the town."

2. **(3)** The third paragraph describes the physical dimensions, the location, and the housing arrangement of the barrio.

3. **(2)** Lines 36–37 state that there are "many, many people living in too few houses." Therefore, you can infer that the housing conditions are overcrowded.

4. **(5)** American Indian reservations are also isolated communities sometimes "stranded in the past."

5. **(2)** Domino's Pizza promises delivery within 30 minutes. Like the Roman god Mercury, the drivers "move with heroic speed" (lines 3–4).

6. **(2)** Like dictionaries, many thesauruses list words alphabetically. Next to each entry are other words with similar definitions. For example, *fast*, *instant*, and *swift* have the same meaning as *speedy*.

7. **(3)** The author states that "what really dazzles them [Americans] is speed" (lines 18–19). Throughout the passage, the author cites examples supporting the main idea: Americans are time-conscious consumers who are attracted to businesses offering fast service.

8. **(1)** Felipe Castro, an assistant professor of psychology, offers a viewpoint related to the main idea of the passage. His quotation is effective because he interprets why Americans value speed: "The more you hustle, the more money you can make" (lines 34–35).

9. **(4)** Using hand-operated meat grinders is a slow method for preparing ground meat. The remaining examples emphasize speed—the main focus of the passage.

10. **(2)** The word *heat* is used figuratively, not literally. The phrase immediately following *heat*—"no delicate little derringer"—is an important context clue. A derringer is a gun. Therefore, you can infer that *heat* also means gun.

11. **(1)** Their business card states that they practice in Washington, D.C.

12. **(4)** Throughout the passage, the author refers to popular images of fictional detectives. The concluding sentence summarizes the author's comparison-and-contrast technique: "In other words, they [Goldstein and Denton] have little in common with . . . the detective novels of the past, and nothing at all with the TV fantasy world of . . . 'Charlie's Angels' " (lines 39–46).

13. **(3)** The majority of engineers, like detectives, are men.

14. **(2)** Al, armed with a sawed-off shotgun, is holding Nick and the cook captive in the kitchen. Max is watching George's every move in the lunchroom. These plot details reflect an atmosphere of tension in the diner.

15. **(1)** Max repeatedly calls George "bright boy." Max is making fun of George and is not complimenting George's intelligence. Another example of a sarcastic remark is "You'd make some girl a nice wife, bright boy" (lines 45–46).

16. **(5)** Earlier in the scene, George says, "He's not coming." Toward the end of the scene, George repeats, "Your friend, Ole Andreson, isn't going to come." Therefore, you can conclude that Max and Al are waiting for Ole Andreson, their intended victim.

17. **(2)** The tough and sometimes threatening speech of the two thugs could be effectively converted into a gangster movie script. This excerpt is from "The Killers," a short story that was made into a 1940s gangster movie.

18. **(5)** The following statement supports this inference: "A white-coated waiter had just brought on the main course of the dinner" (lines 9–11).

19. **(3)** The first paragraph introduces Sylvester, the trainer; Simmons, the bookie; and the rich man.

20. **(2)** Lines 12–13 directly state, "It was Sylvester who first saw the jockey. He looked away quickly."

21. **(4)** Sylvester, the trainer, states the reason for Bitsy Barlow's behavior change: "A accident. A kid got hurt on the track. Broke a leg and a hip. He was a particular pal of Bitsy's" (lines 40–43).

22. **(3)** A young girl, the "I" in the poem, relates her experiences and fantasies.

23. **(5)** The girl states in line 1, "I've stayed in the front yard all my life."

24. **(2)** Throughout the poem, the girl contrasts her experiences in the front yard with other children's experiences in the back yard. The front yard and the back yard represent two different types of upbringings.

25. **(4)** The mother is apparently very strict. She allows her child to play only in the front yard and disapproves of Johnnie Mae and George, children who play in the back yard and the alley. Therefore, the mother would most likely agree that children require close supervision.

26. **(4)** The poet notices that, in just a year, her mother had grown older and weaker due to "age and need" (line 18).

27. **(3)** You can conclude that the poet is saddened by her mother's failing condition.

28. **(4)** You can infer that age and need are the same as "those simple weeds" gathering around Mama.

29. **(4)** Amanda directly states, "I don't believe that you go every night to the movies." The remaining lines of dialogue build on this main idea.

30. **(2)** The stage directions [*wildly*] and [*He bends fiercely toward her* . . .] show that Tom delivers his lines angrily.

31. **(3)** In lines 65–71, Tom states, "Why, listen, if self is what I thought of, Mother, I'd be where he is—GONE! [*Pointing to father's picture.*] As far as the system of transportation reaches!" From these lines, you can infer that Tom's father deserted the family. This action reveals his father's lack of responsibility.

32. **(5)** The scene shows a troubled relationship between Tom and his mother, Amanda. A family counselor is best qualified to analyze the conflict between a parent and a child.

33. **(2)** Chelsea directly states, "There's just something about coming back here that makes me feel like a little fat girl" (lines 14–17).

34. **(5)** The stage direction [*An outburst*] indicates that Chelsea is delivering her lines emotionally.

35. **(3)** The main point of Ethel's speech is "Don't you think everyone looks back on their childhood with some bitterness or regret?" (lines 31–34). The remaining lines of dialogue develop this central point.

36. **(2)** From the very beginning of the scene, you can infer that Ethel finds Chelsea's complaining about the past to be annoying and senseless. Therefore, Ethel would probably agree that people shouldn't bear grudges because they should place their past experiences behind them.

37. **(5)** Lines 15–17 directly state, "Blood donations are taken from unsuspecting commanding officers in their sleep."

38. **(2)** Every sentence in the first paragraph summarizes a comic situation in *M*A*S*H.*

39. **(1)** In lines 32–33, the reviewer directly states, "The routines in *M*A*S*H* are outrageous."

40. **(4)** Because *M*A*S*H* portrays war as "obscene," "offensive," and "a joke," the reviewer predicts that younger audiences may no longer glamorize the patriotism of war.

41. **(2)** *M*A*S*H* presents a serious historical event—the Korean War—as a comedy. Similarly, *Dr. Strangelove* depicts a gravely serious issue—nuclear destruction—as a comedy.

42. **(5)** Lines 18–19 state Stephen King's major question: "What if the fears of childhood were actual?"

43. **(3)** The reviewer states in the concluding sentence that "He [Stephen King] has not shown himself to be a great artist but he has been a powerful entertainer."

44. **(4)** Because terror fascinates Stephen King, you can predict that the atmosphere of his stories is horrifying.

45. **(2)** You can conclude that Stephen King writes stories about menacing situations and supernatural events. He is not drawn to everyday, realistic experiences. Therefore, he is *least* likely to write a story about a typical day in a suburban high school.

POSTTEST EVALUATION CHARTS

Use the chart below to determine the reading skills areas in which you need to do the most review. Circle any items that you got wrong and pay particular attention to areas where you missed half or more of the questions.

Posttest Reading Skills Chart

Skill Area		Item Number	Review Pages	Number Correct
Literal Comprehension	Main Idea/Global	35		_____/1
	Supporting Details/ Specific	1, 11, 20, 21, 23, 29, 33, 37, 39, 42	9–30	_____/10
Inferential Comprehension	Main Idea/Global	2, 7, 26, 40		_____/4
	Supporting Details/ Specific	3, 5, 6, 14, 16, 18, 31, 43, 44	31–54	_____/9
	Figurative Language/ Specific	10, 28		_____/2
Analysis	Style	8, 15, 27, 30, 34	55–84	_____/5
	Structure	12, 19, 22, 24, 38		_____/5
Application		4, 9, 13, 17, 25, 32, 36, 41, 45	47–54	_____/9

If you got fewer than 35 items correct, go back and find the areas in which you had the most difficulty. Then review those pages that you need additional work in.

Now circle the same numbers for the items that you circled in the chart above. This will give you additional information about the literature and the arts content areas in which you need the most review.

Posttest Content Areas Chart

Content Area	Item Number	Review Pages	Number Correct
Nonfiction Prose	1, 2, 3, 4, 5, 6, 7, 8 9, 10, 11, 12, 13	85–109	_____/13
Prose Fiction	14, 15, 16, 17, 18, 19, 20, 21	110–56	_____/8
Poetry	22, 23, 24, 25, 26, 27, 28	157–87	_____/7
Drama	29, 30, 31, 32, 33, 34, 35, 36	188–220	_____/8
Commentaries on the Arts	37, 38, 39, 40, 41, 42, 43, 44, 45	221–54	_____/9

ANSWER KEY

CHAPTER 1: LITERAL UNDERSTANDING

Exercise 1: Main Idea in Paragraphs
pages 12–13

Any six of the following are correct:

1.	the sky	**6.**	birds' nests
2.	the earth	**7.**	the moon
3.	the sun	**8.**	teepees
4.	the stars	**9.**	the seasons
5.	the wind	**10.**	the life of a man

Exercise 2: Main Idea in Passages
pages 14–15

1. cutting lemons
2. She calls him the "boy" instead of the "man."
3. (2) Lines 14–16 state that you won't be respected "if you do work that others don't respect even if you have a Ph.D. It isn't education that counts, but the job in which you land."

Exercise 3: Supporting Details
pages 18–19

1. An Indian's name tells the world what kind of person he is. This statement summarizes the main idea of the passsage.
2. An Indian's first name describes some circumstance surrounding his birth.
3. The Indian woman who was helping his mother heard a wolf howling across the river. When she told his mother what happened, the mother decided to call her son "Howling-in-the-Middle-of-the-Night."

Exercise 4: Facts Relating to the Main Idea
pages 20–21

1. (1) Ellison was born.
   (2) He moved to New York.
   (3) His *Invisible Man* was published.
   (4) He won the National Book Award for Fiction.
2. music and composing
3. Richard Wright
4. White America had to recognize blacks as human beings.
5. *Shadow and Act*

Exercise 5: Identifying Context Clues
pages 25-26

1. **waifs:** homeless children
2. **charisma:** magnetic and charming personality
3. **subpoena:** a legal document requiring a person to testify in court
4. **extraterrestrial:** a creature from another planet
5. **convoluted:** complicated; full of twists and turns
6. **toxic:** poisonous
7. **tuition reimbursement:** payment for the cost of a class
8. **documentary:** a film that shows real events and people
9. **panhandling:** begging
10. **electronic preachers:** preachers who deliver sermons on TV and radio

Exercise 6: Chapter Review
pages 27-30

1. (2) **Main Idea of a Passage**
   The entire passage discusses the young boys' game of imitating a bullfight.
2. (3) **Context Clues**
   Following the italicized word *aficionados* is the phrase "or fans." *Fans* is the English word for *aficionados*.
3. (4) **Main Idea of a Paragraph**
   The second paragraph describes in detail how a boy disguised himself as a bull by using the bleached skull of a steer, horns, and a cactus leaf.
4. (2) **Supporting Details**
   As lines 18-20 directly state, if the bull suspected that he was poked in a sensitive spot on purpose, a free-for-all, or a fight, would follow.
5. (2) **Main Idea of a Passage**
   Lynette Woodard is the only woman on the team. This is the point that is stressed and expanded throughout the passage.
6. (4) **Main Idea of a Paragraph**
   This paragraph describes, play by play, Woodard in action. Almost every move is detailed.
7. (3) **Context Clues**
   The third answer defines the term according to the context. Context clues include "revenues," "attendance figures," and Woodard's importance to the team "financially."
8. (2) **Supporting Details**
   The example of Billie Jean King in tennis is used to support the author's idea that women can be as talented as men in sports.
9. (3) **Main Idea of a Passage**
   This passage describes the miners' faces, walks, builds, and other noticeable features.
10. (2) **Supporting Details**
    Lines 1-3 directly state that their faces are pale from breathing in foul air.
11. (5) **Supporting Details**
    The author summarizes the reasons for this condition in lines 11-14.
12. (4) **Context Clues**
    The word *cheeses* immediately follows the word *Roquefort*. This is a clue that Roquefort is a type of cheese, as are American and Swiss.

CHAPTER 2: INFERENTIAL UNDERSTANDING
Exercise 1: Clues That Support an Inference
pages 32-33

1. **Clues:** The referee blows his whistle to stop the game . . . The quarterback, unable to move, must be carried away on a stretcher.
2. **Clues:** The stone set in an engagement ring is usually a diamond . . . Engagement rings are worn on the left hand . . . The secretary's co-workers are probably congratulating her because she is engaged.
3. **Clues:** An alarm goes off . . . The sweater that falls from underneath the woman's coat is apparently stolen merchandise.
4. **Clues:** Loud claps and cheers and the expression "bravo" indicate the audience's enjoyment.
5. **Clues:** A black limousine is often used as a hearse, a car for transporting a body . . . Cars follow the limousine . . . Cars in a funeral procession often have their headlights turned on.

Exercise 2: Inferring the Unstated Main Idea
pages 36-37

1. (4)
2. *Clues:* There are "no fish in the river" because fish cannot survive in a polluted river. Other clues include the garbage on the bank and in the river.
3. (1)
4. *Clues:* The rope attached to the crossbeam and the noose around the man's neck indicate that a hanging is the central event.

Exercise 3: Supporting Details
pages 40–41

1. (2) Descriptive details that support this response include "elevator doors," "glass doors at the end of the lobby," and "revolving doors." Also, the time is 5:18. Office workers usually leave their jobs at about five o'clock.
2. (4) Lines 3–5 indicate a more intense relationship, like that with an ex-wife, than those implied by the other choices.
3. (2) Feelings of "faint guilt" and "bewilderment" are uneasy emotions.
4. (1) Busy traffic and blowing car horns are usually associated with a city scene.

Exercise 4: Character Descriptions
page 42

Valid conclusions:

1. She doesn't drink, smoke, swear, or wear makeup. She can sense sin. Parker believes that she married him to "save" or redeem his soul. Therefore, you can conclude that Parker's wife behaves as though she has strong religious convictions.
4. Parker has a "suspicion that she actually liked everything she said she didn't like." In other words, he is hinting that his wife's disapproval of sinning may be hypocritical or insincere.
5. The statement "It was himself he could not understand" implies that Parker probably lacks self-knowledge.

Exercise 5: Figurative Expressions
page 43

1. d   6. g
2. i   7. c
3. j   8. e
4. b   9. h
5. f   10. a

Exercise 6: Distinguishing Between Literal and Figurative Language
page 44

1. L   6. F
2. F   7. F
3. F   8. F
4. L   9. L
5. L   10. L

Exercise 7: Interpreting Comparisons
pages 45–46

Compare your interpretations to the ones below. They do not have to be exactly the same, but they should be close.

1. Icicles are compared with a crystal monster's vicious teeth.
   Interpretation: The icicles appear menacing. The comparison emphasizes the shape and sharpness of the icicles.
2. A person is compared with a circus tightrope walker.
   Interpretation: In the person's imagination, the tightrope shows signs of breaking. The comparison conveys a sense of panic and anxiety.
3. An eyelid is compared with a window shade.
   Interpretation: Someone playing with the cord of the window shade makes you picture a window shade snapping up and down. The comparison imaginatively shows what a twitching eye looks like.
4. The sun is compared with a club.
   Interpretation: The comparison emphasizes the intensity and strength of the sun's heat beating on the man's face.
5. Lucy is compared with a general inspecting troops.
   Interpretation: The comparison suggests both Lucy's authority and her attention to details.

Exercise 8: Inferring Applications
pages 48–49

1. No. According to the passage some educational counselors in trade schools are mainly concerned with selling tactics. The counselor could be distorting the truth.
2. No. Some vocational schools tell an applicant that his test scores are amazingly high so that he will enroll in the school.
3. Yes. This personnel director is a reliable source of information.
4. No. Felicia shouldn't judge the educational quality based solely upon Sandra's opinion.
5. No. TV commercials are sometimes deceptive. TV commercials, like salespeople, may falsely advertise the school.
6. Yes. Cindy should not allow the interviewer to pressure her into signing the Enrollment Agreement.

Exercise 9: Chapter Review
pages 50–54

1. (5) **Main Idea**
This statement summarizes the central focus of the passage. All of the paragraphs describe the personalities and the distinctive characteristics of the men.

2. (2) **Figurative Language**
The author uses this figurative language to give the readers a sense of the boomers as wandering adventurers. He implies this comparison to reveal the character of the construction workers. The statement is not literally true.

3. (1) **Figurative Language**
Lines 11–13 explain the meaning of the figurative name "boomers."

4. (3) **Main Idea**
The supporting details are directly related to this statement. The fourth paragraph presents several examples of the dangers that construction workers face.

5. (2) **Supporting Details**
You can conclude from the details describing the construction workers' life and behavior that they would not choose to settle down to a safe life.

6. (1) **Application**
Building railroads most closely matches the construction workers' job skills and outlook on life.

7. (1) **Supporting Details**
Lines 9–11 state that the mother is no longer pretty, and that is why she picks on Connie. Therefore, you can infer that she is jealous of Connie's looks. You can assume the mother's remarks stem from her jealousy.

8. (3) **Supporting Details**
This statement implies Connie's conceit about her appearance. There is not enough information in the passage to support the other conclusions.

9. (5) **Supporting Details**
The mother's constant praise and approval indicates that she favors June.

10. (4) **Figurative Language**
Trash is considered worthless. The phrase "trashy dreams" suggests that her mother thinks that Connie's inner thoughts are worthless.

11. (2) **Supporting Details**
The father does not relate to his family. Since he reads the newspaper during supper, you can assume he isn't talking to his wife or daughters. You also know that he goes to bed after supper.

12. (2) **Application**
A family counselor is trained to analyze the relationships within a family.

13. (3) **Figurative Language**
The author uses this comparison to show how a creative idea is similar to a pregnancy. He carries within him a story that he can bring to life.

14. (2) **Main Idea**
The paragraph describes in detail the way his father told stories.

15. (1) **Supporting Details**
The author respects his father's talents. You can conclude from the second paragraph that his father probably inspired the author to write stories.

16. (2) **Supporting Details**
Becoming a writer seems to be a mixed blessing. The phrase "cursed my fate" suggests the difficulties and struggles that the author experiences.

17. (4) **Application**
Because an artist produces original work, she would most likely identify with the author's struggle for creative expression.

CHAPTER 3: ANALYZING STYLE AND STRUCTURE
Exercise 1: Analyzing Writing Style
page 61

1. conversational
2. conversational
3. formal
4. informal
5. formal
6. informal
7. informal
8. informal
9. formal
10. conversational
11. informal
12. informal
13. informal
14. formal
15. conversational

Exercise 2: Analyzing Authors' Diction
pages 62–63

1. formal
2. conversational
3. formal
4. conversational
5. informal
6. informal
7. conversational

Explanation: All examples of formal diction address a select reading audience and use difficult vocabulary. All examples of informal diction address a general reading audience and use simpler vocabulary. Conversational diction most closely resembles people's speech.

Exercise 3: Analyzing Figurative Language
pages 64–65

1. Any five of the following are correct: cash, check, promissory note, funds, bankrupt, vaults, riches
2. (2) The central message expressed in the passage is that America denies black people their freedom.
3. (3) Dr. King wants to emphasize that black people, like all Americans, value their civil rights. Civil rights is an ideal that cannot be literally translated into dollars and cents.

    However, by comparing civil rights to money, he uses an image that all people can understand. Americans want their money's worth, and King is indicating that black people just want what is due them.

Exercise 4: Analyzing Tone
pages 67–68

1. threatening   3. somber
2. funny   4. scary

Exercise 5: Analyzing Time Order
pages 71–72

Numbers should be listed in the following order: 5, 3, 8, 1, 9, 2, 4, 7, 6.

Exercise 6: Analyzing Categories
pages 74–75

1. d   5. e
2. f   6. a
3. b   7. c
4. g

Exercise 7: Comparisons and Contrasts
pages 76–77

1. The purpose of this passage is to compare and contrast TV shows with the real world.
2. In paragraph 3, a TV cabdriver is compared and contrasted with a real cabdriver.
3. In paragraph 5, an emergency ward on TV is compared with an emergency ward in a real hospital.

4. According to Dr. Applebaum, television shows present children with an inaccurate picture of real-life situations.

Exercise 8: Cause-and-Effect Relationships
pages 79–80

1. (4) Huck thinks killing a spider is a cause of bad luck.
2. (4) Huck says, "I was scared and most shook the clothes off of me."

Exercise 9: Chapter Review
pages 80–84

1. (3) **Tone**
    Throughout the passage, the author expresses anger toward the coffee machine.
2. (5) **Style**
    The author's conversational writing style would also be appropriate for a script of a TV comedy series.
3. (1) **Structure**
    The author explains a process—how to kick a machine.
4. (2) **Style**
    A conversation is the author's primary method for revealing the people's reactions to the coffee machine.
5. (4) **Structure**
    The introductory sentence of the passage states the author's purpose. He categorizes two types of teenagers—ducks and hard rocks—who live in his Brooklyn neighborhood.
6. (3) **Tone**
    You can infer that the author is critical of the hard rocks' behavior. For example, he states that they use drugs, cut classes, and don't work.
7. (2) **Diction**
    Words like *ducks, hard rocks, cheeb,* and *zooted* are examples of conversational speech from the author's Brooklyn neighborhood.
8. (4) **Diction and Tone**
    Although the storyteller admits that he is nervous, he refuses to believe that he is, in fact, mad. The way he repeats certain phrases also conveys that he is emotionally unbalanced.
9. (1) **Tone**
    The storyteller discusses his actions of the week before the murder. The way he sneaks around the old man's room every night causes the reader to wonder how he actually committed the crime. By leaving out

this information, the storyteller builds suspense.

10. (5) **Structure**
In the fourth paragraph, the storyteller organizes his account to show the sequence of his actions preceding the crime.

CHAPTER 4: NONFICTION PROSE

Exercise 1: An Unemployed Steelworker
pages 86-88

1. twenty-seven
2. Wheeling Steel's Yorkville, Ohio, mill
3. (2) In line 15, Jimmy Runyan says, "I get *real* depressed sometimes."
4. seventeen
5. He dreamed of buying a music store.
6. (1) The entire passage explores Jimmy Runyan's response to his own unemployment crisis.
7. (4) The phrase "great tools for a union man" refers to Jimmy Runyan's personality traits—"calm eyes and a hot temper" (lines 24-25).
8. (3) The concluding paragraph states that union members felt a deep bond with one another.
9. (2) Jimmy Runyan gives a first-hand account of the layoffs.
10. (4) By reporting how the layoffs personally affect one individual, the author reveals his concern.
11. (1) The informal writing style used in profiling Jimmy Runyan is characteristic of many biographies.

Exercise 2: A Homemaker's Experience
pages 88-89

1. (5) The passage details the demanding work of a homemaker.
2. Her household chores include (1) preparing her children's clothes, (2) bathing the children, (3) cooking her children's lunch, (4) scrubbing the house, and (5) washing and ironing the clothes.
3. (2) She states, "Welfare makes you feel like you're nothing. Like you're laying back and not doing anything and it's falling in your lap" (lines 8-9).

Exercise 3: Advice to Job Seekers
pages 90-91

1. (1) legal   (6) illegal
   (2) illegal   (7) legal
   (3) legal   (8) legal
   (4) illegal   (9) illegal
   (5) illegal   (10) legal
2. Answers will vary.

Exercise 4: A Tennis Pro's Opinion
pages 91-92

1. (4) When addressing high school audiences, the author's major message is "You will need that diploma" (line 7).
2. (1) **invalid**—The author believes that too many athletes are uneducated. However, he does not suggest that they are stupid but that they have the potential to learn.
   (2) **valid**—In the third paragraph, the author summarizes the realities of professional sports. He implies that athletes seldom foresee these problems.
   (3) **valid**—In the second paragraph, the author implies that high school athletes spend more time on the athletic field than in the library.
   (4) **invalid**—Although the author states that there are some stars "earning millions," he doesn't suggest that they are overpaid.
   (5) **invalid**—You can conclude that some athletes spend sleepless nights worrying about their future. They are not staying awake to study.

Exercise 5: Children and Sports
pages 93-95

1. (4) The entire passage discusses this problem.
2. (2) The author quotes doctors who specialize in sports medicine.
3. (5) This quotation from the passage is meant figuratively, not literally. Doctors are conducting highly detailed examinations of the problem of children's sports injuries.

Exercise 6: Games and Education
pages 93-96

1. (4) The author states this question in line 16. The rest of the passage is devoted to answering it.

2.   Energy Czar "teaches players about the barter and trade-offs involved in contemporary energy negotiations" (lines 30–31).

3. (2) Multiplication tables and algebra are taught in math classes. Adverbs and prepositions are taught in grammar classes.

4. (5) The author states that "games are one of the most ancient and time-honored methods of educating" (lines 7–8). He obviously shows a preference for learning through games over other methods, such as memorizing rules—choice (1). From this you can conclude that the author would view a word game like Scrabble as an educational tool.

Exercise 7: Soap Operas
pages 95–97

1. (1) relaxation
   (2) release from daily stress
   (3) cure for loneliness

2. (2) Dr. Haun states in line 24 that watching soap operas makes college students feel "less homesick."

3. (5) The author cites nothing but benefits from watching soap operas. Therefore, you can infer that she would agree that watching soap operas is therapeutic.

4. (1) **false**—Dr. Haun states that "there doesn't seem to be any relationship between socio-economic levels, occupations, or education among those who watch soaps" (lines 33–35).
   (2) **false**—Dr. Cassata states that "the characters have become so complex, it's hard to tell the good guy from the bad guy" (lines 40–41).
   (3) **true**—Dr. Cassata states, "It gives the person another way of thinking about the problem" (lines 6–7).
   (4) **false**—According to Dr. Haun's research, the number of viewers under thirty is steadily climbing.

5. (2) Using the research and observations of professors Haun and Cassata—experts in the field—strengthens the author's own viewpoint.

Exercise 8: Missing Children
pages 97–98

1.   a Detroit area teacher

2. (5) Lines 7–9 suggest that only paper cartons "bear the pictures of missing children."

3. (2) The author draws this conclusion in the last sentence of the passage.

Exercise 9: Treatment of
Vietnam Veterans
pages 99–100

1. (2) When the police officer says, "They can do what they want," he means that he won't arrest any Vietnam veterans regardless of their conduct. Keeping his handcuffs on his belt emphasizes this point.

2. (5) The veterans' gestures—walking arm and arm, holding hands, kissing or hugging people in the crowd—are the context clues that support choice (5)—that *intimate* means personal.

3. (2) "Mend its fences" is a figurative expression that means to patch up or improve relationships. The phrase is not used literally in the passage.

4. (1) The author states that the sign "fit the mood of the parade" (line 34).

5. (3) From the reporter's comments as well as the veterans' and crowd's reactions, you can infer that the reporter believed that Vietnam veterans deserved the public's recognition.

Exercise 10: John Dillinger's
Violent End
pages 101–102

1. (2) Melvin H. Purvis, head of the Chicago office, organized his men to trap Dillinger. Therefore, you can conclude that the shooting occurred in Chicago.

2. (5) Line 19 states that *Manhattan Melodrama* was a "feature film."

3. (3) The action-packed description resembles the writing style of gangster novels.

4.   Numbers should be listed in the following order: 3, 4, 2, 6, 5, 1.

Exercise 11: A View of
Oklahoma
pages 103–104

1.   Kiowas

2. **Sight:** "tortoises crawl about on the red earth"
      "great green and yellow grasshoppers are everywhere in the tall grass"
      "green belts along the rivers and the creeks"
  Hearing: "grass . . . cracks beneath your feet"
  Touch: "grasshoppers . . . sting the flesh"
      "grass turns brittle"

3. (1) The author uses figurative language to emphasize the intense summer heat. The plants are not literally on fire.

4. (4) The author vividly describes colors and the scenery. He uses words to paint a picture of the landscape.

5. (1) "Rises out of the plain" is the context clue that supports the answer that a knoll is a hill.

Exercise 12: Chapter Review pages 104–109

1. (2) **Main Idea and Structure**
The entire passage explains the procedure that Mr. Hagenlocher follows in sketching a suspect.

2. (4) **Supporting Details**
Line 1 states that "Mr. Hagenlocher tries to put witnesses at ease."

3. (2) **Supporting Details**
Lines 9–10 state, "Witnesses are asked to leaf through these [mug shots] to try to find a similar face."

4. (4) **Supporting Details**
According to the passage, Mr. Hagenlocher poses all of the other questions except this one.

5. (5) **Style and Structure**
Quotations from Mr. Hagenlocher explain the process of sketching suspects from his viewpoint.

6. (3) **Application**
A portrait painter is also skilled in drawing people's faces.

7. (2) **Main Idea**
The first sentence of the passage introduces the main idea. This message is later restated in the most well-known sentence from this speech: "Ask not what your country can do for you—ask what you can do for your country."

8. (1) **Supporting Details**
"Call to service" in line 4 refers to military combat. Therefore, you can conclude that the phrase "graves of young Americans" signifies the soldiers who died in battle.

9. (4) **Supporting Details**
In lines 2–3, John F. Kennedy states that "each generation of Americans has been summoned to give testimony to its national loyalty."

10. (3) **Style and Structure**
John F. Kennedy's speech is intended to be an inspirational message to the American people. For example, by appealing to the power of "energy, faith, and devotion," he attempts to foster the highest ideals. The speech encourages Americans to involve themselves in achieving the country's goals.

11. (2) **Supporting Details**
In line 16, John F. Kennedy states, "I do not shrink from this responsibility—I welcome it."

12. (3) **Style and Application**
The concluding sentence contains religious language such as "blessing" and "God's work."

13. (5) **Supporting Details**
Classes were taught "by instructors who came from such places as Harvard and Boston universities" (lines 2–3).

14. (4) **Supporting Details**
Lines 16–17 state that "an inmate was smiled upon if he demonstrated an unusually intense interest in books." Therefore, you can infer that the prison officials approved of this activity.

15. (3) **Figurative Language**
Malcolm X is using this expression figuratively, not literally. He is describing the "well-read inmates."

16. (3) **Supporting Details**
Lines 26–27 state, "It always seemed to catch me right in the middle of something engrossing." In other words, the "lights out" rule interrupted Malcolm X's reading.

17. (2) **Main Idea**
Throughout the passage, Malcolm X conveys his enthusiasm for "being able to read and understand." He also admires the other inmates who show a desire to learn.

18. (3) **Application**
Malcolm X and some of his fellow inmates are examples of individuals who took the initiative to educate themselves. Therefore, you can conclude that if Malcolm X were alive today, he would believe strongly in self-education.

CHAPTER 5: PROSE FICTION
Exercise 1: Inferring Atmosphere pages 114–15

1. "There must be more money! There must be more money!"

2. the children
the rocking-horse
the big doll
the puppy

3. (3) The haunting, unspoken phrase gives the house a supernatural atmosphere.

Exercise 2: Understanding Setting
pages 115–16

1. (3) References, such as "the punishment block (the stone prison inside the camp)," "barbed-wire fence," and "prisoners," support the idea that this is a prison camp.
2. (5) The details describing the environment of the prison camp and the extremely cold weather create an atmosphere of oppression.
3. Phrases referring to the weather include:
"freezing cold"
"boots crunching on the snow"
"the thermometer hung, caked over with ice"
"freezing weather"
"frost-covered rail"
"they all felt cold"

Exercise 3: Analyzing Conflict
pages 120–21

1. Karlie sits on a railway bench marked "Europeans Only."
2. Karlie knows that legally he is forbidden to sit on the bench. However, he thinks that his human rights and sense of dignity may be more important than the official laws.
3. (2) Karlie shows courage when he defies South Africa's system of racial discrimination.
4. (5) Karlie's actions suggest that he would also support the civil rights movement in the United States.

Exercise 4: Interpreting Character—Author's Point of View
pages 126–27
Part I

1. Tony grew up in a crowded, poverty-stricken neighborhood.
2. sixteen
3. juvenile delinquents
4. He was in a car with boys who robbed a liquor store.
5. Tony would marry Rosa and manage a candy store for her father.

Part II

6. (4) Tony dropped out of school, associated with juvenile delinquents, and ran away to Texas. Consequently, you can conclude that Tony led a troubled life before his marriage.
7. (1) Tony dreamed of escaping from his neighborhood, "but everything had fouled up against him before he could." Therefore, you can infer that he was a victim of his environment.

Exercise 5: Interpreting Character—Another Character's Point of View
pages 128–29

1. riding clothes
2. **Age:** thirty
Hair color: "straw-haired" or blond
3. "hard mouth"; "arrogant eyes"; "cruel body"
4. Words or phrases suggesting Tom's strength and force include:
"sturdy"
"dominance"
"leaning aggressively forward"
"enormous power"
"great pack of muscle"
"body capable of enormous leverage"
5. (2) From the descriptive words in the passage, you can infer that Nick's attitude toward Tom is critical.

Exercise 6: Speakers in Dialogue
page 130

1. Pepi
2. one of the men from Detroit
3. Joe Sansone
4. Pepi
5. one of the men from Detroit

Exercise 7: Interpreting Dialogue
pages 132–33

1. (3) The general topic that the brothers are discussing is Sonny's choice of careers.
2. (1) Sonny's brother says in line 26, "I was furious."
3. (4) You can conclude from these lines of dialogue that Sonny sincerely wants to become a jazz musician.
4. (1) valid   (5) invalid
   (2) valid   (6) invalid
   (3) invalid   (7) valid
   (4) invalid   (8) valid

Exercise 8: Observing a Character
pages 134–36
Part I

Numbers should be listed in the following order: 3, 4, 7, 2, 6, 1, 5

Part II

1. false   5. false
2. false   6. false
3. true   7. true
4. true   8. true

Exercise 9: Interpreting Comparisons
pages 138–39

Your interpretations may differ.

1. Hogs are compared with huge spotted stones.
   Interpretation: The comparison emphasizes the coloring of the hogs.
2. A man is compared with a crow.
   Interpretation: The man makes bird-like movements.
3. A woman's eyes are compared with two chips of green bottle glass.
   Interpretation: The woman has sparkling green eyes.
4. Mrs. Watts's grin is compared with the blade of a sickle.
   Interpretation: The comparison exaggerates the shape of her smile.
5. Windshield wipers are compared with two idiots clapping in church.
   Interpretation: The comparison describes the noise of windshield wipers. The wipers sound like fools clapping their hands.

Exercise 10: Figurative Language
pages 139–40

1. (4) "Painted savages" suggest an image of wildness.
2. (1) Serpents are usually characterized as being evil creatures. The coiled chimney smoke seems wicked.
3. (3) The comparison suggests that the steam engine functions like a crazed animal.
4. (2) The descriptions of the buildings, the chimney smoke, the river, and the steam engines reveal the ugliness of this industrial city.
5. "buildings full of windows where there was a rattling and a trembling all day long"
6. "a river that ran purple with ill-smelling dye"

Exercise 11: Interpreting Theme
pages 143–45

1. (3) Line 12 states that this money from the picker's pay would mean "a huge windfall for Morales." In other words, Morales's greed for profits prompts him to ask the pickers for more money.
2. (3) Hard work and cruel treatment have taken their toll on the men. They seem like "exhausted animals," rather than human beings.

3. (1) Lines 25–26 support this response.
4. (5) Lines 28–30 show the pickers moving toward their own buckets, threatening to knock them over. The pickers' defiance reveals their contempt for Morales.
5. (4) This statement summarizes the author's comments in lines 44–48.

Exercise 12: Reading a Short Story
pages 145–50

1. Waterbury
2. 2, 5, 1, 3, 4
3. **Character:** Famous doctor
   Situation: Performing surgery on a millionaire banker

   Character: Accused murderer
   Situation: Testifying on the witness stand

   Character: Captain during the war
   Situation: Volunteering to fly alone in a bomber plane
4. The following lines of dialogue reveal Mrs. Mitty's bossiness and critical attitude toward her husband:
   "Not so fast! You're driving too fast! What are you driving so fast for?"
   "Couldn't you have put them on in the store?"
   "Remember to get those overshoes while I'm having my hair done."
   "You're not a young man any longer."
   "Why don't you wear your gloves? Have you lost your gloves?"
   "I'm going to take your temperature when I get you home."
5. (4) The commander, the doctor, the accused murderer, the captain, and the man before the firing squad are heroic characters. They all demonstrate strength and courage.
6. (5) The events of the story reveal this theme. Walter Mitty's daydreams add excitement to his life.
7. (2) Walter Mitty is portrayed as a comic character. The tone of the story is humorous.

Exercise 13: Chapter Review
pages 150–56

1. (5) **Supporting Detail**
   The fact that an arrested person was treated violently is supported by the description that away from the crowd, the police "whaled him with their clubs" (line 12).
2. (2) **Structure and Point of View**
   The second and third paragraphs describe the scene from Tod's point of view.

3. (4) **Characterization**
Line 16 states that Tod "began to get frightened."

4. (4) **Figurative Language**
When the author makes a comparison between a reporter and a revivalist preacher, he is using this to create an image of someone speaking in an agitated manner.

5. (2) **Point of View**
References such as "They had enough to do without chasing him" and "he began to get frightened" indicate that the story is being told by a narrator acting as an all-knowing reporter. Not involved in the action himself, the narrator relates the events and the thoughts and feelings of the characters.

6. (2) **Theme**
The author reveals this theme by describing the crowd's behavior as if it were one personality. The crowd is portrayed as a mob out of control. As a result, individual personalities do not seem to exist.

7. (2) **Application**
Newspapers frequently report similar mob scenes at rock concerts.

8. (3) **Setting**
Miss Havisham is surrounded by clothing and jewelry. Since she appears to be in the middle of dressing, you can infer that the scene takes place in her bedroom.

9. (3) **Characterization**
You learn about Miss Havisham's character from her physical appearance and the condition of her surroundings.

10. (1) **Characterization**
Clues supporting the inference that she is wealthy include rich materials and the sparkling jewels around Miss Havisham's neck and on the table.

11. (1) **Setting**
The phrases "faded and yellow" and "withered like the dress" suggest decay.

12. (5) **Point of View**
In answer to the question "Who is it?" the reference "Pip, ma'am" and the use of the pronoun "I" indicate that the narrator is the character Pip. He describes Miss Havisham and the setting from his point of view.

13. (1) **Setting and Characterization**
The author includes this observation to emphasize that the watch and the clock show how time has really stopped in Miss Havisham's mind.

14. (2) **Application**
The camera would focus on Miss Havisham because she is the center of attention in this passage.

15. (1) **Figurative Language**
The purpose of this comparison is to show how the author presents the action-filled plot.

16. (3) **Point of View**
Lines 15–16 support the response that the author tells the novel from Bigger's point of view.

17. (3) **Style and Structure**
References such as "building of a well-constructed book"; "I told of Bigger's life in close-up, slow motion"; and "I restricted the novel" imply that the author deliberately constructed the novel to achieve a certain effect.

18. (2) **Figurative Language**
The author uses the comparison to illustrate how he wants the reader to experience the story. The reader should feel that he is a special audience watching Bigger's drama unfold.

19. (3) **Main Idea**
The focus of this passage is to show the techniques of writing a novel. The author discusses methods of presenting plot, characterization, and point of view.

20. (3) **Application**
It is a journalist's job to report on factual events.

CHAPTER 6: POETRY
Exercise 1: Characteristics of Poetry
pages 160–61

1. **Lines 2 and 4:** play, today
Lines 6 and 8: wild, child
Lines 10 and 12: me, free
Lines 14 and 16: fire, choir
Lines 18 and 20: sweet, feet
Lines 22 and 24: place, face
Lines 26 and 28: wild, child
Lines 30 and 32: shoe, you

2. (1) "For the dogs are fierce and wild, / And clubs and hoses, guns and jail / Aren't good for a little child." (lines 6–8)
"For I fear those guns will fire." (line 14)

(2) "Her eyes grew wet and wild." (line 26)

(3) "She clawed through bits of glass and brick" (line 29)

(4) "O here's the shoe my baby wore, / But, baby, where are you?" (lines 31-32)

3. (1) False
(2) True
(3) True
(4) True

Exercise 2: Reading a Poem
pages 163-65

1. (3) The title of the poem ("Tribal Cemetery"), the description of the tombstone (first stanza), and line 13 support this reponse.

2. (2) The pronoun "I" refers to the father's daughter—the speaker of the poem.

3. (2) The repetition of "English words" emphasizes that English was an alien language for the father, a Native American, to learn.

4. (1) The daughter's tone of respect for her father and his culture reveals her pride.

5. (1) **invalid**—The father was a veteran in World War I. However, no additional details are given to suggest that he was awarded medals for bravery.

(2) **valid**—The father went to the Mission School when he was twelve. He was apparently forced to learn white America's social customs and language. You can conclude that this education gradually removed him from his original heritage.

(3) **invalid**—The father learned "to pray to the Catholic God" (line 26) when he attended Mission school. Therefore, he did not practice only his native religion during his life.

(4) **valid**—In the concluding lines of the poem, the speaker states that she and her children know only English words. Because they don't understand her father's language, you can infer that they are disconnected from an important part of their Native American roots.

(5) **valid**—You can assume that before the father attended the Mission School, he was probably accustomed to going barefoot, eating without silverware, practicing his tribe's religion, and speaking his tribe's language. The training at the Mission School was evidently designed to make him conform to white American culture and "white ways of thinking."

(6) **valid**—Because of their different language and culture, non-English-speaking immigrants are often alienated from mainstream American society. They, too, are pressured to adopt a new cultural identity.

Exercise 3: Understanding Images
page 168

1. The number 5 on the fire engine. The title of the poem, "The Great Figure," provides you with an important clue.

2. in a rainy, dark city

3. (2) The words *moving/tense* immediately follow the word *firetruck*.

4. "gong clangs"; "siren howls"; "wheels rumbling"

Exercise 4: The Language of Poetry
pages 171-75

1. (2) The title of the poem, "I Wandered Lonely as a Cloud," supports this response.

2. (1) Lines 7-9 compare the arrangement of daffodils with the stars in the Milky Way, the galaxy in which our solar system is located.

3. "I saw a crowd" (line 3)
"dancing in the breeze" (line 6)
"Tossing their heads in sprightly dance" (line 12)

4. (1) Like an artist painting a picture, the poet uses words that create vivid images. The comic strip represents these poetic images as drawings.

Exercise 5: A Poem About Family Relationships
page 176

1. two sisters, a father, a mother, and a stepmother

2. These comparisons describe the mother's figure—sagging and out of shape.

3. You know from lines 11-12 that he did not wear a wedding ring during his marriage to the speaker's mother. In addition, you know that her father left her mother to marry the second wife (lines 16-17). These clues, along with the legend on the photo (lines 13-15), imply that his second marriage meant more to him than his first.

4. Your summary should include the following information: Two sisters are looking at an old photograph of their father. The mother, a woman who is apparently showing her age, is also present. One of the sisters mistakenly assumes that the photo was originally given to her mother. The sister then realizes that the photo belonged to her father's second wife. The father divorced her mother to marry this woman.

Exercise 6: A Love Poem
pages 177–78

1. (1)   in the living room
   (2)   record albums
2. He emphasizes how much he is intrigued by the dimples on the woman's cheeks, arms, and legs. The repetition also produces a musical effect.
3. the beer foam making mustaches on her lips, her long eyelashes creating shadows on her cheeks
4. The woman "loves" Johnny Mathis's music and his looks.
5. (4)   "Dances" and "whirls" emphasize the rhythmic quality of Mathis's voice. "Windblown snow" suggests softness. The entire description uses figurative language to show the beauty of Mathis's voice.

Exercise 7: A Poem About a
Person's Work
pages 178–79

1. the barn
2. 8 A.M., lunchtime
3. (2)   These lines explain how the men stacked hay.
4. **textures:** "*splintery* redwood rafters"
       "*Itch* of haydust in the / *sweaty* shirt and shoes"
   sound: "Grasshoppers *crackling* in the weeds"
5. 17, 68
6. He said that he would "hate" to buck hay all his life.

Exercise 8: Chapter Review
pages 182–87

1. (5)   **Supporting Details**
        Lines 13–14 support this response: "He never learned a trade; he just sells gas, / Checks oil, and changes flats."
2. (2)   **Figurative Language**
        The poet is using personification to show the physical appearance of the gas pumps. He implies that they resemble human beings. Specifically, the hoses seem to be "rubber elbows."
3. (4)   **Main Idea**
        The descriptive details relate to Flick's outstanding athletic performance.
4. (5)   **Figurative Language**
        This simile reveals Flick's skill in handling the basketball.

5. (2)   **Drawing Conclusions**
        From descriptions of Flick's actions at the gas station, you can conclude that he misses playing basketball— "As a gag, he dribbles an inner tube." When the speaker says, "But most of us remember anyway," he is referring to Flick's exciting moments on the basketball court. In contrast, his work at the gas station is dull and unmemorable.
6. (3)   **Understanding Words in Context**
        The "bright applauding tiers" in line 23 refer to the racks used by restaurants to display candies for sale. Therefore, you can conclude that Necco Wafers, Nibs, and Juju Beads are sweets.
7. (1)   **Main Idea**
        By comparing and contrasting moments from Flick's past with his present situation, the poem makes a statement about the short-lived fame of high school athletes. The title of the poem, "Ex-Basketball Player," also emphasizes that Flick's sports career is over.
8. (2)   **Application**
        The poem discusses what happened to a star high school athlete after he graduated. An article about this topic would most likely appear in a sports magazine.
9. (2)   **Characterization**
        These references imply that the speakers are poor and hard-working: "So on we worked, and waited for the light, / And went without the meat, and cursed the bread."
10. (3)   **Figurative Language**
        These words are associated with a person who holds a regal position.
11. (4)   **Supporting Details**
        "To make us wish that we were in his place" suggests that the people envy Richard Cory. They would like to be in his position.
12. (5)   **Supporting Details**
        Richard Cory "put a bullet through his head." In other words, he kills himself.
13. (3)   **Making Inferences**
        Most people who commit suicide suffer from serious personal problems. These problems are not apparent to the townspeople.
14. (1)   **Figurative Language**
        The word *light* is used figuratively, not literally. The poor townspeople are referring to their desire for brighter, happier days.

15. (4) **Application**
This answer restates the central message of the poem as the title of a magazine article. Richard Cory's wealth does not protect him from the circumstances that lead to his suicide.

16. (2) **Figurative Language**
The title of the poem, "Daybreak," is an important clue. The first stanza uses figurative language to describe the dawn—the time when "the light starts up / In the east."

17. (1) **Style and Structure**
The poem is addressed to you, the reader. Lines 9, 13, and 18 state that whoever reads the poem does not directly experience the onion pickers' situation.

18. (5) **Making Inferences**
The speaker indirectly explains how picking onions causes painful blisters on the farm workers' hands.

19. (3) **Figurative Language**
The onions lie asleep or motionless underground. The word "unplug" is an imaginative way of saying uproot.

20. (1) **Figurative Language**
The speaker is showing the force of the raindrops striking the ground. The impact seems to break the raindrops like the broken fingers of a hand.

21. (4) **Main Idea**
The poem details the grueling physical work of onion pickers.

22. (2) **Application**
When consumers purchase a factory-made product, they probably don't appreciate the hours of hard labor required to manufacture the product. Similarly, the poem suggests that people who buy onions never think of the onion pickers working in the fields.

CHAPTER 7: DRAMA
Exercise 1: Characteristics of Drama
pages 192–93

1. (1) [*Almost in tears.*] (line 23)
   (2) [*Stands up and throws the mouse as far as he can. . .*] (line 28)
   (3) [*. . .GEORGE puts his hand on LENNIE'S shoulder for a moment.*] (lines 34–35)
2. (1) "Blubbering like a baby. Jesus Christ, a big guy like you!" (lines 32–33)

   (2) "What, George? I ain't got no mouse." (lines 15–16)
   (3) "Don't you think I could see your feet was wet where you went in the water to get it?" (lines 30–32)
3. (1) **invalid**—When Lennie starts crying, George tries to console him. George says that Lennie can get another mouse.
   (2) **invalid**—Both George and Lennie use conversational language and ungrammatical expressions like "ain't."
   (3) **valid**—You can infer that George controls the relationship. He tells Lennie what to do and how to behave.
   (4) **valid**—Although Lennie is a grown man, he thinks and acts like a child. He cries when George scolds him. Lennie depends on George because Lennie's judgment is evidently inferior.

Exercise 2: Reading a Script
pages 197–98

1. (4) Oscar states in lines 3–4 that the two men live in "a big eight-room apartment."
2. (3) All the stage directions referring to Felix describe his physical movements and house cleaning.
3. (2) "Angrily" is in *italicized print* in line 21.
4. (1) clears the dishes, glasses, and coasters from the table
   (2) dumps and wipes the ashtrays
5. (2) The dialogue between Felix and Oscar clearly reveals their different housekeeping habits. Oscar is annoyed because Felix is always cleaning the apartment.

Exercise 3: The Story Elements of a Script
pages 200–202

1. the front desk area of the police station
2. (4) The stage directions directly state, "[*LARUE and WASHINGTON are glad to see him . . .*]"
3. "Heard you guys are questioning bookies 'bout a cop that got hit" (lines 15-16).
4. (1) Harry Garibaldi
   (2) "Black-hair, pretty good looking, maybe thirty-two" (line 19)
5. (3) After pushing Sid against the wall (line 27), LaRue says, "Garibaldi," the name of the police officer who was shot. Therefore, you can conclude that LaRue is pressuring Sid into revealing information about the shooting.

6. (2) Forcing a man against a wall is aggressive behavior.

7. (1) Washington's dialogue in line 10 and line 12 support this response. Washington sympathizes with the readjustments that Sid will experience after being paroled.

8. (2) The dialogue realistically imitates the speech of police officers and a released prisoner.

Exercise 4: Two Characters' Performances
pages 203–205

1. at a table

2. (5) Nora does not mean this statement literally. She is using a financial expression as a figure of speech. She wants to end the marriage.

3. (3) Nora is using a figure of speech to describe her roles as wife and daughter. Helmer and her father have both treated Nora like a doll—a plaything, not a person.

4. Nora plays a make-believe role in an unreal home. (Your answer may differ slightly.)

5. (1) **false**—Nora says, "I'm saying that we've never sat down seriously together and tried to get to the bottom of anything" (lines 20–21).

(2) **true**—Helmer does not criticize the marriage and resents Nora's description of their relationship. He asks in line 35, "How can you speak of our marriage like that?"

(3) **true**—Although Helmer declares his love for Nora, she replies, "You never loved me. You've thought it fun to be in love with me, that's all" (lines 27–28).

(4) **false**—Helmer asks, "You mean I should constantly go and involve you in problems you couldn't possibly help me with?" (lines 18–19). This question implies that Helmer considers himself superior to Nora.

(5) **false**—Nora tells Helmer, ". . . you've never understood me" (line 23).

(6) **true**—Nora tells Helmer, "And you've always been so kind to me" (line 48).

6. Answers will vary.

Exercise 5: A Complete Scene from a Play
pages 206–14

1. (2) As the scene opens, Willy says, "Like to have a little talk with you, Howard" (line 8). By playing with the wire re-

corder, Howard avoids the conversation with Willy.

2. (3) Willy's decision not to travel causes a heated argument between Willy and Howard. Their argument is the central action depicted in this scene.

3. $65, $50, and $40

4. (4) These lines from Willy's speech summarize the main point—the meaning of a sales career when Willy was a young man: "There was respect, and comradeship, and gratitude in it. Today it's all cut and dried . . ." (lines 163–64).

5. Thirty-four years

6. "I don't want you to represent us" (line 219).
"I think you need a good long rest, Willy" (line 222).

7. (1) proud, desperate, and frustrated
Willy's long speech (lines 137–66) reveals his pride as a salesman. He also doesn't want his sons to support him financially. The stage directions—"[*desperation is on him now*]" (line 171) and "[*grasping HOWARD'S arm*]" (line 239)—show Willy's desperate reaction to Howard's refusal. Willy's anger reveals his frustration over a no-win situation.

(2) insensitive, impatient, and bored
Howard is totally insensitive to Willy's emotional and financial needs. Howard also shows no regard for Willy's thirty-four years of service to the firm. The stage directions—"[*barely interested*]" (line 136) and "[*impatiently*]" (line 183)—reveal Howard's boredom and impatience.

Exercise 6: Chapter Review
pages 214–20

1. (5) **Characterization**
You can conclude that Eddie's attachment to May is based on jealousy and possessiveness. He threatens to fight her dates and says, "You'll never escape me either. I'll track you down no matter where you go."

2. (1) **Making Inferences**
A fifteen-year relationship filled with desperation, misunderstanding, and possessiveness is unhealthy.

3. (2) **Characterization**
The word *now* is italicized three times in May's dialogue (lines 14–15). According to May's remarks, you can infer that his feelings for her are unpredictable.

4. (4) **Stage Directions**
You can conclude that taking a drink and slamming a bottle reveal her anger.

5. (4) **Application**
May's immediate problem is how to handle the difficulties in her relationship.

6. (2) **Stage Directions**
The stage directions state that a *tone of politely feigned interest, masking indifference* (line 15) characterizes Brick's speech with Margaret.

7. (1) **Setting**
Margaret says she could "utter a scream you could hear across the Arkansas border an' parts of Louisiana an' Tennessee." All these states are located in the South.

8. (5) **Making Inferences**
The children belong to Gooper and Mae. Mae is Brick's sister-in-law (line 41). Therefore, you can assume that Gooper is Brick's brother.

9. (4) **Figurative Language**
The children slobber and drool over their food.

10. (1) **Main Idea**
Margaret repeatedly calls the children "no-neck monsters" to describe their appearance. She complains about their screaming and table manners.

11. (4) **Application**
Margaret is the only person onstage in this passage. Brick is in the shower. You hear his voice, but he is "unseen." Since Margaret is the center of attention, the camera would focus on her.

12. (2) **Characterization**
Ruth calls Big Walter "a good man," and Mama agrees, "Yes, a fine man." These statements reveal their respect for him.

13. (1) **Plot**
Mama says that Big Walter "grieved hisself" over their baby's death.

14. (5) **Characterization**
Although Big Walter could be "hard-headed, mean, kind of wild with women," Mama accepted his faults and sympathized with his problems.

15. (3) **Making Inferences**
Mama says in the concluding line of dialogue that Big Walter "just couldn't never catch up with his dreams, that's all."

16. (2) **Stage Directions**
This gesture emphasizes the thoughtfulness of Ruth's response to

Mama: "Yes, life can be a barrel of disappointments, sometimes."

17. (4) **Application**
Big Walter once told Mama, "Seem like God didn't see fit to give the black man nothing but dreams—but He did give us children to make them dreams seem worthwhile." Therefore, you can conclude that if Big Walter were still alive, he would agree that children represent the hopes of the future.

CHAPTER 8: COMMENTARIES ON THE ARTS
Exercise 1: Facts and Opinions
pages 224–25

Part I

1. (1) fact
   (2) fact
   (3) opinion
2. (1) fact
   (2) fact
   (3) opinion
3. (1) opinion
   (2) opinion
   (3) opinion
4. (1) fact
   (2) fact
   (3) opinion
   (4) opinion

Part II

1. 3
2. 4
3. 1
4. 3

Exercise 2: Identifying Descriptive Language in Reviews
pages 227–28

Part I

electric, great, spectacular, strongest, most energetic

Part II

big, brash, strong, mature, tremendous, clear, good

Part III

readable, wonderful, best

Part IV

1. predictable
2. dreadful

Exercise 3: Interpreting a Commentary
pages 229–31

1. (4) This statement explains the central message of the passage.
2. Your summary should restate this information: Prompted by witches, Macbeth conspires with his wife and murders the King of Scotland.

3. Scotland
4. Haiti
5. "full of voodoo drums and witches' cries" (line 21)
6. (1) fact   (4) opinion
   (2) fact   (5) fact
   (3) opinion   (6) fact
7. (3) Brooks Atkinson states this opinion in the concluding line of the passage.
8. (1) Atkinson's flattering remarks about the play reveal his enthusiasm.

Exercise 4: Commentary on a TV Show
pages 232–33

1. (2) The passage presents several examples of humorous dialogue and comic situations in "The Honeymooners."
2. (3) The first paragraph details the setting of "The Honeymooners." The Kramdens rented a cheap apartment on Chauncy Street in Brooklyn.
3. (2) The dialogue from the script familiarizes the reader with the show's characters and comic situations.
4. (5) The excerpt from the TV script (lines 25–29) illustrates a joke about Ralph's weight.
5. (4) By highlighting the funny moments from the show, the authors want you to conclude that "The Honeymooners" is an entertaining situation comedy.

Exercise 5: Commentary on a Film
pages 234–35

1. (2) The author uses this technique to arouse the reader's curiosity about the film. By watching *The 39 Steps*, the reader would discover the answers to those questions.
2. (5) The concluding sentence states that an ordinary man like Hannay typifies many Hitchcock heroes.
3. The statements should be numbered in this order: 5, 3, 6, 1, 4, 2.
4. (4) The headline describes an average man who apparently finds himself involved in a murder mystery. You can conclude that Hitchcock would find this man's predicament intriguing.
5. (3) The critic states that "this thrilling espionage adventure was the first film to establish Hitchcock as the Master of Suspense" (lines 1–2). There is not enough information to determine whether the critic thinks that *The 39 Steps* was Hitchcock's best work, choice (1).

Exercise 6: Commentary on Music
pages 235–37

1. blue-collar housewives (lines 4–5)
2. (1) The description "pure, strong, soulful voice" (line 6) suggests that Loretta Lynn's singing is powerful and moving.
3. (5) In lines 22–23, the author contrasts the two singers' messages: "While Tammy Wynette, ever the romanticist, was singing 'Stand By Your Man,' Loretta was saying 'stand up to your man.'"
4. (4) The song titles "Don't Come Home A-Drinkin'" and "You Ain't Woman Enough To Take My Man" were aimed directly at her husband, Mooney. These two examples illustrate that Loretta Lynn's songs are about personal relationships and experiences.
5. (2) Loretta Lynn's quotation states, "We have just as much right to get some fun out of life as they [men] do" (lines 21–22).

Exercise 7: Commentary on Dance
pages 237–38

1. They taught themselves.
2. Harlem
3. (4) Nick Castle, a choreographer, "designed many of the Nicholas Brothers' routines" (lines 22–23). Therefore, you can infer that a choreographer's job is to create or design dances.
4. (2) Throughout the passage, the author directly quotes Nicholas's comments about the development of his tap-dancing career.
5. (1) Leapfrogging down a staircase and landing in full splits are acrobatic moves.

Exercise 8: Commentary on Theater
pages 239–40

1. "The Rickety Wheel Makes the Most Noise."
2. comic, serious, dreamlike
3. Chile
4. (5) Laura Montenegro states in lines 18–19: "What we'd like to accomplish is to make people get a little bit more insight into our humanness."
5. (4) You can infer from the author's favorable description of the Montenegros' creative ideas that he respects both the artists and their work.

6. (1) invalid   (4) invalid
   (2) valid   (5) invalid
   (3) valid

Exercise 9: Commentary on Sculpture
pages 241–42

1. The sculpture shows the influence of her Indian heritage. Edmonia Lewis's mother belonged to the Chippewa tribe.
2. (1) to learn marble-carving techniques
   (2) to pursue her career with greater artistic freedom
   (3) to avoid racial discrimination
3. (2) The author states in lines 6–7 that Indians are often characterized as "brutal and savage."
4. (3) The passage states that the sculpture shows "a moment of quiet reflection being enjoyed by a father and daughter" (lines 3–4). In line 5, the reviewer says the small size of the sculpture expresses the intimacy of the moment.

Exercise 10: Commentary on a Folk Art
page 243

1. (3) The introductory sentence states, "Tattoo artists have always felt that their work deserved more acceptance as an art." A museum exhibit of tattoo art replicas would be a form of recognition.
2. (3) The supporting details in the third paragraph summarize the ancient historical background of tattoo art. The authors specify dates and locations.
3. (5) The authors state in lines 3–4, "It is easy to see the craft, the fancy, the individuality, and the art of the practitioner." Therefore, you can conclude that the authors appreciate the artistic qualities of tattooing.

Exercise 11: Commentary on Fiction
pages 244–45

1. (5) The passage mainly discusses the character of the fictional detective.
2. (2) Line 3 states that the hard-boiled detective "was born in America."
3. (2) Lines 10–11 state that the origins of the detective were in the lonesome pioneer.
4. (3) Chandler states in line 22 that the fictional American detective is "a relatively poor man."

5. (4) Lines 18–19 state that Philip Marlowe used similes. In the chapter on poetry, you learned that similes, a type of figurative language, are direct comparisons using the words *as* or *like*.

Exercise 12: Commentary on Nonfiction
pages 245–46

1. (2) Lines 2–3 state, "No other writer is asked to commit words to paper with such speed, under such pressure." Therefore, you can conclude that the journalist, unlike the novelist or the poet, is pressured to meet strict deadlines.
2. (3) Both Leo Tolstoy and John Ciardi restate the importance of the writing rule "show, don't tell."
3. (1) **(b)**—This sentence specifically states the umpire's decision and shows you the coach's angry gestures.
   (2) **(a)**—The verb "arrested" conveys a stronger action than "took into custody." "Unregistered handgun" is a more precise image than "illegal weapon." "Mayor" is more specific than "man."
   (3) **(b)**—The sentence shows you how the woman developed her skills and specifies both the woman's original position and her new position.

Exercise 13: Commentary—A Book Review
pages 247–49

1. (1) fact   (5) opinion
   (2) fact   (6) fact
   (3) opinion   (7) fact
   (4) opinion   (8) opinion
2. She melts the witch with a bucket of cleaning water.
3. (5) The author uses the introductory sentence of many fairy tales to begin the book review because he is writing about *The Wonderful Wizard of Oz.*
4. (3) Lines 14–15 state the major theme: "The power of Good is greater than the power of Evil."

Exercise 14: Chapter Review
pages 249–54

1. (3) **Supporting Details**
A building designed in the shape of a turtle is unique. The other choices describe the center's less remarkable characteristics.
2. (2) **Identifying Opinions**
Lines 11–12 state that Dennis Sun

Rhodes believed "it was important that modern architecture be adapted to traditional Indian values."

3. (4) Main Idea
The second paragraph describes the building's size, rooms, and spatial arrangement.

4. (1) Style and Structure
Because the author's purpose is to instruct the reader, the tone is informative.

5. (1) Application
Like the Indian Center, churches also show the influence of meaningful cultural symbols. For example, stained glass windows of biblical scenes, statues of religious figures, and the cross are symbols of Christianity.

6. (5) Supporting Details
Bochco is one of the creators of "L.A. Law."

7. (4) Structure
The author's purpose is to compare and contrast the two shows. The third paragraph cites similarities between "L.A. Law" and "Hill Street Blues"; the fourth paragraph cites differences.

8. (3) Making Inferences
Lines 16–17 state that "L.A. Law" is "about well-educated overachievers who do win, who do have impact." Therefore, you can assume that the attorneys are portrayed as successful and influential.

9. (1) Supporting Details
The author states in line 18, "*Hill Street* was generally a very well written show."

10. (2) Figurative Language
Fisher is using figurative language to emphasize why the show's success depends on the quality of the dialogue. In lines 21–23, she further explains the meaning of her statement: "We've learned already

[in the first few scripts] that when the words aren't good, the show is awful, the scenes endlessly boring."

11. (3) Application
Lawyers viewing the show would most likely be especially concerned with the way their profession is depicted, rather than the show's technical characteristics or entertainment value. TV series often shape the images that people have about various professionals, such as lawyers, doctors, police officers, or reporters.

12. (5) Distinguishing Facts from Opinions
This statement interprets how Emily Dickinson's view of the world is reflected in her poems.

13. (2) Supporting Details
Lines 8–9 state, "She seems to have been, more than other poets, writing just for herself."

14. (2) Main Idea
The entire paragraph details the way in which Emily Dickinson observed nature, people, and herself.

15. (4) Supporting Details
You know from the excerpt that Emily Dickinson wrote about death. However, there is not sufficient evidence to support that those poems reflected a morbid fear of death.

16. (3) Making Inferences
Lines 1–2 state that Emily Dickinson "lived a very secluded life. She was alone most of the time; she didn't know other writers." Therefore, you can infer that she was a solitary person.

17. (5) Application
You know from the passage that Emily Dickinson lived in the 19th century; therefore, she could not have written about jukeboxes, which hadn't been invented yet.